Language Testing

Scottish Centre for Education Overseas

RSA/UCCES Collection

edited by Brian Heaton

ISBN 0 906149 29 0

© MODERN ENGLISH PUBLICATIONS LIMITED 1982

First published 1982
Reprinted 1984

Set by Illustration Services Limited
Printed in Great Britain by David Green Printers Ltd, Kettering.

Cover design by Martin Miller

Table of Contents

Preface

The publication of this collection of articles on language testing comes at a very opportune time, as recent developments in communicative language teaching are now resulting in a widespread reappraisal of language tests and techniques. Not only have the many shortcomings of the structuralist and behaviourist approach to language teaching been strongly attacked, but the whole psychometric basis of language testing has been seriously questioned. Fierce arguments still rage over such established criteria as test validity and reliability. Consequently, it is now necessary to take stock of our present-day tests and examinations in English and to re-examine many of the basic premises so much cherished in the past. However, we should take care not to discard every well-tried and proven method of testing in our search for some magic formula or new technique which will enable us to solve our problems in the assessment of language used as communication. All too often in language testing, as in language teaching, there seems to be a tendency for many to jump on any current bandwagon, accepting half-formed theories and applying them hastily and uncritically. As most articles in this special issue of *MET* clearly demonstrate, considerable critical judgement is necessary in evaluating all the various types of tests and the principles on which they are based. It is always important to keep the best of established methods while, at the same time, seeking to develop where necessary new and more appropriate techniques to reflect the different emphases now being placed on language learning.

In the first article in the collection, **Carroll** points out that testing for any programme should be compatible with the ideas behind the teaching method used: hence communicative teaching programmes should be assessed by communicative tests. The main aspects of communicative tests treated by Carroll are: the test-curriculum relationship, a purposive test framework, test content and procedures, levels of performance and methods of analysing test data. **Davies** pursues this topic in discussing criteria for the evaluation of tests of EFL, and examines three kinds of validity with special reference to six examples of published tests in Britain. The question of validity and reliability is taken up again by **Underhill** in an article which identifies problems in assessing the productive skills of speaking and writing. Underhill uses the terms *direct, semi-direct* and *indirect* to classify tests of speaking and writing ranging from highly realistic tasks to unrealistic tasks. In the next article, **Fabian** reminds us that *studying* a language is vastly different from acquiring its communicative facility, and suggests that teachers can exert a beneficial influence on examining bodies by a more critical and creative participation in the design and construction of examinations.

However, the solutions to the many problems facing test constructors and administrators are neither as simple nor as straightforward as many might at first imagine. This is illustrated in an article by **Shephard**, who traces the development of the Cambridge EFL examinations from 1913, with their emphasis on the formal correctness of language use, literature and translation, up to a functional test currently under consideration, with its one-third oral component. Throughout the article, he shows the importance which the Cambridge Syndicate constantly attaches to public opinion, referring to questionnaires, correspondence, queries, and important public relations aspects of the Syndicate's work. **Seaton** also refers to the problems encountered in constructing examinations which will be administered on a large scale throughout the world. He describes the various difficulties met and overcome in the specification and design of the battery of tests set up and administered by the British Council and the University of Cambridge Local Examinations Syndicate.

Practical considerations in the use of progress tests by teachers and people directly concerned with the running of particular courses are touched upon by **Ward** in an article on the preparation and analysis of progress tests, while **Rogers** approaches this topic in a different way by providing several examples of ways in which test items can be devised so as to provide interest and even amusement on language courses.

It should be emphasised at this stage that a concentration solely on such aspects of communicative competence as authenticity, appropriacy and register is wrong if the testing of the grammatical system of the language is neglected and regarded as subordinate or inferior in any way. Language still consists of grammar, as **Rea** points out in her article on an alternative approach to the testing of grammatical competence within a model of language learning. She gives examples of ways in which the selection and production of a language form is determined not only by its grammatical correctness but also by its function within a given communicative area.

While it is always important to experiment with new testing techniques, it is also essential to attempt to develop existing techniques much further. After falling into disrepute in the 1960's, the long-established dictation test has been the subject of considerable research during the past decade. **Whitaker** examines the flexibility of dictation as a testing device and the various language skills involved, giving numerous practical suggestions for making dictation a relevant and realistic test. In a similar way, **Frantzis** touches on the skills involved in understanding spoken English, describing in detail the use of a radio news bulletin for improving such skills in a systematic way.

After discussing problems experienced by teachers in constructing tests of spoken language, Morrow gives some suggestions for devising appropriate realistic tasks, recommending the testing of students in groups. He then gives a number of criteria for evaluating spoken language before providing an example of the way in which these criteria are used in a basic level examination.

Following **Morrow's** article is a comprehensive account of cloze testing by **Johnson**, who questions several assumptions commonly held about cloze procedure. Johnson draws our attention to the intellectual, cultural and linguistic biases which may militate against attempts to measure a candidate's understanding of a particular text. He then proceeds to show how it is possible to identify much more precisely what each item in a cloze test is measuring, arguing that a random selection of items is not desirable. He adds that such a selection has in any case been largely responsible for the development of tests which are far too difficult and which do not discriminate sufficiently amongst candidates, especially as far as actual comprehension of the text is concerned. An article by **Nation** then deals with advanced reading tests and begins by examining multiple-choice items and reference-word items as techniques for assessing performance on advanced reading tests. These and other test items described in the article direct attention towards the structural features of a reading text and to analytical strategies. **Heaton** draws attention to the more communicative aspects of writing, first examining types of controlled composition before discussing briefly the classification of errors according to global/communicative errors and

local/linguistic errors, and the implications of such a classification for the marking of compositions. He concludes by questioning the validity of composition tests which concentrate only on first drafts written within severe time constraints. This subsection is then concluded by **Boyle** with an article discussing various kinds of tests of language for students of literature. Examples of types of items testing reading, writing, listening and speaking are given in an attempt to foster an awareness among teachers of the relevance and educational values of the literature they teach.

Inter-dependence of verbal and non-verbal information both in the classroom and in the world outside suggests that visuals have a valuable role to play in language testing — provided that it can be ensured that candidates respond to language rather than find the meaning in any accompanying visuals. **McEldowney** shows how visuals compensate for fragmentary verbal comprehension questions on a text by helping to test objectively an awareness of the text content as a whole, without overt clues from the questions and eliminating the need for verbal production on the part of the candidate. McEldowney concludes by showing how visuals can also be used to test production skills, providing basic information for candidates in a non-verbal form and thereby avoiding situations in which prior knowledge of the subject is tested.

Godman deals with problems of assessing performance on academic subjects examined in the medium of English, providing specific examples of the types of difficulties encountered by examiners assessing science examination scripts written in English. In his article, Godman proposes three schemes for the scoring of such answers on a subjective scale, taking into account lexis, syntax, morphology and semantic content.

Pilliner next examines important aspects of the evaluation of language programmes, reminding us that student achievement is only one element in the process of evaluation. In showing that the fundamental purpose of evaluation is to produce information in order to make decisions about an educational programme, Pilliner cites the work carried out by Robert Stake, describing in detail the way in which his model for evaluation can be applied.

In a concise article with highly practical applications, **Chaplen** relates his experience of measuring student achievement in ESP programmes at Kuwait University. He shows how it is possible to convert raw scores by giving appropriate weighting to take account of the different components in a programme, and how a student's final grade can be calculated and decisions taken when several teachers are involved in the process of assessment.

It is only fitting that this collection of articles should end with some brief comments by **Oller**, whose research has contributed so much to the development of language testing over the past decade. Although maintaining that there appears to be a large general factor of language perfor-mance in all the various tests studied, Oller states that there is no basis to conclude that a single test such as a dictation or a cloze test is the best way to measure that general factor. He concludes that a multiplicity of testing methods concentrating on the kinds of language tasks which language users will be expected to perform makes the best language test in any given set of circumstances.

ACKNOWLEDGEMENTS

We wish to express our gratitude to the following for allowing the inclusion of copyright material.

SEAMEO Regional Language Centre for permission to reprint R. Keith Johnson's article *Questioning Some Assumptions About Cloze Testing*, which originally appeared in *Directions in Language Testing*, edited by John AS Read, Singapore University Press 1981; TESOL for permission to reprint Dr. John W. Oller's research notes *A Comment on Specific Variance Versus Global Variance in Certain EFL Tests*, appearing in TESOL Quarterly 14, 1980; the Joint Matriculation Board for permission to use two essay-type questions taken from their Test in English (Overseas), March 1968 and July 1968.

Brendan J Carroll

Language Testing

Is there another way?

THE COMMUNICATIVE APPROACH

Over the last three years, I have been taking part in an evaluation consultancy for a Middle East teaching programme in which new communicative teaching materials are being devised to replace the structural materials in use there for many years. It is interesting to look back on an early report of the evaluation team which commented on the programme as follows:

'The communicative approach stands or falls by the degree of real life, or at least life-like, communication that is achieved in the foreign language in the classroom situation. In our observations of classes in progress, it was not often that pupils communicated naturally and unselfconsciously with one another. Perhaps this is not surprising and should not be expected at such an early stage in the project. However, it is worth stating that pupil-initiated communication should be one of the project's key aims, and the necessary provision should be made in the materials and teaching methodology that it comes about . . . . . We feel that there is still a tendency for teachers to talk too much and, correspondingly, for the pupils to talk too little and that a major aim of the teacher training programme should be to correct this imbalance. We noted that the teachers whose classes were visited dominated the flow of communication and allowed too little communication by and between pupils.'

These words are no doubt true and are often repeated by observers of classroom practice in many subjects and in many countries.

A second area of comment by the evaluation team which bears on our problem is the important question of *correctness* of children's language performance. The team mentions the tension between fluency of language use and accuracy of language usage, recommending a more sensitive and tolerant attitude to student error. Language accuracy and language fluency, it is maintained, should rightly have varying priority at various points in the teaching/learning sequence and the final aim should be that the learners perform both accurately *and* fluently to certain agreed levels.

In the programme we are discussing, there was an obstacle to achieving these enlightened aims of greater pupil activity and a balanced attitude to correctness in that the tests being used to measure the children's progress tended to be traditional ones such as those focussing on the accurate mastery of lexical and structural items by individual pupils. We thus had the position in which the children were being taught, as far as was possible, by one approach − a 'communicative' one − and being tested in terms of another approach − a 'structural' one. In truth, there were at the time no suitable, properly constructed tests for the programme, and this case is just one example of the dilemma we face at present. To test the accuracy of a learner's knowledge of lexical and grammatical patterns is a very different matter from testing the degree to which he has acquired the language so

1

that he can use it in the communicative settings he is likely to face. The effectiveness of a person as a communicator will depend on a wide range of language and non-language skills, and an effective test will have to specify and assess them — a much more complex task than the assessment of his mastery of lexical and grammatical items, which can be much more easily pinned down and counted.

It was at one time widely believed that a person's language competence could be adequately tapped by requiring him to respond to a string of separate multiple-choice items, sometimes as many as 200 in one sitting. Later, it was hoped that the assessment needs could be met by presenting testees with the task of filling in randomly-selected spaces in a written or spoken text. We will examine more fully later the value of such techniques for testing language, all we will say now is: would that measuring communicative performance were so easily done! To approach the problem methodically, I would like now to examine major problems raised by the current structural-objective approach to language testing under five headings.

1. The counting of bits.
2. The four-skill model.
3. The place of correctness.
4. The role of purpose.
5. Justification by correlation.

Later on, I will put forward five considerations for broadening the approach to testing.

1.   The counting of bits

If language performance is to be described by means of numbers, it would be most helpful if such performance could be broken down into small, discrete parts which could be easily judged as to correctness or incorrectness. Then the bits could be put together in a test to provide a numerical score, such as 35 out of 50. The tasks are unambiguous, the marking introduces no element of capriciousness and a person's final score is clear for all to see. Here is an example of such a test item:

> Yesterday I (A. be B. were C. was) very tired.
> (*Instruction — choose the correct option in the brackets.*)

Clearly, option C is a good candidate for choice according to standard English usage. A test made up of a chain of such items could be accurately and objectively marked, possibly by mechanical scanning methods.

So far so good. But the testing problem has not yet been completely solved. For one thing, it is often very difficult to decide if a sentence is correct or incorrect without knowing the context in which it was said. There are, for instance, certain communities in which *I be* and *I were* are accepted forms. For another, an utterance can be quite flatly incorrect from any formal point of view, and yet be perfectly intelligible to the ordinary listener. The French speaker who says 'I have been in London since three days' is certainly incorrect in his English usage, but there will be little disagreement among his listeners about the length of time he has been in London. Much will depend on the amount of tolerance we are prepared to extend to such a speaker. Finally, the suitability of any utterance will be closely related to the relationship between the speakers: whether it is very close and informal, or distant and formal, and so on; and what would be quite proper in one circumstance could be quite offensive in another.

Who, then, was our sample sentence spoken by, and who was the listener? Who are the mysterious 'she's', 'he's' and 'John's' of these pseudo-utterances? Where are they? When was 'yesterday'? The plain fact is that, from the point of view of the tester, it just doesn't matter; these are not real utterances at all, but just vehicles for providing lexico-grammatical traps for the unwary.

All this is just to say that an independent, de-contextualised sentence is a very tenuous basis for making accurate judgements about a person's mastery of a language. It may well be that such snippets will allow us to examine certain limited details of language performance, but I believe that any adequate test must consciously encompass in its design wider strategies and purposes of language use. Adding up the separate bits of performance, however many, cannot tell us the whole story.

2.   The four-skill model

One readily intelligible model of language description, and one widely used for many years, is that of the four skills of listening, speaking, reading and writing, certainly observable aspects of linguistic performance. It is tempting, therefore, to specify our test content in terms of these skills — productive/receptive and oral/graphic. We could, then, devise separate tests of listening, speaking, reading and writing, and thus map a person's language competencies. The trouble is that language is interactive, so that there is interplay between speaking and listening, between reading and writing, and so on. The total communicative situation cannot be adequately described by these separate categories. Furthermore, any test tasks must elicit some responses. Even an objective listening test required the testee to record some response — verbal or graphic; a speaking test must be a response to some verbal or written instructions. To resort to 'objective' techniques of ticking alternatives must trivialise the interaction, debasing one side of what is an essentially double-sided process.

The bases of four-skill assessment — usually spelt out in terms of pronunciation, spelling, vocabulary and grammar — have also been deficient insofar as they rely on features of formal usage rather than on effective use, and thus can be faulted on the grounds of the criticism we have already made of discrete-item, objective-type tests.

3. The place of correctness

We mentioned at the beginning of the chapter the matter of the *correctness* of children's language performance. There are few more emotive educational topics. In the one camp are the purists for whom any mistake — in spelling, grammar, pronunciation, punctuation — is regarded as a personal affront. To them the learning process boils down to the rooting out of errors, accompanied by indignant letters to *The Times*: 'What is our education system (or our country) coming to?' they

tain agreed levels of performance, and within agreed levels of tolerance. It is one thing to differ about ultimate aims regarding accuracy, it is quite another to differ about emphases given to accuracy and fluency whilst pupils are still struggling towards those ends.

What features other than formal accuracy might one consider in building up assessment criteria? It seems to me that we can work at three levels, macro-scopic, meta-scopic and micro-scopic along a spectrum from the broad effectiveness of the message in given settings, through the strategies used in achieving this level of effect, to the linguistic minutiae of spelling and pronunciation through which the strategies are realised. This three-level hierarchy, arbitrary though it may be, can provide a framework for a comprehensive assessment of performance. Below are listed a number of factors subsumed under each of the three levels.

In one of our recently-framed writing assessment scales, a number of performance levels were spelt out in terms of this hierarchy. The macro-scopic features, referred to as *Message*, included clarity of presentation, coverage of points, validity of conclusion and the overall 'flow' of the work. The meta-scopic features, referred to as *Text*, included format and lay-out, coherence of theme, use of cohesive devices, appropriacy of style and neat-

Macro-scopic	Meta-scopic	Micro-scopic
purpose	strategies	spelling
message	interaction	pronunciation
setting	text	grammar
effectiveness	appropriacy	vocabulary
affect	style	correctness
	fluency	
extra linguistic	size of text	intra-sentential
performance	range of skills	
pragmatics	flexibility	
	cohesion	
	coherence	
(Communicative value)	inter-sentential	(Signification)

cry. In the other camp are the permissive ones who have little time for rules, and who see any attempt to insist on their observance to be an assault on the liberty of the individual and his right to free expression. Merely to describe these two extreme positions in this way is to imply that somewhere between them lies a sensible attitude to correctness; the ultimate aim is to produce students who can perform both accurately and fluently to cer-

ness of appearance. And the micro-scopic features, referred to as *Language*, concerned the control of grammar, suitability of vocabulary, accuracy of spelling and intelligibility of handwriting.

Few would deny that such features as those listed are very pertinent to the measuring of language performance. To confine our assessment criteria to formal correctness would subtract greatly from the breadth and depth of our assessment. To sum up on accuracy, then, we can say that it is an important criterion, but by itself cannot form the basis for an adequate judgement of performance — it is necessary but insufficient as a criterion.

4.   The role of purpose

I believe that any measurement of language competence which lacks a detailed and systematic specification of the purposes for which, and the contexts in which, the language is to be used by the person concerned is highly suspect. At the best, ignorance of such purposes and contexts will risk a waste of time and resources; at the worst, it will pervert the very object of our testing. And yet there are those who, believing that 'language is one', think it can be adequately tested by a single set of procedures and with a common content regardless of the specific aspirations of the individual testee; it is immaterial to them whether he requires to use the language to practise Medicine, to teach Architecture, to fly Concorde or to sell Jelly Babies.

But there must be *some* purpose behind a person's choice of the language to be learnt. If he is learning English, why is he paying his money? Why is he devoting considerable time and energy to the task? Why has he chosen English and not Telegu or Spanish? There must be some reasons for his actions; these reasons must be specifiable in some terms, however broad; and his purpose can thus be taken into account in the test content and procedures. Even if one were to accept the monolithic, unitary theory of language, there would still be massive practical reasons for devising context-sensitive testing, and surely no educationist would hope to earn extra points for deliberately ignoring discoverable factors which must be highly significant for his pupils.

5.   Justification by correlation

In this section we will, unfortunately, have to turn to a discussion of statistical issues — not usually a popular topic, but certainly at the centre of any discussion of measurement. Even to those not interested in statistics, the following section could be useful.

The most commonly quoted statistic in discussing the analysis of abilities is the correlation coefficient. A high degree of positive correlation between traits is shown by a coefficient of $+1.0$, a high degree of negative correlation is shown by a coefficient of -1.0, and absence of correlation would be indicated by a co-efficient in the region of 0.0. In practice, however, human traits and abilities tend to be related positively, that is, a person good at one task (say, Maths) tends to be good at another (say, Essay Writing), and many correlations fall in the area from $+0.4$ to $+0.9$ or thereabouts.

Using such correlation coefficients, we may make a statement about language abilities going something like this: 'In our sample of testees, scores on Test A (Writing) correlate highly with scores on Test B (Reading). There is therefore no need to have a special test of Writing because performance on the Reading test will tell us what we want to know about the person's language competence and, moreover, the test of Reading can be marked much more objectively'. This argument is also extended to matrices of correlation coefficients which, when factor analysed, produce factor patterns of the abilities being studied.

To me, this argument is highly suspect, not only because of its practical, educational dangers, but also on theoretical grounds. When I was a teacher, I knew that Sarah Williams, aged 10, was likely to be at the top of the class, or near it, in Arithmetic, Geography, History and English. Had we introduced classes in Industrial Relations or Atomic Physics, I have little doubt that Sarah would have been at or near the top of the class in those subjects as well. By the same token, John Bennett would, in every test (except swimming), have consistently trailed behind the rest of the class. To conclude from such observations that it was thus necessary only to set one or two tests and even to teach only one or two subjects, such as Reading and General Intelligence, in order to foster and measure the children's ability would, I am convinced, be the height of educational naivety. If one were to cut out most courses in Medicine on such 'correlation' grounds, we would finish up with a singularly dangerous generation of doctors. It may well be that for rough, snap decisions we can reduce our testing to the lowest common denominator of elements but, if we want our tests to make accurate and sensitive decisions about our learners, we can ill afford to rely on this type of correlational thinking. We must decide a priori on educational grounds what our test must contain, and use statistics merely as an ancillary process to check whether the tests are doing what we wished them to do.

It is not always appreciated that correlations depend on co-occurences of variance in the responses of the sample being tested. If there is little variance in one or more traits, then their intercorrelations are most likely to be small. Furthermore, even if a correlation is sizeable, it is extraordinarily difficult to trace the precise reason for its being so. It is often found, for example, that it is similarities in testing method between the two tests rather than any relationship between the two traits which lie behind the correlation. Even with the use of factor analysis techniques, there are many ways in which a factor pattern can be explained. It is only recently that sophisticated methods of analysing factor patterns have been used in language studies (see Palmer, A. and Bachman, L., 1981). If these techniques are not used, unless every precaution is taken to identify sources of trait and method variance and unless discriminant as well as convergent features are taken into account, it is very easy to leap to unjustified conclusions from our correlationally handled data.

One particularly disconcerting assertion is one which says that such and such a correlation is 'a good one'. But how can we tell what is a good, or high, correlation and what is a poor, or low, one? Is, for example, a correlation of 0.60 high, medium or low? And what about 0.85, or 0.52? There are three basic ways of answering these questions:

One: to ascertain whether the coefficient is statistically significant and unlikely to be due to chance. A coefficient of 0.60 with 100 subjects would be highly significant in that the odds against it having occured by chance are better than 100 to 1. Clearly, then, there is almost certainly something behind a correlation of this kind.

Two: to calculate the percentage of shared variance between the two variables. This is done by squaring the correlation, so that the 0.60 correlation indicates that 36% of the variance is shared. By this criterion, the correlation is looking decidedly shaky as we have now left unexplained no less than 64% of the variance.

Three: to estimate the forecasting efficiency indicated by the correlation. Using Kelley's coefficient of alienation, we find that a correlation of 0.60 has a forecasting efficiency of only 20%; that is, we are only 20% better off than we would have been if guided by pure chance. (Indeed, even a 0.90 correlation is only 56% better off than pure chance.) Our 0.60 correlation is now looking most decidedly chancy.

All this goes to show that it would be wise to treat apparently 'high' correlations with the greatest caution. A correlation is useful for comparative exploratory studies, but too flimsy a basis for absolute value assessments. And, if the individual correlations themselves are open to question, so much more so are the elaborate factor analyses based on them. This is not to say that producing correlational statistics and analyses is necessarily a fruitless operation; correlational approaches have

their contribution to make in exploring the nature of linguistic-communicative transactions. By all means, let us use them whilst recognising their limitations, but let us not give up the more radical probing of the social, psychological and linguistic entities involved in inter-personal communication. There is a place for descriptive and observational studies as well as quantitative, experimental ones.

We have now discussed five problem areas associated with traditional language testing and reach the following conclusions:

a What we need to do is to look at the whole field of communication in devising our tests and not restrict our task to the counting up of easily-devised and easily-assessed bits of language performance.

b We need to give systematic consideration to purpose and strategy in our task design and not just rest with the simplistic framework of four de-contextualised skills.

c Our important assessment feature of accuracy, or 'correctness', must be put in the context of a range of broad and context-specific criteria.

d We need a direct study of the dynamics of linguistic-communicative behaviour and should not just rely on the circumstantial and *post hoc* evidence of correlational statistics.

The question now is — if a new emphasis is needed — what should it be, and will it produce workable tests? It is all very well to list the alleged defects of a current method of setting about things; it is also expected that the critic outline an alternative approach and show that it has the potential of producing better results. Is there another way?

THE COMMUNICATIVE ALTERNATIVE IN TESTING

The main aim of the new approach must be to widen the basis of our tests from a narrow grammatico/statistical focus towards a broader, multi-disciplinary and multi-level approach which can yet maintain essential features of measurement, always remembering that language testing is much too important to be left to grammarians and statisticians! The way we achieve this broadening, or opening up, is outlined below under five headings — to help provide answers in the problem areas already discussed:

6. The test-curriculum relationship
7. A purposive test framework
8. The test content and procedures
9. Levels of performance
10. Methods of data analysis

6. The test-curriculum relationship

The close relationship of tests with other elements of the curriculum has already been touched on. One way of ensuring their relevance to each other is to see that they both come from a common source, such as a specification of linguistic-communicative needs; thus the programmes of the curriculum aim to meet those needs, and the tests aim to indicate how far the needs are being satisfied. In this way, there is no 'general proficiency' test, as this title would imply lack of specification of the language skills actually needed. Nor would there be a separate 'achievement test' element, such as when a test springs exclusively from a syllabus, because the spelt-out needs are there for direct use in both syllabus and test design.

Without some spelling out of language-communication needs, and of related student aspirations, it is all too easy to base the language programmes on existing tests or examinations, which are usually described in the vaguest of terms, so that students spend their time either on past examination papers or on a course book designed to help students to pass the examination with the minimum of effort. A recently published book of tests, for example, contains strings of items (disguised here for security reasons) such as:

(a) Her mother died when she was young, so she was . . . . . by her aunt.
(4 options presented, the accepted one being 'brought up')
(b) The lion fell into the . . . . . set for it.
(c) When he . . . . . the age of 65, he will retire.
(d) I stood in a . . . . . for half an hour to get my theatre tickets.
(e) Roses are the . . . . . flowers in our garden.
(f) You could tell from his big feet that he . . . . . his father. (*etc.*)

The hapless examinee, had he not been conditioned to such a sequence, might well ask who these mysterious 'he's', 'I's' and 'she's' are, and how he can plausibly be expected to consider in one breath a dead mother, a retiring employee, an unfortunate lion, a slow-moving ticket queue, a rose garden and a boy with big feet. Apart from the inherent absurdity of this juxtaposition of topics, the testee has to struggle through masses of options which are either inappropriate or quite incorrect in the context of the sentence.

Nor is the suspension of disbelief much less in demand with those so-called integrative tests which ask the testee to insert suitable fillers in texts from which words have been eliminated at random. Although much in vogue at present, and

justified on correlational grounds, such tests are only a little more credible than the separate-item test described above. Who, for example, would write a book, report or letter omitting every 7th word, expecting the omissions to be remedied by the unfortunate reader?

If we are keen to see that our tests, in their content and tasks, are meaningful in themselves and can be seen to reflect features of the settings in which the testee will operate, we will, I fear, have to look further than these barren, eduationally-destructive techniques.

7. A purposive test framework

To meet learners' needs and to ensure a benign relationship between the test and other elements of the curriculum, a justifiable approach is to make a clear and detailed statement of the purposes and settings of language use, and of the skills and functions to be called on, and from this statement to generate the language, content and tasks which a comprehensive test will have to encompass. All these design operations must be carried out without losing sight of the specified purposes for learning and using the language.

The framework for approaching our test design may be adapted from such models as those of the Council of Europe (see Van Ek, 1975) and J. Munby (see Munby, J., 1978), to name but two. One of the problems of these models is that they are extraordinarily detailed and lengthy, and it is difficult to fit even a fraction of the specified elements into a test of anything like an acceptable length. Thus, a decision has to be made at an early stage in test design as to how accurate and how delicate, or detailed, the instrument must be. If we required a quick decision for rating students in broad categories for programme placement purposes, if any misplacements caused by the tests could be remedied easily and if the applicants had a wide range of purposes for learning the language, then a fairly short general test of competence could well fill the bill. If, however, the decisions to be made are very refined ones, if the chances of remedying them are small, and if the applicants' language needs are very job-specific, then a detailed needs specification, careful test development and an allocation of time and resources for test application will be called for.

It will, therefore, be for the organisers of the testing operation to decide what scale of delicacy, what tolerance of mistakes and what resources shall be devoted to that operation. The object is to devise tests which will give the necessary answers more economically.

To assist in making a reasonably exhaustive test needs analysis, we have prepared working papers under the following headings which we illustrate by excerpts from an actual specification for a test in English for Computer Programmers.

JOB: Computer programming (English for occupational purposes)

1. Main Events, with their Activities

I   Attending classes in principal subjects
— listening to lectures
— observing demonstrations
— taking notes for further study
— questioning and discussing lectures/demonstrations

II   Making field visits to computer centres
— understanding functions of computer centre
— touring various divisions
— observing sample running programmes
— questioning programmers in centre
— reporting conclusions of visits
— discussing results in groups

III   Studying at home and in library
— carrying out reading assignment
— doing written exercises
— writing reports and critiques
— preparing for classwork and examinations

IV   Carrying out practical computer assignments
— selecting appropriate guidance information
— testing and amending each phase
— general run of programme

Note: the *events* are the main focusses of work during the course, the *activities* are component parts of the events. Further specification is done in terms of each event.

2. Language skills (for Event I)

50 - 1 and 2*. Transcoding information in diagrammatic display involving conversion of diagrams/tables/graphs/ into speech or writing.

48 - 1, 2 and 3. Maintaining discourse; how to respond, to continue and adapt as a result of feedback.

40   Extracting salient points to summarise: the whole text, a specific idea or topic, the underlying point of the text.

39   Distinguishing the main idea from supporting details by differentiating: the whole from its parts, fact from opinion, and a proposition from its argument, (and so on for this and the other events).

*The skills believed to be critical to each event are specified along the lines above, in this case in terms of the Munby model (as described in Munby, J.L., 1978 and Carroll, B.J., 1980). The numbers are those in the Munby taxonomy of language skills.

3. Language functions

To appreciate the functions:
certainty, probability, conjecture, intention, obligation, evaluation; to inform, report, agree, endorse, prove, assume, ratify, conclude, generalise, demonstrate, explain, classify, define, exemplify.
(Taken from the categories of function as described in the two references above.)

4. Topic areas

As in computer programmer training syllabuses:
— special English for computers
— introduction to computer hardware
— advanced Mathematics
— systems analysis
— C O B O L
— management
— human relations.

Text books and instruction manuals will contain the details of the above topics and provide appropriate samples of the language likely to be needed. These topic areas may be general for the programme or allocated to particular events if appropriate.

5. Medium

The events are now categorised according to the medium involved, i.e. listening, speaking, reading, writing and mixed media.

6. Target performance level

On a 1-9 Band system, the level of performance for each medium is specified. In this case, a minimum target level of Band 7 in all media was established (i.e. 'Good user' on a continuum from 'Expert user' to 'Non-user' — see below).

7. Channel

Selected from the following channels:
Face-to-face, phone, radio, TV, film, tape, groups, public address, print, telex, print-out.

8. Other parameters

— *socio-cultural*: (roles and relationships)
learner — instructor
insider — insider
native speaker — non-native speaker
professional — professional

— *attitudinal tones*
assenting — dissenting
cautious — incautious
formal — informal
friendly — unfriendly
inducive — dissuasive
respectful — disrespectful
patient — impatient
certain — uncertain

— *dialect*
Understand British English dialects including RP or near RP accents.
Produce standard English dialect of own area with appropriate regional accent (but generally intelligible to colleagues).

By compiling the above compendium of communicative needs, the tester will have gained considerable insights into the demands of the computer programmers' course, its content, the various activities to be undertaken and the language skills and functions which will have to be mastered to the appropriate target level.

8. The test content and procedures

The events and activities already specified will provide the basis for the balance of tasks contained in the actual test, and the topic areas should point to the main semantic fields to be covered. Similarly, the other parameters of the eight-fold specification will give guidance about skills, functions, tones, dialect and so on. Of course, it will not be necessary, or possible, to provide in any one test a complete coverage of all the specified features but, having selected the main events to be replicated in the test, we will be able to include key features implied by these events.

Test items themselves will fall broadly into three main categories:
Open-ended items for which the testee is allowed a fair measure of latitude in carrying out the task, his performance being assessed on a graded scale probably with accompanying actual samples of different levels of performance.
Closed-ended items, where the testee selects from a given set of responses the one he considers the most appropriate, from a 'Yes–No' dichotomy to anything up to five possible options.

Restricted-response items, which allow a response to be composed by the testee, but on very restricted grounds. Probably the answer will consist of one or two words or, at the most, of a short sentence.

The most effective test instrument will contain a good balance of the above three types of item, allowing the authenticity of the open-ended tasks to be supported by the objectivity (in scoring) of the closed-ended items, bearing in mind the serious limitations of such 'objective' items discussed in earlier sections.

The computer programming test derived from the above specifications included tests of:
Listening Comprehension, using lecture texts with multiple-choice items.
Group discussion, with individual roles provided by guide cards; performances to be assessed by observers according to a graded scale.
Study skills, in which a range of information was provided both in ordinary English and in computer language (with explanations), using multiple-choice items.
Report Writing, responding to written and oral presentations of information; rated by assessors according to a graded scale, with examples.

We have found that, by these test design and development techniques, we can gain insight into the language needs of specialist groups of testees and give ourselves an opportunity of selecting an authentic basis for devising test tasks and items.

9. Levels of performance

For centuries, examiners have made use of scales, or grades, of performance describing successive levels of behaviour in the particular areas being examined. We have, for example, examinations in Pianoforte which range from Beginners to Advanced Level specifying as many as 12 levels of piano piece and the kinds of performance an examiner is to expect when awarding grades. Although basically subjective, this examining procedure is surprisingly reliable and has a good backwash effect on the piano-playing of the pupils. To attempt to improve reliability by breaking up a piece of music into small countable bits would, of course, lead to all sorts of musical absurdity, as the unit of performance *is* the piano piece, which must be judged as an artistic whole.

In language assessment, probably the most widely-used scale has been that of the American Foreign Service Institute (FSI) oral interview, which has proved to result in reliable, consistent judgements whilst retaining some of the naturalness of oral interaction. In the same tradition, we have devised scales of all sorts of communicative activity described at several levels according to the main parameters of level, activity and descriptor. The *levels* range from 1 to 9. The *activities* are, in effect, important communication focusses as described in our category of event/activity above, and can be based on the 'four skills' categorisation if appropriate. The *descriptor* consists of a label (e.g. 'non-writer' through to 'expert writer') followed by a brief thumbnail sketch of the critical features of a typical performance at that level, which can be elaborated in terms of up to a dozen performance criteria for detailed design purposes. The scales are usually accompanied by photostats or tape recordings of performances judged to be representative of each level. For objective, scored tests, conversion tables are provided to convert raw scores into levels on the 1 to 9 band system.

Initial figures for reliability and validity for such tests compare very favourably with those for current widely-used language tests and, more important, authenticity and testee motivation are much more in evidence.

10. Methods of data analysis

A perennial problem in measuring human behaviour is how to describe the target behaviour unequivocally, and to assess accurately how far an individual reaches, or falls short of, that level. The demands are for valid, systematic description, for accurate observation of responses, and for reliable measurement and data analysis procedures. In the main, language-communication tests have suffered on all three counts, description having too often been vague or based on limited, linguistic, features of performance, observation methods being such as to destroy the very communication processes under scrutiny, and data handling being focussed on counting the bits with analysis by correlational means. Thus the measuring devices have tended to demean the very processes they were trying to measure causing the results, however precise in appearance, to be of very little significance.

In the absence of direct measurement based on carefully spelt out, relevant criterion behaviour, much reliance has been placed on sampling and probability theory, the scores obtained from selected samples of performers being arranged in order.

Crucial importance is given to measures of central tendency (mean, median, mode) and dispersion (standard deviation, range, quartile and mean deviations). Norms of performance are established on internal criteria, a 'good' score being expressed in terms of standard deviations above the mean, a poor by standard deviations below the mean; or by

deciles or centiles. Thus the most accurate information obtained is about where in the population any individual lies — in the top 10%, or at the 50% point, and so on. What are so often lacking in such approaches are detailed descriptions of test content and of the exact nature of a 'good' and a 'bad' performance. Briefly, the basis of performance assessment has been the relative performance of individuals in a sample rather than on links with pre-determined behavioural criteria. We thus have the constant danger of vague and circular reasoning behind our testing.

It would be wrong, however, to decry these 'norm-referenced' techniques because, as methods of exploration, they can give us many initial insights into behavioural problems. For instance, some years ago it began to be suspected that cigarette smoking and lung cancer were related. What doctors wanted to discover was the actual causes behind the observed correlations of cancer and smoking. So there came a time when correlational, circumstantial evidence had to be reinforced by more precise, and direct, techniques for describing, observing and measuring the related phenomena. In short, it is crucial that we move as soon as possible to a more authoritative test basis and do not remain shackled in the permanent relativity of norm-referencing.

CASE STUDIES IN COMMUNICATIVE TESTING

There are now interesting developments in the direction of communicative testing in various parts of the world, and I will mention some which I have been connected with. Others are no doubt being reported on as I write.

The Royal Society of Arts examinations in the communicative use of English. (RSA London, 1980).

The English Language Testing Service set up by the British Council and the University of Cambridge Local Examinations Syndicate, (descriptive Handbook in preparation, 1981).

The 'Crescent' English Course and the Mid-East projects associated with it. (O'Neill, T. and Snow, P., Oxford University Press, 1979 onwards).

British Council Course in Testing, testing for communicative programmes, Course 040 (report in preparation by the British Council, 1981).

The Pergamon English Tests in both general and specific areas of English, (in production by Pergamon Press, Oxford starting in 1981).

It is suggested that the above reports be referred to and, when early versions of the tests are released from security, the actual tests be studied. It would be a rash person who would claim to have resolved the incompatibilities between the terms 'test' and 'communication', but at least we can claim to have made genuine efforts to produce tests which contain identifiable communicative features.

Pertinent references

Canale, M. and Swain, M. (1980), 'Theoretical bases of communication approaches to second language teaching and testing', *Applied Linguistics 1.1.*

Carroll, B.J. (1978), *An English language testing service: specifications*, The British Council, London.

Carroll, B.J. (1980), *Testing Communicative Performance*, Pergamon Press, Oxford.

Carroll, B.J. (1980), *Communicative tests for communicative programmes*. Paper given at TESOL Convention, Detroit, 1981.

Fishman, J. and Cooper, R.L. (1978), 'The socio-linguistic foundations of language testing'. In Spolsky, B. (Ed.), *Advances in language testing series No. 2*, Washington D.C. Center for Applied Linguistics.

Morrow, K.E. (1977), *Techniques of evaluation for a notional syllabus*, Centre for Applied Language Studies, University of Reading. Study commissioned by the Royal Society of Arts.

Munby, J.L. (1978), *Communicative Syllabus Design*, Cambridge University Press.

Palmer, A.S. and Bachman, L.F. (1980), *Basic concerns in Test validation*. Paper for RELC Seminar of April 1980 (to appear in proceedings). More recent developments of this project were reported in TESOL, '81, Detroit.

Alan Davies

Criteria for evaluation of tests of English as a Foreign Language

In this paper I want to make some general comments about test choice and test construction, and then to discuss six examples of (British) published tests referring particularly to use in an English as a Foreign Language testing situation.

I plan to begin by making a series of very large but, I hope, gnomic generalisations. Even if nothing else in this paper sticks, I hope that one or two of these statements will.

1. Most linguistics is normative.
2. Language teaching samples by guesswork.
3. Language testing levels are intuitive.
4. Criterion and norm referenced tests are the same thing.
5. Language teaching operations need language level systems.
6. Language level systems need external validation.

Let me examine each of these briefly.

1. Most linguistics is normative

The rules of grammar, the observations of language acquisition and discourse analysis, the selections for language teaching and testing, all present language as if it were unvaried and thus they are all a kind of necessary idealisation: they all set a limit on what the language is (and by definition isn't). Typically, all such descriptions, all such norms, hold up internally, but, as we shall see, what is urgently needed is some measure of external validity. Here, paradoxically, it is easier for the more applied parts of linguistics in language teaching and language testing to provide such buttressing for the hypotheses of descriptive linguistics.

2. Language teaching samples by guesswork

This is even more of an exaggeration, but it is likely that, until we know far more about second language acquisition, the construction of a syllabus and a textbook will be more art than science. It is not surprising that so many language teaching materials should resemble one another. What is noteworthy for language testing is that *first*, the achievement test cannot improve on the syllabus: the test simply reports, it doesn't teach; *second*, and more optimistically, the test can be used as a check on the guesswork. I do, of course, admit that in the sense in which I have used guesswork, language proficiency tests are also guesswork; but it does make sense, I suggest, for new courses, syllabuses, etc. to be piloted — which they are — and tested — which they are only rarely. Testing and teaching have the same interests if not the same purposes.

3. Language testing levels are intuitive

I am thinking here of the ease with which examiners allot test papers to categories (High, Mid, Low, etc) and then, commonly, convert into some numerical score. It is part of the professional judgement of the teacher to grade thus. Even when we provide the apparatus of an itemised test which distributes students widely, it is still necessary to decide the *meaning* of a particular score or band. Sometimes this is done internally (or historically): such and such a score will allow 50, 60, 70, 80% to pass (or fail) and that's what is wanted or how it's always done. Or it may be possible (it is a pity it isn't done more often) to make use of expectancy tables and an external criterion of some kind, and show the effectiveness of a particular cut off — this is using a norm referenced test for criterion referenced purposes.

4. Criterion and norm referenced tests are the same thing

Again an overstatement. But what I mean is what I have just explained. *Intuitively* examiners do work to a Pass/Fail (etc.) criterion, i.e. we always do work in a criterion referenced way. Imposing a series of equal interval scores (1–10, 1–100, etc.) just extends the curve and distributes types of Fail and Pass. So from this point of view a norm referenced test is a use of a criterion referenced test just as we have noted the reverse. They do the same job, in the one case emphasising the distribution, in the other the cut off.

5. Language teaching operations need language level systems

What criterion referenced test uses may have, but what language level systems lack, is a criterion or series of criteria outside the system. Of course language teaching operations do need internal logic so that it is possible to relate each level to the ones below and above. The recent new life in foreign language teaching in the UK has come precisely from the inspiration of the Council of Europe unit credit courses leading to the graded levels of achievement schemes (which are rather like music examinations, as we shall see later). Educational systems characteristically operate in terms of educational levels. Language teaching operations need this ladder security just as much.

6. Language level systems need external validation

It is striking that most of the EFL exams I will be discussing set themselves up as systems of language levels, through grades, etc. This is — as I have just suggested — excellent. But what is lacking is the validation I have called for. In spite of the emphasis I have given to *guesswork, intuition* and so on, I urge that language tests can provide some necessary objective indication of the validity of a system of language levels — and should attempt to do so.

The first question to ask in language testing is always *for what?* There are degrees of query, from the most lay (I want to know how much English they know) through the more refined (How good is their spoken English? Have they mastered that communicative language syllabus?) to the precise (Does she/he have adequate English to work as a secretary in a travel agency? What are the main errors that need remedying in this unit of the syllabus?). Note that the precision is more apparent than real, in that the content of a test is necessarily based on the earlier sampling of the syllabus or other universe of discourse. The test specifications need to be as precise as possible in language content validity, and they must attempt some kind of external validation. Thereafter, the question is properly circular, and the test exists as its own criterion, viz. Do they have enough English for this test?

I want to propose that we use three kinds of validity in our evaluation of EFL tests. They are as follows:

Validity 1 is concerned with the internal logic of the system, making use of levels or grades, each one dependent on and interlocking with the others, such that the use of one element implies all the others (as in, for example, a printed circuit). It is no doubt the case that there is more at stake than harmony or use in setting up a system of levels; there is also the political, publicity, financial aspect in the sense of capturing an audience, as in

a *course* of textbooks, or a *series* of volumes on a similar theme.

Validity 2 is the acceptance of a new test as the equivalent of an existing measure. There are two sides to this — the first the matter of content validity, i.e. the 'experts' must be satisfied when they look at the test that it consists of the right bits, units, combinations and so on — in other words, that it is a test of what it says it is. The second aspect is the reputation of whose test it is: and as in other things, the more prestigious that institution, the more quickly will the new test gain its equivalences. This must be the case — otherwise you or I would write a new test (series of tests) perfect in terms of content validity, but we don't, because it won't gain acceptance. Similarly, it would be possible for a prestigious institution (like a successful author) to produce any old test and claim it valid. And if the producer is the Cambridge Syndicate or whatever, it would work, but not for long because on the whole we rely with good reason on the integrity of our prestigious institutions (PI) — and we recognise, as they do, that they would be found out. Such institutions have everything in their favour — the reputation, the contents, the money (and staff) for research and development and also the acumen to be at the forefront of new ideas (although on the whole testing is fairly conservative). It is probably the case that test development is much more a matter of administration than of ideas. If you or I have those ideas, we'd be much better off selling them expensively to one of the prestigious institutions I have mentioned so often. This makes it really very difficult for an organisation which is only partly (or locally) prestigious to see its way forward. Without full government authority (as in state education systems, which tend to be very nationalistic) such an attempt has no chance of success unless it can cleverly gain some sort of tie up or sub-contract with one of the major, internationally known prestigious institutions. The West African Examinations Council did this, as have others, with the Cambridge Syndicate; and it is interesting to see a more recent tie up between the Oxford Examinations in EFL (Oxford Delegacy of Local Examinations) and ARELS (of which more later). However good an examination may be produced, it will just not gain equivalences, acceptance, credibility unless it has such backing. There may be one exception to this, and that is by making use of Validity 3 — though I am sceptical even here.

Validity 3 — the examples of EFL tests I will mention are all *examinations* rather than *tests*, and while these terms tend to be used quite often the one for the other, it is in Validity 3 that they differ. Validity 3 is the appeal to some external criterion, i.e. the establishing of validity statistically through concurrent or predictive validity. I am unaware of this being done — normally — for EFL examinations; it is, however, done *as a matter of course* for EFL tests. There are various reasons — examinations tend to be less clearly directed at a given population; they change more frequently; they are less objective (in terms of items); and they are more *public* altogether, in the sense that there is less attempt to control their use, and less concern generally with their security. The kinds of criterion that may be appealed to (which would provide exactly the external assessment of the self justifying system I have referred to, and would provide exactly the support needed for promotion of a new test from a non-prestigious institution) are (concurrent) already existing tests or measures. I am sure it would not be too difficult for a PI like the Cambridge Syndicate to provide this kind of evidence, but I am unaware that it has done so. (The annual statistical survey of Cambridge Examinations in English for 1978 certainly does not do anything like this.) Cambridge could use its older formats and other PIs could use Cambridge. Of course, it will be said, why bother to match (or correlate) a new test against an existing one? New tests are new because (e.g. the present Cambridge FCE or the new RSA exams) they are trying to be different. Correlation with existing formats — which have been rejected — is exactly what is not needed. Yes and no; although it will not be very satisfactory, the new test and the old one both test English. But since this is a problem, then the other criterion type, established by (usually though not always) predictive validity, can be employed. Here we require a criterion which is accepted by 'experts' and which is regarded as an operational measure of the required English. Teachers' judgements, observation of language use by judges, performance on various defined scales, even school and college exams, these can all be made to work. Although it is time consuming to do the work, it is essential because, if new tests are needed, then presumably they are doing something better than the old test — and what they are doing better is predicting the criterion that one has selected. The alternative is to fall back on Validity 2, and say I know it's better and I'm an expert. This is certainly respectable, but I want to maintain that it is not enough. It is, perhaps, a little better to provide verbal descriptions of performance at various cut-off scores (e.g. students can . . . . .) but once again

what we look for is some evidence that justifies the cut off, the test and the levels of which they are part.

So what we look for in our tests of EFL are these three validities. (Incidentally we also look for indications of reliability, and I can say now that no indication is given — the word is not mentioned.)

So back to a 'typical' EFL situation and against such a situation I want to consider five tests of EFL, viz.:

1. RSA Examinations in the Communicative Use of English as a Foreign Language.
2. Cambridge Examinations in English as a Foreign Language.
3. Trinity College, London: Examinations in Spoken English as a Foreign or Second Language, and Written English (Intermediate).
4. Oxford Examinations in English as a Foreign Language.
5. ARELS Oral Examinations.
6. PALSO Examinations.

1. RSA Examinations in the Communicative Use of English as a Foreign Language

Characteristics of the Examination (quotations from RSA information)

'The examinations are designed for students wishing to operate independently in Britain. They may be living, working, or studying here, or intending to visit the country on a long or short-term basis. The language and skills tested are thus clearly and explicitly those of 'in-Britain English'. . . . . . the audience envisaged is adult (16+).'

'The exam is offered at three levels — Basic, Intermediate and Advanced. . . . . . it is difficult to match the levels to an external yardstick. Instead we see the levels as being defined internally.'

'. . . . . Candidates will be able to choose different combinations of levels and areas to meet their own requirements or abilities (therefore three levels X four skills).'

'The tests are operational in nature, i.e. they are intended to measure whether or not the candidates can do certain things in English. The 'things' they are asked to do are specified at each level and represent authentic tasks of the sort which confront language users in real life.'

'Authenticity is thus of major importance. It affects not only the tasks which the candidates are asked to perform ('Is this the sort of task which a real person in real life might want to do?') but also the type of texts which the candidates use in the Reading and Listening tests and produce in the

Alan Davies

Writing and Oral tests ('Is this a real English text being used for a relevant purpose?').'

Content Areas   What are the general areas in which candidates taking this exam will want to use English?'

Levels   What will candidates want to *do* in each general area? How *well* do they need to do these things? What sort of *texts* will this involve the candidate in handling?'

This is a new examination, the 'result of a conscious effort on the part of the RSA Examinations Board to develop new testing procedures to match recent developments in the communicative teaching of foreign languages'.

In terms of our three validities, it has Validity 1, with its three levels of Basic, Intermediate and Advanced, not defined, as is pointed out, by an 'external yardstick', but 'defined internally': the interlocking becomes clear when we look at the Reading tests at Intermediate and Advanced levels, and of the 30 questions at Intermediate level, 15 (at least) are repeated exactly at the Advanced level.

Validity 2, very much so: it has the backing of its own PI (the RSA) and the rubber stamp of content validity from its own 'experts'. The desire to 'match recent developments in the teaching of foreign languages' seems to me very proper and may be one way of evaluating ideas about communicative language teaching.

But there is — so far — no Validity 3, though we are told the Exam Board intend 'to monitor closely the validity of the tests'. I hope this will come and it is, of course, too early to expect it yet since this is a new examination. However, we are not expected to see the examination as relevant to the typical EFL situation since, at the beginning we are told — 'the language and skills tested are . . . . . clearly and explicitly those in in-Britain English'. This is fine if you intend to visit Britain in the near future, but I am less sure of using that as the criterion. It is interesting to observe the tendency in recent years to make life in Britain, interaction among native-speakers or at least with them, the focus of attention in language teaching materials, again perhaps one of the unexpected (and not altogether welcome) results of the communicative movement.

2. Cambridge Examinations in English as a Foreign Language

The most PI and still the one best known. The Cambridge examinations are offered at three levels:

the First Certificate in English (FCE) containing Reading Comprehension, Composition, Use of English, Listening Comprehension, and Interview; the Certificate of Proficiency (CPE) in English containing the same sections; and the Diploma of English Studies comprising Language and Appreciation, Literature, Life and Institutions. We are told that the CPE alone bears the official approval of the Department of Education and Science and is recognised by the University of Cambridge as part of the examination requirements for matriculation.

Description (quotations from the Cambridge information booklet)
'Provision for the foreign learner began specifically at the teacher rather than the pupil level, with the introduction of the Certificate of Proficiency in 1913. The modest examination then offered . . . . . test in phonetics, translation tests in French and German, and its Literature paper . . . . . (now) a range of examinations providing . . . . . a highly structured assessment of essential communication skills.'

The new syllabus introduced in 1975 'has been received with general approval . . . . . making the best use of machine scoring and computer facilities and at the same time maintaining those features which have characterised the Cambridge examinations over the years: an accurate, valid and comprehensive test; an examination standard in form, marking and general procedure wherever taken; an administrative procedure which allows for a reasonably short time between entry examination and issue of results, yet gives each candidate individual attention where needed'.

'Although only Proficiency and the higher examination for the Diploma of English Studies have any official recognition or equivalence with the GCE or foreign counterparts, the main demand is for the lower level examination and in its own right rather than as a preparatory stage for Proficiency as it was designed in 1939. The attraction seems to be its simplified yet adult character and its attempt at an international flavour and freedom from over-literary emphasis.'

'. . . . . Proficiency (is) . . . . . recognised as a quite demanding test of general literacy and maturity.'

'. . . . . has state recognition . . . . . as an English qualification for teachers in a number of countries, notably in Southern Europe and South America, and it is in these areas that demand is biggest.'

How do the Cambridge examinations measure up to our Validation? It looks, in spite of disclaimers, as though Validity 1 is there: we are told that there is no connection between FCE and CPE and that very few people go in for the Diploma, but the system exists, and although FCE is not officially required for CPE, its parameters will certainly be used as informal measures when assessing a potential CPE entrant. (It is interesting that Cambridge think too many people enter for CPE who shouldn't. Perhaps an intermediate level between FCE and CPE is needed, and a lower Preliminary examination in English is now under discussion.)

What of Validity 2? The PI backing is certainly there. What of content validity? I am less sure here. Little indication is given, and we need to look at past examination papers, or trust the Cambridge judgement. But I am not too happy about being told that this is 'an accurate, valid and comprehensive test' without being told why and how.

Validity 3 — lacking again. As I have said before, I think there is less excuse for Cambridge precisely because they are the leaders and the most PI. Perhaps they do validate in this way, and I should be grateful to be pointed to those statistics.

3. Trinity College, London. Grade Examinations in Spoken English as a Foreign or Second Language and Written English

The following quotations have been extracted from the Trinity College information booklet:
'The examinations are recognised by the British Council as comprising a useful series of graded tests in oral communications ability.'

'This syllabus . . . . . has been compiled to meet the needs of children and adults learning English as a Foreign or Second language. It reflects the theory and spirit of modern foreign language teaching.'

'The principal aim is to find out how well the student understands 'educated' spoken English within the limits of each Grade, and how well he or she can speak it. Importance is attached to the candidate's pronunciation, readiness, fluency, and comprehension, and to the appropriateness and grammatical accuracy of the English used, but above all to the ease with which the candidate can communicate by means of English.'

'Progress is made by small steps from a very elementary level of achievement (Grade 1) to a very advanced one (Grade 12) . . . . . the grades are best regarded as milestones along the road towards an advanced oral command of the language.'

'Particularly in the lower grades the syllabus is formed chiefly on a sequence of basic English structures and usages. Because they *are* basic they are important to communication by means of English.'

As we might expect from a College of Music there is very clever use of the internal system of interlocking grades — 12 in all. 'The grades are regarded as milestones along the road towards an advanced oral command of the language'.

So 'yes' to Validity 1, the *most* valid (in this sense) of all our EFL examinations.

As to Validity 2, Trinity College is less of a PI, but still well-known, and so it scores reasonably there. Does the test have content validity? It claims that it reflects the theory and spirit of modern foreign language teaching, and the syllabus information for each grade is the most detailed of all five examinations. The problem I wonder about is whether the syllabus is really a *spoken* English syllabus or a *written* one. 'The principal aim', we are told, 'is to find out how well the student understands educated spoken English within the limits of each Grade, and how well he or she can speak it'. Now there is a dilemma here. For native speakers, there are substantial differences between the spoken and the written language: what the communicative language teaching mission has attempted is to extend this difference to EFL speakers. I am not sure (and I suspect others are not) that this is a proper or feasible aim for TEFL; it may be that we should accept for EFL spoken English a limited goal which is written English spoken aloud. This is what (I think) Trinity College is doing, and I wish it would say so.

Again there is no evidence of Validity 3.

4. Oxford Examinations in EFL (the Oxford Delegacy of Local Examinations) (quotations from Oxford Delegacy information sheet)

This is another new examination.

'The examination . . . . . is principally concerned with assessing performance in a very practical way by using test items from among the reading and writing tasks candidates might be expected to have to perform whilst in England (sic). . . . . The level of the exam is below that of the Cambridge FCE.'

'There are two papers:
1. practical writing skills
2. practical reading skills
3. ARELS preliminary Oral Examination (optional)

Validity 1 can be claimed only by the attempts to equate the test to other measures, e.g. 'the level of the examination is below that of the Cambridge First Certificate' and again 'the Delegates' English Committee is happy to recommend (the Preliminary Oral Examination of the ARELS Examinations Trust) as a counterpart to its own written examination.

Otherwise there is no internal system.

Validity 2: the PI backing is there. As for content validity, again there is (in the specimen items shown) an attempt to capitalise on the communicative movement – 'test items . . . . . from among the reading and writing tasks candidates might be expected to have to perform whilst in England'. (Notice that, as with the RSA, we are right away from the 'typical' EFL situation.)

Again, Validity 3 is not mentioned.

5. ARELS Oral Examination (ARELS Examination Trust) (the quotations below are from the ARELS information booklet)

There are three levels, Preliminary, Certificate and Diploma, 'designed specifically as a reliable means of assessing ability in the use and comprehension of Spoken English'.

The ARELS examination has a lot going for it. It has Validity 1 (three interlocking levels), and it has Validity 2: PI backing and content validity, which is certainly approved of by teachers and is *not* limited to Britain or, as Oxford quaintly put it, England: so it is available for the typical EFL situation. I must enter a caveat here though, which is that the cultural requirements of some parts of the ARELS examination make it quite difficult for someone who is not actually in daily contact wtih native speakers in their own environment.

Validity 3: if there is none, it is not for want of trying, since I did myself agree to look into the statistical validation of the ARELS examinations and I hope to get round to this soon. In the meantime I offer my apologies and note that the ARELS Examinations Trust are aware (unlike the others we have discussed) of the need for Validity 3.

6. The PALSO Examinations (Panhellenic Association of Foreign Language School Owners)

Last year the PALSO organisation carried out its own trial examinations at three levels, Basic, Standard and Higher, so there was the attempt to achieve Validity 1. The other validites were more difficult: for reasons I discussed earlier, PALSO is not a PI – if it wishes its examination to gain equivalence widely; and the content validity of the test needed earlier expert advice – though that is understandable in a trial examination. So far as I know there has been no attempt to establish Validity 3. The PALSO attempt showed what can be done with enthusiasm (not unlike the ARELS enthusiasm inspired by Peter Fabian). But if my argument is accepted, then enthusiasm is not enough.

Conclusion

The question *what for* remains central. Is the test for life in Britain, for communicative interaction, or is it meant more generally (with the implications of perhaps a Trinity College-like syllabus)? And does it provide the validities I have listed – ways of helping us to evaluate and choose a test for our own use?

I have not mentioned other examinations like the Joint Matriculation Board, the new Associated Examining Board, the Stages of Attainment Scale from the English Language Teaching Development Unit, the English Speaking Board, the Regent's School Test and the new English Language Testing Service of the British Council (interesting, I suspect, because it represents a move away from the previous test to a more examination-like instrument, more comparable therefore to the measures I have spoken of today).

There is a paradox in the *what for* question. A test must be related to local demands – but it must also have wider currency: the best test manages to serve both ends, the local and the global or international.

Nic Underhill

The great reliability validity trade-off:
problems in assessing the productive skills

The two principal criteria for evaluating any kind of test are reliability (whether it gives consistent results) and validity (whether it measures what you think it does).

The main problem with tests of speaking and writing may be stated simply: high reliability and high validity are seemingly incompatible. The situation is complicated by the existence of several different kinds of validity, some theoretical and intuitive and others empirical and quantifiable. As a result, what may be valid for one school of thought may not be for another.

If you are of the 'onward march of science' frame of mind, you may be convinced that it's just a matter of time before the ultimately reliable and valid productive test appears. If you believe that real language use only occurs in creative communication between two or more parties with genuine reasons for communicating, then you may accept that the trade-off between reliability and validity is unavoidable. Testing is an inherently artificial situation; the question is, how artificial can it be, and yet still be considered valid?

This article outlines some of the attempts to resolve the reliability/validity trade-off, and considers the influence of a third criterion, practicality. It examines the chronological development of productive testing and the test types in vogue at each stage. For the sake of brevity, examples of test items are kept to a minimum — all the standard works on testing contain numerous examples (i).

First, in the interests of successful communication, some definitions are in order.

WHAT MAKES A PRODUCTIVE SKILLS TEST DIFFERENT?
Considering for the moment only the oral interview and written composition, the following characteristics distinguish tests of productive skills:

(a) they are *integrative* tests
(b) they are, on the whole, *subjectively scored*
(c) there are *serious doubts* about their *reliability*
(d) they are, or can be, *direct* and pretty *realistic* measures of performance in *real-life situations*; therefore
(e) they have high *face/content validity*.

So how do they contrast with other tests?
Consider this item from a multiple-choice test:
'The opposite of *strong* is 1. short 2. poor 3. weak 4. good'

Compared with the characteristics listed above,
(a) this is a *discrete-item* test — it aims to test
   — only one component of language (vocabulary)
   — through only one skill (reading)
   — and one aspect of that skill (receptive recognition)

An oral interview, on the other hand, requires the testee to listen (receptive) and speak (productive), using many components of language — grammar, vocabulary, pronunciation, stress, all at the level of discourse rather than the single word or sentence.

(b) this item is *objectively scored* — the teacher/tester does not need to exercise his judgement in marking it; the decision has already been taken for him about the correct answer. In tests of productive skills, by contrast, he may have detailed guidelines to help him assess the testee's performance, but ultimately he must use his judgement to decide on the value of a particular response. (It is worth noting that of the three stages common to language tests, viz.

   1. the compilation/construction of the questions
   2. the answering of the questions by the testee
   3. the marking/scoring of the testee's answer,

only in 3. can the objective/subjective distinction be maintained; all tests are 'subjectively' compiled and 'subjectively' answered) (ii).

(c) although any particular question must be tried out in practice, this type of item is generally considered *highly reliable* — from one administration to the next, without intervening tuition, the same testee will answer the question in the same way and the marker will mark in the same way.

In an oral interview or written composition, there are three principal sources of unreliability:

   1. the testee may produce different answers to the same task from one day to the next — he may be feeling uncommunicative, morose, uncomfortable, deaf, antagonistic to a particular interviewer or composition topic, or just lacking in the confidence necessary to produce connected self-expression.

   2. a single marker may score a particluar response differently from one day to the next (for similar reasons!) (a problem of *intra-marker reliability*).

17

3. two or more markers may give different scores to the same response (a problem of *inter-marker reliability*).

(d) the multiple-choice item is a thoroughly unrealistic measure of language performance. It does not reflect actual language use — there is no real-life situation in which we go around asking or answering multiple choice questions. Productive skills tests are not necessarily ultra-realistic — few adults have the inclination or the incentive to produce written compositions, and the atmosphere in an oral interview can be notoriously strained — but they should nonetheless be more realistic than discrete-item tests.

One way of tackling the question of realism is to use the terms *direct, semi-direct* and *indirect*. These can be defined for speaking as follows:

> '*Direct* speaking tests . . . . . include any and all procedures in which the examinee is asked to engage in a face-to-face communicative exchange with one or more human interlocutors . . . . .
> *Indirect* are those tests which do not require any active speech production on the examinee's part . . . . .
> *Semi-direct* tests, although eliciting active speech by the examinee, do so by means of tape recordings, printed test booklets, or other 'non-human' elicitation procedures.' (*iii*)

While these labels cannot be maintained as rigorously clear-cut categories — and this problem will be discussed below — they form a useful classification for comparing tests.

The straightforward oral interview, such as that used by the US Foreign Service Institute (*iv*), the BETA Test (*v*), and many schools as an informal placement procedure, is a direct test; the use of a conventional written cloze test to assess speaking ability would be indirect; and tests such as the Cambridge FCE and Proficiency oral interviews, the Ilyin Oral Interview (*vi*), Upshur's Oral Communication Test (*vii*), and many others would be semi-direct, as they elicit speech by means of visual, recorded or printed stimuli. Because the nature of the language is thus controlled, such semi-direct tests are easier to score than direct tests and show higher reliability, and hence their popularity with examinations boards.

In written production terms, one could call direct a composition where only subject, audience and purpose are specified; a semi-direct test would be any task that requires writing, but elicits it by means of taped, visual or written cues (e.g. guided or picture composition, gap-filling, re-ordering exercises, etc.); an indirect test requires no writing at all.

(e) because of its lack of realism, the discrete-item, for the majority of students and teachers, has *low face validity* — it is decontextualised, non-creative and generally doesn't look like a valid test of language ability. While criticisms can certainly be made of specific productive tests in this respect, the option is open to the tester to make the testing situation as realistic as he has time and money to spare. The more effort is expended in this direction, the better the testee will respond by treating it as a valid task.

The question of *content validity* is more complex, and depends on the theoretical assumptions of the tester; if you believe that language can reasonably be broken down into discrete components and skills, and that language learning can be tested in the same way, then you may well consider the discrete-item given above to have high content validity.

The important point to make about face/content validity is that it can be determined only by non-quantitive criteria, such as introspection and informed judgement; unlike predictive or concurrent validity, it cannot be assessed in statistical terms. This non-quantifiability should not in any way be allowed to detract from its importance. Of all forms of validity, it most directly answers the central question: does this test item measure what it's supposed to measure?

'AS YE TEACH, SO SHALL YE TEST':
(i) COMPOSITION AS AN ESSENTIAL SKILL
Traditional methods of language teaching ('the grammar translation method') emphasized the importance of written rather than spoken language. Learning a language involved learning a set of grammatical rules which were applied to the analysis of certain texts. These texts, which were usually of a literary nature, were supposed to embody those aspects of 'good' writing which the learner was to imitate, or at least show awareness of, in his own written production. The ability to write English clearly and effectively was seen as an essential skill, and written composition was considered the most valid test of this skill. (No clear distinction was drawn between teaching and informal testing; dictation, translation and composition were simultaneously teaching strategies and testing exercises.)

It was realised that serious doubts could be raised about the reliability of composition as a testing device from the point of view of the testee the task and the marker. Few would argue that their performance on a creative writing task will vary more from day to day than their performance on a multiple-choice test; or that a particular composition subject will suit some people better than others, irrespective of their writing ability. From the examiner's point of view, a partial solution is to offer a choice of composition topics; but this compounds the problem of the comparability of student responses.

In the 1930s and 40s, when TEFL scarcely existed as an independent profession and took its methodology from first- and foreign-language teaching in schools, examiners of English schoolchildren agonised for many years over how to reduce these sources of unreliability, and their conclusions laid the foundations of the composition marking schemes in use today.

1. Standardisation of marking schemes

Two principal marking schemes were used: the method of general impression and the analytic method. The first is exactly as it sounds — the marker reads the composition and awards it a mark on a single scale, without picking out any special features for consideration. The analytic method uses a pre-determined marking scheme listing a number of sub-scales and specifying the weight to be given to each in totting up the overall score. For example, the FSI Oral Interview scales are Accent, Grammar, Vocabulary, Fluency and Comprehension, weighted approximately in the ratio $1 : 9 : 6 : 3 : 6$ respectively.

Within the analytic method, there are again different systems used to assign marks within each category: (i) Impression; (ii) Additive (giving one mark for each of a number of pre-selected features); (iii) Subtractive ('from a sub-total of 10 for mechanics, subtract ½ mark for each error of spelling or punctuation'); and (iv) Marking Protocol, which is a pre-defined scale of levels, e.g. for Vocabulary:

10 points — no errors
8 points — occasional misuse, but expression hardly impaired
6 points — fairly frequent misuse, which may limit full expression
4 points — limited vocab. and frequent errors clearly hinder expression
2 points — vocab. so limited and so frequently misused that reader must often rely on own interpretation
0 points — limitations so extreme as to make comprehension impossible.

Such marking schemes are in wide use today; they are difficult to construct and often hard to interpret, but many assessors feel happier with some sort of written protocol for assessing both oral and written work. In 1949, the battle lines were already drawn up:

'Among teachers of English, a constant battle is waged between supporters of analytic marking, and those who believe wholeheartedly in general impression . . . . . it should be noted that the analytic schemes were born out of a realisation of the general unreliability of essay marking, and some schemes have gone to extraordinary lengths to achieve 'objectivity' and thus consistency'. (*viii*)

Already an association, if not an equation, was being made between reliability and objectivity. Although neither method was proven in experiments to be clearly superior, the analytic method tended to be more popular, partly because of the appearance of greater objectivity. To counter this, it was recommended that three or four markers, whose scores are averaged out, should be used to improve the reliability of the impression method.

2. Standardisation of markers

As a corollary of standardising the marking method, the principle was established that regular meetings should be held to brief assessors on the marking scheme, and by 'test-marking' sample compositions and comparing results, to standardise the way all the markers applied that scheme.

3. Increase the number of questions

(This is a well-established way of improving the reliability of any kind of test, within the limits of fatigue and endurance.) For composition, it was suggested that two or three shorter pieces give a more reliable indication of the testee's performance than one long one.

4. 'Task-realism'

The importance of task-realism was another notion to be discussed long before it became fashionable in the field of TEFL. Hartog said:

'In real life, a person does not just 'write'. He writes for a given audience and with a given object in view, which may be to explain, to persuade, to give an order . . . . . or indeed fulfil any other purpose or combination of purposes.' (*ix*)

He carried out an investigation to compare performance on 'Directed' versus 'Undirected' essay subjects; for example, one of the Directed essay subjects for English schoolchildren was:

> 'Describe a school speech day at which you have been present as if you were writing to a boy or girl who has been prevented by illness from being present.'

compared with the Undirected essay topic 'A School Speech Day'. (Note that, for the purposes of this paper, I am not drawing a distinction between 'essay' and 'composition', as some authors have done). (*x*). Hartog concluded:

> 'The majority of examiners were decidedly of the opinion that a Directed essay subject yielded an essay of better quality than the corresponding Undirected essay subject, and that it could be marked with greater confidence.' (*xi*)

(ii) COMPOSITION AS THE PERPETRATION OF INJUSTICE

With the advent of the audio-lingual methodology in the fifties and sixties, there were a number of important changes in the teaching and testing of the productive skills. Principally:

1. Speech was considered primary; the aural/oral skills became the main objective of language teaching.
2. Language was learnt by habit formation, mainly through repetitive oral practice. Written work, of a rigorously controlled nature, was permitted only after the patterns had been properly established. This was because of 3 below.
3. Making mistakes set up wrong patterns and could lead to the formation of wrong habits. As far as possible, materials were constructed to reduce the chances of error, by careful sequencing of structures and adequate practice of each structure before moving on to the next.
4. Not only was language proficiency composed of a number of discrete skills, but tests could and should be constructed to assess these skills and their sub-components separately. (In fact, genuinely discrete-item tests were a rarely achieved ideal.)
5. Little emphasis was given in the classroom to meaning, and hence to the role of genuine communication.

The unguided composition, in these terms, is all wrong; it is a meaningful written task, employing numerous inseparable language elements and skills which cannot be constrained to fit a structural syllabus, and which is an open invitation to the testee to commit all kinds of errors. The interview fared slightly better by virtue of being oral; but as unstructured elicitation procedures, niether was acceptable to audio-lingualism.

Both could be made more acceptable by asking a pre-determined series of questions designed to elicit one-sentence answers containing specific structures or functions. This technique of structured interview and guided composition is in widespread use today and has the advantage of eliciting comparable speech samples from each testee while still being productive; but in the process, of course, the exercise becomes progressively less life-like, ending up with a string of unconnected, decontextualised stimulus-response questions.

Another big disadvantage in audio-lingual terms is that the unstructured interview and unguided composition are not amenable to the objective-test format, such as multiple choice, where only one correct answer is possible. This was another incentive to restrict the creativity involved in production tests; written gap-filling or sentence transformation, and simple oral question-and-answer could be marked objectively and thus reliably.

There was certainly an awareness of what was being lost in the process:

> '. . . . . often we have to choose between more apparent validity but less objectivity and more objectivity but less apparent validity' (*xii*)

but reliability was, and still is, considered to be logically prior to validity. Following the assumption of the discrete nature of language skills, numerous tests were devised to assess particular elements of language via oral production — pronunciation, grammar, vocabulary, intonation, stress, etc. — Valette (1977) gives many good examples of this genre. Because these questions were composed of unrelated questions with a single correct answer, e.g.

> 'The man who flies an aeroplane is a _____ '

they fitted the desired objective test format, tested one item at a time, and left little room for serious error.

The solution to the reliability/validity trade-off being offered here was part of the audio-lingual package — if you accepted the discrete-item philosophy on which it was based, then the content validity of such tests could be very high, due to the close correspondence possible between the items on the syllabus and the items in the test.

This argument is fine for a test of achievement of a specific syllabus, but not for a proficiency test. In order to maintain the same content validity, it had to be shown that the items tested were in some sense representative of the testee's overall proficiency; a lot of hot air was generated trying to establish adequate sampling techniques before it was realised that this task was a linguistic as well as a statistical impossibility.

Written composition became an outcast — one author saw its only value as avoiding an undesirable 'washback' effect:

> 'Tests of composition are necessarily unreliable and of doubtful validity. Since, however, it is important that composition should be taught, and since if not examined, it may not be taught, it should be included in a language examination.' (xiii)

Others were more extreme in their rejection of composition:

> '. . . . . attention should be drawn to the consensus that injustices are prepetrated every time an essay is set at an examination . . . . .
> it is widely recognised by linguists that an essay is not an adequate test of knowledge of the language. If the student is cunning, he will avoid constructions he is not sure of and create situations in which he can use his pet phrases.' (xiv)

This, surely, is the essence of communicative ability: to make the best use of those language elements and structures which one does command and to avoid those which are likely to be communicatively ineffective. Some people do this better than others; they are better communicators. See the cunning student twist and turn to avoid the third conditional!

(iii) RETURN OF THE PRODIGAL INTEGRATIVE TEST

As the communicative emptiness of the audiolingual approach was recognised — students being able to produce complex structures given the correct stimulus, but unable to transfer this fluency to real communicative situations — integrative productive tests made a cautious return. There was now a place for both objective and subjective tests in a proficiency battery:

> '. . . . . the more subjective evaluation of the composition will complement the grade for the more circumscribed items, just as the mark for the oral interview was shown to do in the area of oral production.' (xv)

Inevitably, there was a resurrection of the arguments about the best way to score such tests; Rivers, along with many others, was in the analytic camp:

> 'an overall intuitive grade for written composition can be seriously influenced by neatness and clear writing. The grade should be a composite one . . . . .' (xvi)

Heaton was in the overall impression camp:

> 'It is impossible to obtain any high degree of reliability by dispensing with the subjective element and attempting to score on an 'objective' basis.' (xvii)

During the seventies, the realisation spread that language could not be divorced from its contexts-of-use for purposes of teaching and testing. New tests of productive skills were consciously task-oriented, aiming for the best possible face/content validity; for example, letter writing became a popular choice for written composition, and situational role-plays for oral interviews.

Experiments to find ways of improving the reliability of the more direct and realistic tests came up with the same results as before — increase the number of markers, hold standardisation sessions, use an analytic scheme — and the reliability claimed for some productive tests is high by any standards. However, such tests are expensive and time-consuming to administer and mark. This criterion of practicality is especially important if you want to construct a test battery to be given to large numbers of testees all over the world and then marked as economically as possible. The search was on to find a valid and reliable method of testing productive skills accurately without the practical disadvantages of highly realistic tests.

Two possible solutions were offered: semi-direct tests, which give much greater control over what the testee says or writes; and indirect tests, where he doesn't actually say or write anything at all.

(a) Semi-direct tests

The distinction between direct and semi-direct tests, as defined above, seems at first glance intuitively reasonable; a face-to-face conversation without printed or recorded stimuli is more natural than one in which one participant asks questions about a picture and the other answers them.

Again, the reliability/validity trade-off can be clearly seen; by asking questions about a picture or other stimulus, the tester is restricting the number of possible correct answers, and taken to its limit, there will only be one correct answer. There is an immediate gain for reliability; with only one possible answer, all the marker has to do is to decide whether that answer has in fact been given or not. At the same time, the testee is deprived of the opportunity to be creative or to display his communicative proficiency in a realistic manner.

However, there are many real-life situations in which we *do* hold a natural conversation about a visual, recorded or written stimulus; and such a conversation in an oral interview can be a lot more realistic than a so-called direct speaking test in which the interviewer is controlling and structuring the conversation so as to elicit particular structures or functions.

Direct and semi-direct tests should be regarded as being on a continuum from the most realistic to the least; and the position of a particular test on this scale can only be determined by an intuitive examination of the test itself. Consider the following description of an oral test:

> 'The examinee is presented with four pictures differing significantly on one or two conceptual dimensions. These may represent, for example, a person performing four different actions, or the four conjunctive possibilities of a man with or without a hat walking up or down a staircase.
> The examinee is instructed to provide a single sentence description to a visually remote audience of one picture which is randomly selected from the set.' (*xviii*)

The audience (i.e. the examiner) then decides which picture he thinks is being described, and compares this with the instruction given to the examinee. It is genuinely productive, arguably communicative and highly reliable. How valid would you consider it?

(b) Indirect tests

The other solution to the trade-off is to stop worrying about face/content validity, take a step backwards from realistic, life-like tests and take refuge in concurrent validity. The argument goes like this: if you can show that there is a high correlation between the same students' scores on a realistic oral interview and on an indirect but more easily administered test, then you can safely say that the second test is measuring the same as the first, and can be used as a test of oral proficiency in its place. The relationship is entirely statistical; there is no place for intuition, except in subsequent attempts to justify the relationship theoretically.

An enormous amount of research has taken place, mostly in America, into constructing and using easily administered but indirect tests. For example, a lot of work has been done to promote cloze tests, both conventional and in many variations, as tests of global proficiency, including speaking and writing skills.

The new Test of English for International Communications (TOEIC) is entirely receptive; it consists of two hundred multiple-choice items, half reading comprehension and half listening comprehension. But the Educational Testing Service felt able, by means of concurrent validity correlations, to interpret the scores in terms of speaking and writing ability:

> 'The correlation between the TOEIC listening part score and the direct Language Proficiency Interview is 0.83. This high degree of correlation would seem to indicate that the TOEIC part score is a good predictor of the candidates' abilities to speak English. . . . .'

and again . . . . .

> 'The direct writing measures correlated 0.83 with the TOEIC reading part score. This high correlation suggests that the TOEIC reading score is a good indication of the examinee's ability to write in English' (*xix*)

This use of concurrent validity studies to justify the interpretation of indirect tests of productive skills has become common. What are the arguments for and against this procedure?

FOR

(i) All tests are artificial situations. The testee is under a strain to perform well, and the interviewer/marker is under pressure to make the best assessment in the short time available. Neither is acting naturally. In these terms, there is little to choose between direct and indirect tests.

(ii) Where the aim is to measure achievement rather than proficiency, indirect or semi-direct tests give the tester more control over the language generated and hence permit a more accurate determination of the testee's mastery or otherwise of the specific syllabus contents.

(iii) They are more practical and usually more reliable than direct measures.

AGAINST

(i) Intuitively, direct tests are better.

(ii) The value of the concurrent validity depends entirely on how good the criterion test is — if the direct test used to validate the indirect measure is open to question in terms of either its reliability or validity, then the concurrent validity correlation is meaningless.

(iii) Although the nature of the correlation coefficient itself forms the basis of *all* numerical reliability and validity calculations, the interpretation of correlations is far more complex (and subjective!) than the calculations themselves. Especially in the field of language testing, a person's interpretation of a set of statistics may depend entirely on the assumptions of his particular theoretical viewpoint; the statistics have no inherent meaning other than as a purely mathematical relationship between two sets of numbers.

CONCLUSION

The only possible conclusion to be drawn on the virtues and problems of different methods of assessing the productive skills is that what kind of test you use should be determined pragmatically by the purpose for which the test is to be used, the resources you have available for construction, administration and marking, and what you intuitively feel will have the highest face/content validity for testees and testers alike.

Prognostic/Predictive Tests, by definition, are not concerned with present ability but with some future criterion performance, which may itself not be particularly realistic. Therefore, whatever test most successfully predicts that performance is the best test to use — and only experimentation will reveal that.

Achievement tests are easier to set up and control using indirect or semi-direct measures. Since the syllabus itself is an artificial construct, there is no point going to great lengths to reduce the artificiality of tests of attainment of that syllabus. On the other hand, any experienced interviewer can tell countless tales of trying to elicit a particular structure from a testee who answers the question perfectly well while avoiding that structure completely. Does he get a point or doesn't he?

Proficiency tests are concerned with the testee's ability to carry on sensible and realistic communication, and this is where the argument is strongest for using direct tests of productive skills. Secondly, the question of availability of resources (time, people and money) may exert a significant influence on the choice of tests.

The last word has been reserved for a researcher who, apparently under pressure from all the concurrent validity studies giving the kiss of death to direct productive tests, felt it necessary to preface her findings on improving the reliability of oral interviews with the words:

'. . . . . it has generally been recognised that the best way to test for oral proficiency is to have a subject speak.' (*xx*)

(*i*) e.g. Lado (1961), Heaton (1975), Valette (1977), Oller (1979).
(*ii*) see Pilliner in Davies, A. (ed.) *Language Testing Symposium*, Oxford University Press.
(*iii*) Clark, J.L.D. (1979) in Briere, E.J. & Hinofotis, F.B. (1979) *Concepts in Language Testing: Some Recent Studies*, TESOL.
(*iv*) U.S. Foreign Service Institute Oral Interview.
(*v*) Businessmens' English Test & Appraisal International Language Centre, Japan (1977).
(*vi*) Ilyin, D. (1976) *Ilyin Oral Interview*, Newbury House.
(*vii*) Upshur, J.A. (no date) *Oral Communication Test*, Ann Arbor; University of Michigan.
(*viii*) Wiseman, S. (1949) *The Marking of English Compositions in Grammar School Selection*, B.J. Ed. Psych., p. 204.
(*ix*) Hartog, P. (1941) *The Marking of English Essays*, MacMillan, p. 1.
(*x*) Heaton, J.B. (1975) *Writing English Language Tests*, Longman, p. 127.
(*xi*) Hartog, op. cit., p. 17.
(*xii*) Lado (1961), p. 29.
(*xiii*) Grieve, quoted in Pilliner in Davies, op. cit.
(*xiv*) Forrest, R. (1968) 'ELT versus the Examiners' *ELT*, V. 22, No. 2, p. 121.
(*xv*) Rivers (1968), p. 305.
(*xvi*) ibid., p. 257.
(*xvii*) Heaton, op. cit., p. 135.
(*xviii*) Clark in Briere & Hinofotis, op. cit., p. 36.
(*xix*) Woodford, P.E. (1980) *The Test of English for International Communications*, paper delivered at ESU Conference, London, November 1980.
(*xx*) Mullen in Oller, J.W. & Perkins, K. (1980) *Research in Language Testing*, Newbury House.

Peter Fabian

Examinations-why tolerate their paternalism?

An examination is a formal and unnatural ritual. In theory, it sets out to gather information about a person and passes it on to interested parties. It is to all intents and purposes a dialogue between Supplier and Consumer. The *suppliers* are those who, in response to a need, create examination structures and strategies: the Examining Boards and their fellow-conspiritors (i.e. teachers, schools, publishers, course planners, educational institutions), and the meek and passive victims of their paternalistic power (i.e. parents and student candidates). The *consumers* are those who need the information: employers, selectors, Further Educational establishments, governments — and again parents and student candidates, though for different reasons.

Examinations are commonly expected to reflect attainment as well as potential in further skill development. They thrive on faith. So long as the consumers believe that an examination is a mirror of something, it can withstand the grumbles and bloody-minded 'objections in principle' that abound these days. But when examinations cease to be a communal act, in other words when some of those involved opt out, as they will and do, then examinations begin to deteriorate, to become distorted and eventually irrelevant except to those who get their living out of them, whether they be examiners or schools. In our society, obsessed as it is with qualifications and specialisation, even the worst examinations — and there are many — manage to survive long after they have ceased to be firmly rooted in the community's needs. This happens because those who have resigned their active, creative and critical participation do unfortunately continue to give their unquestioning confidence to an examination as a qualification; mostly they no longer know anything about it: how it is run, what it contains, how it is weighted, validated, what it is really for. With blind but dangerous faith they surrender their vital role to distant and increasingly isolated 'experts'. Only when they find themselves at the receiving end of inadequate applicants for a job, do they discover how dubious the syllabus must have been that led to such a qualification: then they complain that they

aren't getting the people they need. It is more tragic when the foreign employer, say, discovers no inadequacies because he has to trust the examination implicitly.

A community gets the examinations it deserves. If it fails to take an interest, to be vigilant about what the examining boards are up to, it will soon find that someone else has taken over: a vacuum is invariably filled.

Examinations — like democratic institutions — do not thrive in isolation. When the consumer and the community at large surrender to academic technicians their right and duty to be involved, they also surrender the right to check on the teaching strategies that are the direct result. They cannot then turn round and complain about 'straightjackets', or pontificate about pressures, unfair competition, the conduct of examinations and their 'remoteness' to real life. Such are the frustrated grumbles of children and they have about as much impact. Whether we like it or not, examinations are here to stay. Their rejection for the time being in revolutionary or reactionary situations — times of social upheaval — does not alter this a bit. They always come back again. No one has come up with a really workable alternative way of measuring attainment on which the selector must depend to get round pegs into round holes. Parents, by and large, accept meekly, if not exactly with reverence, the requirements of GCE. Perhaps they do not realise — or do not want to — how much their children have to sacrifice to the annual ritual, and what a huge chunk of a never-to-be-repeated educational experience is affected, even destroyed. There is a reluctance to cross swords with experts, though it is abundantly clear that experts all too often suffer from the constrictions of their own expertise. But they do often have an awesome weapon: professional jargon and impressive woolliness.

Yet that jargon is often surprisingly imprecise, even in language teaching. Take the words 'examining' and 'testing' which are so often used as if they were synonymous and interchangeable. How many people are aware that they are in fact very different in kind and have different aims?

Tests are almost entirely diagnostic; they belong in the classroom and are the teacher's most constantly used tool. They help to close gaps, clarify, prescribe individual treatment, and build confidence. You can *act* on tests. They do not shape a syllabus but draw on existing techniques with the clear-cut purpose of edging and nudging the learning process along some controlled path. In examinations we have nothing so constructive because they are final. Based on a controlled system of spot-checking, they are more superficial and global. Examinations tell us if a student has succeeded rather than why he has failed. It is often very difficult to get specific diagnostic information from examinations.

Who Improves What?

As we have learned from bitter experience, teachers, directors of studies and principals do not as a rule take an active part in engineering the structure or contents of examinations. They are content to be passive and to follow a leader. They may moan, of course, about what examinations contain and how they interfere with what they want to do, but on the whole they accept what is profered and are reluctant to interfere. If for some reason — worthy or otherwise — an examination is considered prestigious, impressively mounted, and professionally validated, that seems good enough for most of them. The American TOEFL test is universally admired in the States, not for what it does to teaching but for its technical and administrative gloss. Cambridge examinations are generally supported because 'everybody wants them'. Much of the teaching syllabus takes its lead both from them and from their numerous textbook satellites because it is convenient, not because the learning strategies they prescribe are realistic or evenly balanced.

The view that a school is the servant of a string of such examinations is deplorable. A school simply cannot opt out of its special responsibility for this link in the Learning-Teaching-Testing-Examining chain. It owes that much to its students, whose faith lies in the entire teaching-testing system. Nor can a school ignore the simple fact that examinations influence to an unacceptable and unreasonable degree what is being taught on its premises and why.

The result of this easy-going relationship, this friendly conspiracy between examining boards and schools, is that in the end examining boards are practically all-powerful. They invade the classroom and saturate the staffroom without a murmur of protest. And for all the pretence to the contrary (schools are jealous of their independent role), the indifference of schools — of consumers generally — has isolated the boards more and more. Since they are not perpetually exposed to the sort of criticism which they are bound to note or act on, that isolation extends far beyond educational establishments so that finally the boards go one way while the rest of us go another. Only when there is wholesale disenchantment amongst thousands of students does the whole problem come to light. Many British schoolchildren do not feel motivated to learn foreign languages because their courses and examinations seem remote from their real needs. The extremely costly exercise of foreign language teaching (despite gimmicks like language laboratories and the sparse contingents of 'assistants') is largely a waste of money; and this is due mostly to that friendly conspiracy between professionals.

Unworkable Progress

Until 1965, the emphasis in language teaching was on Writing and Reading, on definitive grammar even within the 'direct method', and on what in the case of the native tongue might be called 'language study and definition in retrospect'. It tended to pull in the same direction as the treatment of the native tongue. The reason why we all put up with this lop-sided prescription was that it was easier and more economical to handle. If examinations are best conducted in Writing and Reading, then the preparatory work is bound to take on the same slant. One supposes that if the driving test could be carried out by answering questions from an examination paper, driving schools would sell their cars, sack their instructors and revert to the classroom for driving instructions.

The pretence that the major part of communication was on paper, as it were, was bound to lead to the neglect of oral work. Apart from not being required for examinations, teachers were often not too hot in speaking and understanding the language they were teaching. The miserable appendages purporting to examine speaking and understanding in EFL commanded little respect. They were — and continue to be — tolerated because the school follows the leader, and the leader found it too complicated and too expensive to make the urgently needed improvements. The examining boards which enjoy the greatest respect and prestige today know full-well that their oral 'interviews' are negligible in comparison with their written sections. But instead of improving them, they simply down-grade their status in the examination. In the act, however, they also down-grade the associated learning-teaching activities in schools. Cambridge, for example, still awards only 25% of the total weighting to speaking and understanding; and that in a situation and at a time when oral skills are most urgently sought after throughout the world.

Such examples from the past protrude into the present; they illustrate the power and influence wielded by examining boards. The need, therefore, for upgrading oral/audial skills to the same level of thorough examining as written and reading skills must be painfully obvious to anyone. But so long as examining boards fail to give the lead here, all attempts to infuse systematic training will remain sporadic, localised and superficial.

There are those today — and I am one of them — who suggest that oral/audial skills are really the central and determining aspect of language acquisition and that no one should be put in a position of having to decide whether or not to 'study' a language until they are orally and audially proficient up to a point.

Fads and fashions like Programmed Learning or Skinnerian lab drilling have come and gone. Since 1965, the classroom has accepted speaking as the real goal: a spontaneous development and for once independent from examinations; but it has remained unreinforced by the disciplines of a recognisable end-objective. The effects of the shift have thus been abortive to some extent because, after all, the pressures and traditions of orthodox examination-based language teaching proved too great.

The Fourth Skill: Aurality?

In all this hullabaloo, the fourth skill — listening comprehension — was the cinderella. The spontaneous Speaking Revolution has itself down-graded it. Neither 'Threshold' nor 'Waystage' has given it much attention in depth. Few schools have done much about installing such things as Listening Libraries to counter-balance the Reading Library. While ad hoc syllabuses in speaking have been devised, the entire problem, of listening comprehension has remained largely unfertilised, unresearched, and neglected. Such aspects of listening comprehension practice as audial drilling, ear conditioning and aptitude testing, exposure to accents and dialects, intuitive comprehension and guesswork are still in their infancy. People do not talk about them: linguisticians write each other the odd paper which explains why there is still no universally accepted word to replace 'aural', which is in effect indistinguishable phonemically from 'oral' and therefore has to be mispronounced. The new word

'audial' springs from an urgent need and was introduced by the architects of the Arels Oral examinations. Mentioning this small point may look pedantic but in fact it is symptomatic of an attitude.

A Lever — Not Just an Exam

Arels Oral examinations — introduced in 1967 — are an attempt to rock the foundations of orthodox academia-bound language learning. As examinations are powerful, the attempt had to be made through them. But it should not be thought that they were introduced merely to offer yet another examination. The role of the Arels Oral is still widely misunderstood. Of course, the field was wide open for reform; oral testing had not yet progressed far, and any improvement was a purpose in itself. But it was wrong — and still is wrong — to say that these are no more than specialised 'extras' which you can decide to use or ignore. Or that in the context of English in Britain the student can pick and choose because it really does not matter which examinations he takes; it has to be bluntly stated that schools claiming to teach English in Britain should very seriously consider making these examinations their central theme. Preparation for most other examinations can be had at home; the advantages of taking them in this country are marginal. But not so with the ARELS examinations. Practical and sustained exposure to the language, which is then systematised and monitored in a school, can only be achieved in the country of the language and in the context of a multi-national student body.

The ACEs are a manifesto, a statement of practical objectives which are today indispensable. True, the examination makes additional demands on a school. An oral/audial examination cannot be textbook-bound in the way written examinations are. It can only give a lead; through its past examination scripts and tapes it can say: 'Here are samples of all the oral and audial skills we test, NOT because we find them easy or convenient to test but because you cannot perform in practice without them. Now you go and elaborate on these; draw on your own daily experience and observations in how we use the native tongue; use our past papers as models and to remind you of what must not be forgotten, and the syllabus will look after itself.' Is that asking too much? Yet, any school claiming to take advantage of English in Britain which fails to cover the Arels Oral range may actually be guilty of gently and innocently misleading its students. And that is putting it mildly.

An Oral Century

We live in an essentially oral century. The telephone has made the entire world more accessible; correspondence is becoming too expensive and inconvenient when you can ring your business partner in Sydney. International conferences are increasingly conducted in English and that means a smooth command of social English as well; if the asymetric language system is adopted in the EEC, the only languages for listening comprehension will probably be French and English. Negotiations, social contacts are both drifting fast into English, while the sophisticated hardware technology from tape recorders to video and internationalised TV is helping to shift the emphasis further away still from writing and reading. A school which ignores these trends is in danger of getting out of touch, while its brochure may be promising by vague implication what it is ill-equipped to do.

It is *not* a matter of forcing examinations down students' throats: far from it. The Arels examinations are a mere by-product designed to set off a new and systematic approach to the two neglected skills, just as the Cambridge examinations are admirably designed to initiate the 'study' of English, which points them elegantly in the ESP direction.

No more than a fraction of students coming to Britain have the slightest wish or desire to 'study' English. Twenty years as Principal have taught me this. It is a modern tragedy that they are so often encouraged to think that studying language is synonymous with acquiring communicative skills.

Pendulum of Fashion

Nor is it a question of a pendulum going this way and that. A pendulum only exists where there is uncertainty of purpose. To suggest as some do these days that 'we have gone too far in oral directions' is nonsense. In fact, we have not begun to bring oral and audial work up to the lavish levels of the other two.

There is a theory that man's ability to practise a multiplicity of language disciplines is infinite; that we are all of us capable of practising a dozen languages at least. This seems to be supported by the millions of bi- and tri-linguists who acquired their skills by accident or circumstance, not because they were gifted or in love with language. They speak these languages naturally in their multi-lingual environment, and the only inhibition that exists comes from nationalistic pressures. It is likely, therefore, that the vast majority of language learners are not students so much as people naturally receptive to the right environmental treatment.

Democracy in Examinations

Arguably the most democratic virtue of an examination concept like the Arels Oral lies in the fact that it aims truly to reflect current usage: it has to do this. Written language remains static for several decades. Oral language changes quickly. English especially adapts constantly to the ever-changing flow of influence across the English-speaking world: not by decree of ossified grammarians but by popular inclination. Usage precedes acceptance. The pedant and the linguistician may deplore this as a concession to fashion or vulgarity. But, then, pedantry is always a little ridiculous in oral language which springs from spontaneity and from the heart. Examinations must respond swiftly to these changes and if they do, then language will never be consigned to the museum.

But they will only adapt if everyone who is involved in the process of language acquisition, whatever it may be, participates in making examinations come close and stay close to the reality of the day.

W G Shephard

The Cambridge Examinations-an exercise in public relations

Examinations stultify and constrict, emasculate the new and perpetuate the old, and appeal to the lowest motives on the part of all concerned. Every teacher is sufficiently convinced of the efficiency of his methods, and every student sufficiently full of faith that the standard reached will guarantee him the ability to function in the job of his choice, for examinations not to be necessary. All this is believed, and repeatedly asserted. Yet entries for the Cambridge EFL examinations are increasing at an average rate of nearly 5% on already large numbers (80,000 plus annually since 1979) in over sixty countries. Their central position as a target and a definition of standards can be seen in any school or college brochure or publisher's catalogue. The organisers of the examinations, in Cambridge and at the 400 local centres, are in a unique position to observe day-to-day and year-to year the interplay of attitudes, assumptions and desires in the fields of teaching and testing. Some details of this experience, and particularly of a large-scale consultation with the centres just concluded, may be of interest, therefore, read in association with the discussion elsewhere of basic aims and models in testing.

The Cambridge examinations have reflected the fluctuations in views of what a relevant and effective test in a foreign language should be since extremely primitive times. The Local Examinations Syndicate was one of the first two examination boards established in Britain, based autonomously on what Victorian social and educational conservation termed 'the universities' and providing quality control of the range of schools existing before compulsory education came in. General education, geared to the needs of the world's most highly-industrialised state in respect of operatives and officials, was tested in line with contemporary notions of content and method, and had its Dickensian moments. A properly conducted local examination, leading to a Cambridge certificate, began with the ceremonial arrival by train in a given town of a solemn don in charge of a black box. A little of this aura clings even to today's vast operation, coming out in awestruck responses to suggestions or instructions, particularly where

these appear more humane and practical than august authority is expected to be.

For Cambridge, the specifically linguistic problems involved in the absorbing and regurgitating of knowledge came up early, through the expansion of activity in what are now called the ESL areas. The Cambridge School Certificate examination survived in these areas both the UK transition to the GCE in 1951 and in many cases the far-reaching political changes, and is still one of the Syndicate's major activities. A specifically EFL commitment began in 1913, with the introduction of the Certificate of Proficiency in response to the demand for a qualification for non-native-speaker teachers of English.

In 1935 this examination was first set in December as well as in June. In 1937 it was recognised by the University of Cambridge as an English qualification for matriculation purposes and by Oxford in the following year. The Lower Certificate was also introduced in response to demand in 1939. The more appropriate title of First Certificate was adopted in 1975, when both examinations appeared in a totally revised form following a long period of research and consultation.

Long-standing collaboration with the British Council was formalised in 1941 by the establishment of the Joint Committee of the Syndicate and the British Council. The Diploma of English Studies was introduced in 1945 at the request of the Council. The Executive Committee for these examinations includes representatives of a wide range of interested bodies; institutions of further education, ARELS, universities, the British Council and, when possible, visiting overseas representatives.

The early pattern for EFL testing was merely to carry over the skills thought appropriate for the first-language or second-language aspirant towards 'educated native speaker' status. The expression of proper sentiments with formal correctness and the study of literature were the main features, with translation as the revolutionary 'element of functional relevance'. The Syndicate is still sometimes involved today in consultation with education officials from countries who are applying the same axioms in their developing local examining systems. Very gradually came the move to the present system of a five-paper series of written and spoken tests, covering productive and receptive skills and as internationalised and functional as it can be made by teacher participation in syllabus design, marking and test setting.

Translation and literature remained integral parts of the syllabus until 1975, with a quasi-compulsory status not much affected by widening the range of alternatives. Translation was heavily favoured overseas because it was a softer option for candidates and teachers than literature, and the reverse applied in the polyglot British centres. Even the lower level examination had its scaled-down literature paper, essentially a composition and factual recall test still remembered favourably for its encouragement of extended reading — and its 'indoctrination value'. When a structure and usage paper, introduced in 1970 along with objective comprehension tests at this level, quickly became the most popular alternative, the way became clear to establishing a standard pattern of tests at each level. It is on record that a consultation in 1961 with a university department of applied linguistics, interested in the riches of Cambridge candidates' answer scripts as a research source, produced the first suggestions that a semi-objective, well-designed Use of English type paper should be the core of the Proficiency examination rather than one among a mixture of ESP alternatives. In a striking contrast of tempo highly revealing of the dynamism of the EFL teaching field, a further revision is now planned only five years after the introduction of the current syllabus in 1975. The inspiration for this came from a straightforward administrative need to take general opinion on the feasibility of conducting listening comprehension tests on recorded material. As well as this issue (which has proved inconclusive, in view of the teachers' equal distrust of examiners and machinery), the Syndicate's enquiry invited comments on all aspects of the standard and content of the examination. It is interesting to note some of these in the context of the historical development of the Syndicate's examinations and of discussion elsewhere in this collection of articles.

The teachers, nearly 250 of whom replied from 24 countries, have endorsed the move away from culture and background testing, and shown approval for a very large proportion of the objective and semi-objective elements introduced. The old 'guessing game' criticisms of multiple-choice batteries are now as tiny a minority as the pleas for a return of prescribed reading, with its charac-teristic teaching pattern, to an integral place in the scheme of the examination. Other minority comments argue equally pressingly backward to dictation, or forward to video. Information retrieval exercises on a variety of visual stimuli are suggested, together with criticisms of every such exercise so far set and pleas to 'keep the examinations Cambridge' and 'avoid railway timetables'. Above all, the clamour for individual paper grades instead of the present aggregate result, formerly widespread, has died down significantly. The replies give a strong impression of approval of the present syllabus and its aims, though linked with forthright comment on failure in particular question types to realise these aims fully, on the part of a sophisticated profession able to unite well-disseminated linguistic theory with comprehensive experience.

Above all, the body of expert opinion represented in our replies has made out a strong case for moving much further in the direction of functional testing, as a way of aligning the examinations with modern teaching methods and also as a way of re-defining their role internationally. The most strongly-argued method of achieving this is a substantial increase in the oral weighting of the examination. This emerges clearly out of the traditional doubts expressed about examiner reliability, timing and general administration. Recognition of it is a leading element in the detailed consideration the Syndicate now proposes to commission, with a view to a basic re-design of syllabus taking effect possibly in 1984. Oral/aural activities deserving of a place in an extended interview and listening comprehension session will be tried out, and their actual contribution to the candidate profile matched against that of the present range of tests, in order to establish which new, and which old, features most qualify. 1975–1981 experience suggests that, in spite of incidental criticisms, the picture stimulus for conversation achieves its modest aim, that of evoking something more individual and lively than 'How long have you been learning English?' between total strangers. Experience also suggests that 'reading aloud' is not basically an unclean concept, as it does reflect, when suitably non-literary, a realistic skill and does help the tempo of an interview which is, after all, a marking exercise as well as an extended role-play. Current experience has borne out, however, the criticisms of the present three-passage, examiner-read listening comprehension test, and we shall be drastically re-vamping here, greatly assisted, it is hoped, by the ability to use appropriate recorded material: material with more dialogue and general variety of text and delivery, and a good many steps nearer to the ideal of total eaves-dropping realism, probably in colour video, which will be the next demand. Only one centre put in for a 100% oral, in the ARELS manner, and no-one felt a separate examination with no oral component, (in the Oxford manner?) to be viable. In assessing a possible weighting, we were thus somewhere between 0% and 100%, with considerable pressure to go above our present 25%. The current model, now being considered by the centres and as stated already the subject of trial working, has gone for a one-third oral component, not so much for neatness in an examination for which our computer cheerfully allows 39 as a (raw) maximum oral mark along with marks scaled to one decimal place in the case of two written papers, as for a combination which can be meaningfully filled in the right proportions. To increase the openly oral element simply on demand has not seemed, over the years, necessarily the way forward, or the only way to give true and complete credit to oral-based fluency, though the day is clearly coming when Cambridge can increase the oral weighting both because it is good to help to define the teaching syllabus and because it can be done more reliably.

The recent questionnaire was a special operation, emerging as explained from particular needs. The Syndicate's contacts with the EFL teaching public, and the candidates themselves, are however constant through the year, and highly revealing of the variety of aims, emotions, misconceptions, etc. associated with EFL. By means of yearly issues of regulations and documents aimed at candidates, local secretaries, supervisors, oral and written examiners, all revised and resharpened in the light of the previous year's experience, the plain message is conveyed about the timing and cost of entries, conduct of the examinations, and issue of results. A vast amount of correspondence, telephone enquiries, questions at conferences, etc., indicate however, that much of this material is not received, not read, or not understood either through language difficulties or because what is laid down is not what is desired. Late entries, for instance, simply cannot be accepted under a computer-processed control system which apportions question and answer documents and provides statistical data for the monitoring of marking for the entire entry, yet provides also personalised documents, from timetable to final result, for each candidate. At the other end of the process, results once issued, though subject to a check when requested by teachers who feel a grading is significantly out of line, are final and related to a carefully-maintained general standard.

From teachers, the range of queries is also wide. 'What is the pass mark?' is a basic question, but a confused one. It cannot be answered in a standard way, as it is asked from an approach to testing concepts which varies according to country. Questions on the length of essays, and the relative importance of content and language, also need to be answered other than by formula to be helpful, though we have our series of general reports with illustrative extracts from candidates' work to send out. 'How many mistakes are allowed?', another 'backward' question usually related to rigid pass-mark concepts, is heard now and again, and shows little appreciation of the prominence given to communicative competence, which, as was suggested above, is much more basic.

One very productive aspect of public relations with the teachers, in terms both of the general mounting of the operation and because the only effective answers to many queries on marking standards and procedure are gained in this way, is their active involvement in our marking panels. For the present large and increasing entry, a total team of over 1,000 examiners is appointed in the year, and the vast majority of these are teachers with extensive and current specialist experience. The largest proportion of these are the oral examiners at overseas centres, some responsible only for small numbers at isolated centres working with the aid of instructions, sample recordings and occasional feedback, but a much larger number as part of an organised teaching/examining operation on a large scale. A panel of over 250 oral examiners deal with the interestingly polyglot U.K. entry, and many of these double as markers of Composition or Use of English papers. The 'hard core' of this group are the 50 or so who in addition to marking current examinations participate in the setting of future examinations across the whole range of objective and open-ended test types, written and oral/aural. These are our best allies in the public relations field, those who know that perfection in testing is not a matter of realising heart's desire once, but over and over again in a way that will satisfy the demands of security, consistency, discrimination and still not offend against a wide spectrum of methodological or ideological feeling.

In general, the Syndicate's contacts with the EFL teachers, whether as regular collaborators, or occasional enquirers or critics, indicate in a highly interesting way the current degree of acceptance of various concepts in language attainment and the teaching approaches based on them. Over a period of ten to fifteen years we have seen a swing away from the revealingly formulated cry, heard at an ARELS conference, of 'Too much objectivity!' against multiple-choice testing, and the 'Crossword puzzles!' criticisms of material in structured answer-book format. A question setter, quite eminent in course-book production circles, did once actually submit a crossword puzzle as part of a semi-objective paper, having temporarily taken his eye off mundane considerations of marking techniques and values.

The Syndicate would claim that, by and large, its good relations with the EFL teaching public are based on recognition that its role and procedures have caught the whole testing process, from reliable theory to consistent practice, somewhere near the right point of balance.

Ian Seaton

Proficiency testing for tertiary level study and training in Britain

1. Beginnings

The British Council, either directly through its own scholarship schemes, indirectly for the Overseas Development Administration training awards or as service to international bodies such as the United Nations agencies, administers overseas students from their initial selection through their study or training to their return home. A crucial part of this administration is ensuring that the English language ability of these students is such that they can fully profit from their stay in Britain. Over the past twenty years, therefore, the Council has operated language tests to provide such information for all concerned: students, teachers, the Council itself, sponsoring bodies and British institutions. Clearly, such tests operating all over the world and informing all interested parties have heavy demands placed on them. The tests have to select, diagnose and predict to enable the various people involved to take a variety of important decisions.

Some five years ago it was decided by the Council, together with other interested bodies like the Committee of Vice-Chancellors and Principals, that the tests used hitherto — the Davies English Proficiency Test Battery and the Council Subjective Test — should be changed. The reasons for this decision fall into three groupings. First was the recognition that views on what language is and how it is used had changed in the 1970s. In syllabus design and in the classroom there was more emphasis on presenting language in use and ensuring that the learning was more specific and appropriate. It was felt that the new test system should derive from the same concern, account for the communicative use of language and complement and integrate with the general shift in ELT. Second was the desire to achieve a balanced system whereby a central and controlled test system could provide a reliable and valid measure yet be flexible enough to allow for local (national) differences. The previous tests had been operated on an increasingly local basis, leading to unreliable scores which could not be consistently interpreted by all those involved in the long and often complex chain of getting the student to and from Britain

successfully. Another reason in this second grouping was the need for a stable and monitored system that could be developed on the basis of evidence, and not anecdote, with the back-up of statistical analysis and provision of parallel and improved versions. Third was the need to make the test system more transparent. Tests of the formal language system often present their information in unitary scores with cut-off levels for standards determined by norm-referenced analysis. As such, both in 'face' terms and the way the scores were arrived at, they meant little to the ELT teacher and less to the student. A transparent test system would — it was agreed — organise its shape and content, and present its results in a way easily understood by the non-specialist.

2. Requirements

The committees and working parties that met during this period soon came up with a formidable list of requirements for the new test system. It would have to deliver information on three counts. Had the student reached a minimum level of adequacy which would indicate that his/her planning to come to Britain within a year or so was reasonable? Had the student reached a level where a period of one to six months English language teaching would bring him/her to a fairly adequate level? Had the student reached this fully adequate (target) level already? The test system would therefore have to be criterion referenced or linked, testing those language skills likely to be needed for the specific purpose of studying or training in Britain. It would have to establish the various levels of adequacy in these skills validly and reliably. Its content and item types would have to have at least a beneficial backwash into the classroom and its results accurately predict the part language ability would play in the outcome of that student's actual course.

Then the test system would have to be capable of being marked locally or centrally as certain decisions would have to be made in the student's own country and certain in Britain. It would have to be a comprehensive test, and yet not so complex as to inhibit its uniform administration in some seventy countries. It would have to be a testing *service*, flexible and 'on demand', not a formal twice-a-year examination. The results would have to be presented in a way that gave a picture of the student's ability so that different levels of performance in different skills could be seen and acted on by all involved in the process.

3. Problems

With such a list of requirements, the working parties that began the work of survey, specification and design in 1976 obviously ran into problems. All involved knew they would have to account for a large number of variables that had never been adequately identified — let alone described — and that any solutions would be partial. The survey had to account for the wide range of teaching and learning practice and levels of tolerance in British institutions, and yet organise and order this variety to control the design of a 'manageable' test system. To specify the content of the test to the degree of delicacy and validity that would control the organisation of text, activity and item types required a theoretical model of language in communicative use. Previous tests inherently relied on the formal system of language — grammar, syntax, lexis, etc. to act as such a model with more or less agreed descriptive terms to label the components. There was, and is, no such commonly agreed model to describe the communicative use of language; yet without it the specifications could become too loose and unfaithful to the criterion behaviour. A six-month language course can allow the process of teaching and learning to fill in the gaps between syllabus, materials and methods; a two-hour language test claiming to be a valid and reliable measure cannot. The idealisations of theory and design can be constantly adjusted as they are exposed to the reality of practice in a course. However, how can this be done in a test that is so much more constrained and which has to remain stable for a longer period?

The next series of problems came in converting the specifications (assuming that they were agreed, appropriate and detailed) into a language test. The activities specified had no immediate item-type in the test designers' repertoire to carry them. Delicate and detailed specifications of the communicative use of language might have to be constrained into the strait-jackets of multiple-choice items to satisfy requirements of objectivity and reliability.

If one ignores the issues of validity and the detrimental effect on language learning of the discrete-point tests of language structures solely with paper and pencil, it remains a fact that such tests can be reliably scored wherever and whenever the test is given. How could a test system emphasising the communicative interaction between text and person or person and person be so 'properly' scored. The item-types would inevitably call for whole, integrative performances which would have to be subjectively assessed. And, finally, even if the transparent reporting of results was laudable, could we as yet be fully explicit about what constituted language performance at this or that level and describe it using commonly agreed terms?

4. Solutions

By 1977/78 solutions to these and other problems were coming from the teams set up by the Council and the Cambridge Syndicate. Some solutions were more 'solid' than others but all had to contribute to getting the test system operational. It was agreed that, given the size and nature of the task, however, it was essential that where a solution was clearly interim, procedures had to be set up to allow its improvement over time and actual operation. The model developed by John Munby and set out in his book *Communicative Syllabus Design* was used flexibly for both survey and specification by the six teams who investigated the language demands made on students in the academic subject areas of Physical Sciences, Life Sciences, Technology, Social Studies, and Medicine. This use of a common procedure, supplemented by the data collection, observations and intuition of the specialist teams allowed the survey/specifications to be consistently presented. Thus the inevitable variables of such a wide survey could be systematically extrapolated to enable an explicit and justifiable link to be made within and between the separate parameters. For example, the communicative event specified as 'taking part in an academic tutorial' could be broken down into component activities such as 'note-taking' and then further into groups of component language micro-skills such as 'use of cohesion devices in discourse'. At each level of specification the teams could describe significant variables affecting performance and in particular use the dimension and tolerance levels in Munby's parameter six to assign different standards of performance.

The editing team then set about the organising and condensing of these specifications into a core of EAP activities, text types, skills all with assigned levels of language realisation and performance to allow realistically the writing of the tests. Although the specifications organised the language skills in groups of mixed-mode activities, it was decided that the test system should select and organise its sub-tests around the single modes of 'reading', 'listening', 'study skills', 'writing' and 'speaking'. This re-organisation recognised that both students and teachers still think in these terms, and that such a test system could not afford to be too innovatory. Again there was a compromise on item-types. The system would need the 'anchor' that discrete-point items provide while testing the more integrated activities specified, and so three of the sub-tests are multiple-choice and the other two task-based. Although the editing produced 'common-core' skills it was decided that, particularly to make the test more acceptable in 'face' terms, there should be six modular tests with 'source booklets' (collections of texts) particular to the five specified subject areas — with an extra module for 'General Academic'.

The solution to the administrative problems set by such a large-scale system was there from the outset in the decision to run the Service jointly. The Council would provide its unique network of ELT qualified staff through its office world-wide, while the Cambridge Syndicate provided its experience and facilities in running examinations and tests in Britain and overseas. The Test Development and Research Unit at Cambridge would provide the analysis and computing services while the Council set up a Liaison Unit to combine these various resources in operating and especially validating the test system.

It was decided to report the results by presenting them as a five-point profile of language ability; the scores on each sub-test are converted to a band, or level of performance, on a scale of one to nine with each band having the appropriate description of what it means in terms of ability. This framework already has interim validity but will be refined through the 1980s to improve both its definitions of target levels and its predictions as to the average time and type of language tuition needed to reach target levels. The Council has its own unit, the English Tuition Coordinating Unit, which is now interpreting these profiles and advising students, sponsors and institutions on placement and/or pre-sessional English language tuition. This means that, although there is only one test system, it can be used to inform on the varying levels demanded on a whole range of courses.

5. Operation
After two years of pretesting, analysis and revision with large samples in Britain and overseas, the Service went into operation in 1980 in forty British Council representations and certain regional

offices in Britain. It is now available in all Council offices throughout the world for both sponsored and private students, and parallel versions of four of the sub-tests are being phased in. In countries like the Sudan it is used by ELT Institutes preparing students for study in Britain, while in Australia, the University of Melbourne has contracted to use it for its own pre-sessional and concurrent service English courses. To meet 'local' requirements where some students may already have a good English language background or may be planning only a short period of study not necessarily in Britain, one of five combinations or patterns of sub-tests can be taken, as appropriate.

The Liaison Unit, as well as monitoring the use of the Service worldwide and controlling some of the subjective assessments, plans the development of the tests on the findings of the various validation studies. These studies currently focus on basic reliability features, construct and content validity and most importantly predictive validity. The Unit also publishes occasional information on the Service together with the User Handbook (for prospective candidates) and the Specialist Handbook (for the professional ELT community). As part of the development of the Service, the Unit plans to bring into operation in 1982 a series of modular tests for the increasing number of students coming to Britain for vocational technical training. The first versions of these tests were ready for trialling in the Autumn of 1981.

6. Directions
Although it is a complex and comprehensive test system using a lot of specialist resources, all of those involved in its design, operation and validation recognise that we are at the beginning of the business of describing and measuring the communicative use of language rather than at the end — particularly so in attempting to define the role language plays in academic study, vocational training or any learning process. The English Language Testing Service more than fulfils the standard requirements of a language test, but beyond that should provide in the next ten years a systematic and stable procedure to investigate the use of language in the areas in which it operates. Validation studies such as the one recently set up with the Institute for Applied Language Studies at Edinburgh University, which will run for the next five years, will support such investigations while, of course, contributing to the improvement of the decisions that have to be taken in arranging in-Britain study or training.

Many surveys over the years have pointed out that other factors such as personality, motivation, cultural background, etc. play a crucial role in determining the outcome of study or training in Britain. It is hoped that, when research into these factors has reached a certain stage, it might be possible to extend the framework of profile reporting to build a more whole profile of a student's learning style and language ability. Such a step would fit in well with the whole development of the Service, which has been one of applying current thinking as rigorously as possible to working systems which can then be increasingly validated and improved.

Key references:

The English Language Testing Service, User Handbook, 1981; Specialist Handbook, forthcoming, The British Council.

Graded Objectives in Modern Languages, 1980. Centre for Information on Language Teaching and Research.

Testing Communicative Performance, An Interim Study, 1980, Carroll, B.J., Pergamon.

Communicative Syllabus Design, 1978, Munby, J., Cambridge University Press.

C S Ward

Progress testing:
preparation and analysis

One of the main tasks of any educational institution and its teachers is to check on the success of their courses with reference to particular students and the whole group. In the case of the individual student, there is a need to know how well he is keeping up with the programme. Should there be difficulties, he needs to be provided with a remedial programme or moved to a more appropriate course. Checking on group progress enables a check to be made on the course itself and can provide clues as to how it can be improved.

The importance of the progress test will vary from situation to situation. In the small institution, where there are close contacts between staff and students, the teacher's assessment of students will probably have much greater weight than in the large institution with many classes running at the same time or where circumstances impose a considerable number of teacher changes. In the latter case, there will be much more pressure for a common yardstick by which to judge students' progress. However, even in the small school a double check, such as provided by a progress test, will help the teacher to review his assessments and will help to indicate what areas of the course have yet to be mastered. A good progress test can also help the student to understand where his weaknesses lie and build confidence by indicating the areas he has mastered.

Many of the principles for preparing good progress tests are similar to those for preparing achievement and proficiency tests. Instructions to the students should be clear so that they have no difficulty in understanding what they have to do. Trick questions should be avoided. These are more likely to trick the better students than the poorer ones. However, in other ways, the principles will be quite different, reflecting the different purpose the test is to serve. A quotation from J.B. Heaton's *Writing English Language Tests* (Longman, 1975) will serve to summarise these differences.

'Good performances act as a means of encouraging the student, and although poor performances may act as an incentive to more work, the progress test is chiefly concerned with allowing the student to show what he has mastered. Scores on it should thus be high (provided, of course, that progress has indeed been made). Whereas in standardised achievement and proficiency tests, a wide range of performance should be indicated, the progress test should show a cluster of scores around the top of the scale.'

This difference has important consequences when preparing and analysing progress tests, and the techniques used for standardised testing are not completely applicable. This has not always been sufficiently emphasised. Some suggestions are now offered which may help produce good progress tests as defined in the above quotation.

Preparation

One of the requisites of a successful syllabus is a clear statement of aims and methods, which is also a requisite for successful testing. As the progress test should reflect the syllabus, the statement of aims and methods prepared for the syllabus will largely dictate the form the progress test will take.

Each course syllabus, except those for an absolute beginner in a particular language, will assume an ability in certain areas of the language. On the basis of this previous ability, the course will aim to develop abilities in new areas. In the progress test that follows such a course, the design and content will seek to show that the students have attained those abilities the course sought to develop. The test may include questions that involve students using the ability they were assumed to have at the beginning of the course, but it should not be central to the test. Nor should the test include anything which was not considered a necessary previous ability, and which was not covered in the course. In other words, the content of the test should be such as to result in any student who has successfully mastered the course content getting perfect or near perfect scores.

Once the content of the test is decided, the testing method will have to be decided. The types of possible questions are well described in the standard texts and need not be discussed here. The choice will again reflect the course as much as possible. We need to use the testing method that will indicate as near as possible that the student has attained the target ability. For example, it would be inappropriate to ask students who have attended a course which emphasised *reading* business letters to *write* a business letter as a test of their successful completion of the course. Similarly, it is not advisable to depend on reading comprehension tests when checking the success of a course in writing. This is true of other forms of tests, but it needs to be emphasised even more for progress tests for two reasons. First, students will tend to concentrate on areas of the course in which they know they will be tested. Second, the correlations between different types of tests that are quoted as a basis for accepting standardised tests, the contents of which do not completely sample the language, may be suspect when progress tests are considered. A course which emphasises a particular skill over others will probably cause such correlations to be reduced substantially. However, in large institutions or where time is limited, a machine markable test may well be used as a common yardstick. If combined with, for example, a teacher's assessment (hopefully, a continuous assessment) of areas not covered by the test, and if the students are aware of this, then the disadvantages of using such tests may be avoided while the benefits are retained.

Finally, the questions need to be written and the test booklet designed. These should always be at least double-checked. A second opinion will often see flaws that the first writer cannot see until they are pointed out. The following questions need to be asked:

1. Are the instructions clear?
2. Is the content restricted to course content or what might be reasonably thought as a prerequisite to the course?
3. Are the tasks in open-ended questions sufficiently defined? Are they likely to provide the student with an opportunity to show his ability in the relevant skills?
4. In multiple-choice questions, is there clearly one and only one correct answer?
5. Is the marking scheme for the subjectively marked tests clear? Does it emphasise areas stressed in the course or does it emphasise other areas? For example, if the course has stressed communication over accuracy, does the marking reflect this?

Analysis

Once the test has been used, there is unfortunately a tendency for it to be put to one side. An analysis of the test results can be done fairly rapidly and can provide a lot of information about the students and the course. It can also lead to the development of better progress tests for the future. Often the use of a test can show flaws in it which cannot be seen by inspection.

One of the first steps in the analysis of the test would be to seek wherever possible the opinions of the teachers and students who have used it. If the progress test has been a good one, most students will be satisfied that their results reflect their progress. They will have seen the course reflected in the test and will see that any loss of marks was due to their lack of mastery of sections of the course. General discontent with any section of the test will usually indicate that either the instructions were not clear, or the question was obscure, or the students did not feel that particular area was covered in the course. Teachers who have seen the test in operation will also often be able to give helpful advice.

A fairly easy second step is to look at the distribution of marks. As stated in the earlier quotation, the scores on a progress test should be clustered towards the top end of the scale. If they are not, something has gone wrong. There are several possibilities: for example, either the course design needs to be revised or the test needs to be redesigned, or both.

The final step is to investigate each question. It is useful to keep each question on a separate card with a summary showing when it was used and how successful it was. This may take a little time at first, but will save time later when making up new tests. It will also provide any successor to the present administrator a useful guide when he, in turn, has to prepare progress tests.

In the case of subjectively marked papers, the best check available is to find out how well students did on each question. The scoring scheme will depend a lot on the type of question, and thus hard-and-fast rules are difficult to give. However, generally the question scores should reflect our expectation of the total score, i.e. the students should generally do well. If they have not performed well, a discussion among those involved in teaching the course and preparing the test should help to identify the problem, and either lead to a revision of the question or a revision of the course.

In the case of multiple-choice tests, an item-analysis can be done. This process is clearly described in several texts. It need not take a long time and the information that can be obtained can be very useful. However, the item analysis as described in most texts was developed for checking items in standardised testing and, if used in the same way for progress tests, will not help to develop the type of test that is needed. Thus, the process will be described in detail and any differences of approach needed will be pointed out.

The first step is to rank all the answer booklets according to the total score obtained by the students. The lower and upper 27% are then set aside for analysis. There should be an equal number of papers in the upper and lower piles. Thus, if there were 100 candidates, there should be 27 papers in each pile. Sometimes there are several papers with the same score at the point where we have to make the cut-off. For example, there might be in this group of 100, 24 students with scores above 88% and 5 students with scores of 88%. We would then choose 3 of those 5 randomly for the upper group. We could then prepare a table for each item as follows:

	A*	B	C	D	NA	TOTAL
U	24	0	0	3	0	27
L	22	3	0	1	1	27

Key:	A to D	– Choices in the item.
	*	– Indicates correct answer.
	NA	– No Answer.
	U	– Upper group.
	L	– Lower group.

From these tables we can easily work out two statistics: the difficulty coefficient (= simply the proportion of people who got the item right) and the discrimination coefficient (= a figure which tells us how well the item discriminates between the upper and lower groups). The formulae are:

$$Difficulty\ coefficient = \frac{UR + LR}{2n}$$

$$Discrimination\ coefficient = \frac{UR - LR}{n}$$

Key: UR – The number of people in the upper group who got the item right

LR – The number of people in the lower group who got the item right

n – The number of people in one of the groups.

(N.B. There is a more complicated and accurate formula for discrimination for those contemplating using a computer.)

For the above example, difficulty is $\frac{24 + 22}{2 \times 27} = \frac{46}{54} = 0.85$ (to 2 decimal places). In standardised testing, this would generally be regarded as too easy as an attempt is made to spread the scores along the whole scale. Items that all or nearly all candidates get right or wrong do not help to do this, and so items with difficulties over 0.80 and less than 0.20 are rejected from such tests. However, in progress tests we expect the items to represent areas the students have mastered, and thus easy items should be retained. On the other hand, items which the majority of students get wrong are suspect. Any item that has a difficulty of less than 0.50 may have been badly written or may test an area not covered sufficiently in the course. In the first case it should be rejected. In the second, either the course should be revised or the item rejected.

The discrimination coefficient for the above example would be $\frac{24 - 22}{27} = \frac{2}{27} = 0.07$ (to 2 decimal places). Again, in standardised testing, such a low discrimination would be regarded as unsatisfactory. Low discrimination indicates low agreement with the other items in the test. As much agreement as possible is needed between items to help spread the candidates along the whole scale. Thus, generally items with a discrimination of less than 0.20 are rejected for such tests. However, in progress testing this is not such an important consideration. Indeed, it can be proved mathematically that, when using the formulae given here, an item with a difficulty over 0.90 cannot have a discrimination above 0.20, and a question that students all get right can only have a discrimination of 0.00. Furthermore, it is unlikely that an item will have the maximum discrimination theoretically possible. Thus, few items with difficulties over 0.80 will have discriminations over 0.20. In a progress test, as we wish to retain these 'easy' items, we will have to accept lower discrimination coefficients.

However, the discrimination coefficient remains useful. In progress testing, as in standardised testing, we use the total score rather than the score on individual questions, and so it is still important that particular items do not work against the rest of the test. If more of the lower group get the answer right than the upper group, then the discrimination coefficient will be negative and the item will be working against the rest of the test. Such an item should be rejected or revised. A suggested approach is to reject all items with a negative discrimination coefficient, and reject items which have both a difficulty coefficient of less than 0.80 and a discrimination coefficient of less than 0.20. In this way we would build a test that could identify the weaker students while continuing to have a cluster of scores towards the top of the scale.

Following this, we should check the distractors in the table previously given. The distractors are the incorrect choices (B, C and D in the example given). Distractor B would be acceptable in any test as more of the lower group chose it, and it thus helps to identify the lower group. Distractor D would be rejected or revised as more of the upper group chose it, and it thus confuses the issue. Distractor C is more difficult. It would be rejected in standardised testing as it does not help to discriminate and is thus just a waste of candidates' reading time. However, in progress testing, if it represents a common error which students completing the course have mastered, it is worth keeping. If, on inspection, however, it proves to be a distractor that is so ridiculous that no-one would think of choosing it, it is worth revising.

The final stage is to go through all the reject items and try to establish why they are rejects.

Many will simply be badly written, but others will provide keys to where the course is failing to cover certain areas or failing to clear up misunderstandings (or where it is actually creating misunderstandings). Where it is decided that the course is at fault, the course can be revised and the item retained.

The above discussion has been an attempt to suggest an approach to the preparation and analysis of progress tests that emphasises such tests as a tool for the educational administrator or teacher, a tool to encourage students and a tool to help check and revise the course so that the aims of the course will be realistic aims for both students and teachers. Such tests cannot function properly if they are divorced from those who are responsible for the courses. Used wisely, progress tests will lead to better designed courses. Progress tests are an adjunct to courses. They should never supersede them.

John Rogers

Tennis plays Nha – or how to humanise tests

Nha (/na/) was a Vietnamese member in one of the courses for the English Language Institute's Diploma in the Teaching of English as a Second Language. He spent a lot of his time on the tennis court. (He doesn't mind my saying this.) So when it was time to give a test on a linguistics unit, it seemed the sensible thing to change the wording of Chomsky's 'Golf plays John', and make the question of immediate, personal relevance to Nha and his colleagues. In addition, of course, the course members all smiled – some laughed – when they came to this question. I cannot prove that more people got the question right because of the personal reference, but at least the examinees relaxed a little and the name Nha triggered a memory.

This same technique worked equally well in usually feared Grammar tests. In a so-called *Simple* Sentence Patterns test, course members were asked to classify sentences into SV/SVC/SVO/SVOO/ *There* VS types. Previous tests included the usual dreary classroom/grammar book sentences. We found that sentences referring to individual course members and to some of the things that they had actually said in conversation or in tutorials caused considerable visual and audible amusement in the examination room. Apparently, these personal references evoked vivid, and therefore easily retrievable, memories of grammatical explanations. This may have been an interesting example of the involvement of both the right and left hemispheres, and their distinctive thinking or heuristic styles, in problem-solving. Here are a few examples. (The situation is explained before each test item.)

a. We had some discussion about 'taste' and a class joke developed about a certain course member's exploits.
   'Lim has tasted the night life of Wellington.'
b. During a very cold spell, there were complaints about the beds in a university hostel.
   'The university hostel wouldn't give them any Dutch wives.'
c. One course member had been described as a very romantic person.
   'Ibrahim gave her his heart, body and soul.'

Other test sentences were intended to remind course members about what had been said in class and about possible traps in the test itself, which then taught as well as tested. Other items were about the test itself. All of these helped to take some of the tension out of the test and to provide some interest and amusement in the actual test paper. Again, it would be difficult to say whether the results were better or not. Perhaps it was more important that items like the following provided some primary motivation. They might even have stimulated course members to try something similar in their own testing programmes back home.

For the classifying sentences test, we usually had a sentence like this as an example:

    S   V   O
    We/like/tests.

In the re-test, the example becomes:

    S   V   O
    We/(still) like/tests.

Scattered through the tests were sentences like the following:

    'I hope you avoid the traps.'
    'There aren't any problem sentences.'
    'So far this test doesn't seem very difficult.'
    'I think number 15 was a trap.'
    'There won't be any more·*there* sentences.'
    20. I can't remember the difference between SV and SVC sentences.
    21. This is an SVC sentence.
    22. This isn't.

The last item in a test: 'I've begun to enjoy classifying sentences.'
Another final item: 'I don't want to make up another test!'
The conclusion to another test:

    'You will lose a mark for every minimum requirement mistake you make.'
    S   V   C
    You/have been/warned! (or SV, if we haven't brainwashed you)
    S V   O
    I/hope/you all pass.
    S V   C

(This/is/) THE END

At the beginning of our Study Skills course we usually administer the following 'Can You Follow Directions?' test. First of all we show the following flashcards:

> *Can you follow instructions?*

> *Are you sure?*

> *Let's find out.*

> *Let's have a test!*

> *You have only 5 minutes*

Then we give the following test:

Can you follow directions?

(*Speak to no one. Do not look at anyone else's paper. Work very quickly. You have only five minutes.*)

1. Read everything before doing anything.
2. Put your name in the upper right-hand corner of this paper.
3. Circle in the word *name* in sentence two.
4. Draw five small squares in the upper left-hand corner of this paper.
5. Put an 'X' in each square.
6. Sign your name under the title.
7. After the title write, 'Yes, yes, yes'.
8. Put a circle around each word in sentence number seven.
9. Put an 'X' in the lower left-hand corner of this paper.
10. Draw a triangle around the 'X' that you have just written.
11. On the back of this paper multiply 703 by 9805.
12. Draw a rectangle around the word 'paper' in sentence number four.
13. Call out your first name when you get to this point in the test.
14. If you think you have followed directions properly up to this point, call out, 'Yes, I have'.
15. On the back of this paper, add 8950 and 9850.
16. Put a circle around your answer. Put a square around the circle.
17. Count out loud in your normal speaking voice backwards from ten to one.
18. Now that you have finished reading everything carefully, do only sentences one and two.

(Have you been caught out by this test? The editor of this collection of articles was caught out not many years ago!)

At the end of the Study Skills course, we gave a Reading Comprehension Test. The opening instructions contained the following:

> 'Can you follow directions? Do you remember the test on following directions? Read all the instructions first. This isn't a test of reading speed. But there is a time limit for the whole test.'

Course members smiled, heads nodded and they started work on page 1. It was a long test, intentionally, and when they got to the end, on page 7, they found this final instruction, which, of course, the majority had NOT read before they started on page 1:

> 'Now that you have read all the instructions and now that you know how to follow directions, do NOT answer questions 1, 5 or 9 on *The Stolen Letter* (question 1).
> If you have already circled a, b, c or d for questions 1, 5 and 9, you will lose three marks. Do NOT ask for another question paper. Do NOT rub out any marks you have made.'

John Rogers

Quite a number of course members laughed out loud at this point, shook their heads and sat back resignedly. I think they then learnt how to follow directions. Tests CAN teach. And they CAN be made more human.

Finally, an example of a cloze test that provided a great deal of amusement and entertainment. It proved to be challenging, but the inherent human interest of the material kept motivation high. And there was an instant clamour for the 'official' answers. The follow-up 'correction' lesson was as entertaining as the original test. I offer it to anyone who would like to try it out. Making and taking tests CAN be fun. Enjoy yourself!

All you need is love . . . . . and oxygen

It's anyone's guess how many people have joined the Mile High Club by making love in an aeroplane.

'I mean, who knows what _____ do under blankets when the _____ are turned out,' said an Qantas spokesman.

'Love-making in _____ is certainly possible and our _____ and hostesses have caught people _____ the act.

'If the couple _____ quite happy and not disturbing _____ else, we'd probably say a _____ 'Sorry, sir' and leave them _____ it. We've nothing in the _____ on it.

'Incidentally,' the spokesman _____, 'it's time the terminology of _____ Mile High Club was updated — _____ planes fly at six miles high.'

One report caused Mr. Norman Tebbitt, _____ British MP and former B.O.A.C. _____, to state that passengers should _____ instructed to 'fasten your chastity _____ before boarding.'

'It is not _____ for people to become bored _____ over-emotional on long flights. After _____, what else is there to _____ ? '

Airlines offering in-flight movies are _____ help to impatient lovers who _____ keep their hands off each _____. 'You'd be surprised what goes _____ when we darken the cabin,' _____ stewardess said.

'If there's a _____ scene in the movie it _____ starts someone off. People get _____ on long daylight routes.'

As _____ the dangers in six-mile- _____ love-making, medically speaking, there _____ none, says Professor John Llewellyn-Jones, _____ professor of obstetrics and gynaecology _____ Sydney University. 'It is O.K. _____ a pressurised aircraft, in the _____ of the deepest mine, or _____ the Moon, with the right _____,' he explained. 'All you _____ need is oxygen.

'The only _____ against it are the reactions _____ the other passengers. I suppose _____ would either object or be _____.'

(Adapted from an article by John Sims, in *The Dominion*, Wellington, New Zealand. August 21st, 1971)

Pauline M Rea

An alternative approach to testing grammatical competence

The main thrust in language education today is on the teaching of language as communication. The terms 'notional', 'functional', and 'communicative' are labels frequently used to describe current approaches to language teaching. In other words, the central concern is with the imparting of language skills which will enable our language learners to engage more efficiently and effectively in natural communicative activities. Whereas at one time the focal point has been on the learning of the grammatical patterns of the target language, it is now claimed that the primary aim of most language programmes is to develop learners' 'communicative competence' in the target repertoire. There is, however, a tendency to interpret a 'communicative' syllabus as one which is organised primarily around a set of notional and functional categories, which subordinates the role of grammar as an organising principle to second place. This sharp swing in the pendulum in the orientation of language teaching programmes will certainly lead to considerable difficulties in the foreseeable future if the imbalance in present trends is not redressed.

There are two inherent dangers with some interpretations of the communicative approach to language teaching that are relevant to the present discussion. The first is associated with the rather unsystematic and unprincipled presentation of the grammatical system of the target language. Indeed Wilkins (1976), as one of the major contributors to discussions on the notional syllabus, stresses the importance of the acquisition of the grammatical system of a given language (p. 66). The second, related problem stems from the emphasis which many communicative courses give to the acquisition of socialising skills during the early stages of the language learning process. The likely outcome from both these factors is the emergence of groups of learners whose language proficiency, at best, demonstrates an adequate degree of fluency at a basic level of communicative interaction, but whose knowledge of the underlying target language system is grossly inadequate. Cummins (1979) has found that basic interpersonal skills may be acquired fairly rapidly whereas literacy-related language proficiency, involving a wider breadth of vocabulary and more sophisticated manipulation of language structures, takes a longer time to develop. One can therefore anticipate difficulties when second language learners try to operate at a higher level of understanding and communication in the language but find they are unable to do so because of an inadequate formal linguistic generating mechanism.

When we say that someone 'knows a language', we mean that this person has acquired certain abilities. These include the ability to produce grammatically acceptable sentences in the target language, together with an ability to use these correct forms appropriately, as the occasion demands. It is essential, therefore, that both these aspects of communicative competence are taught, and that the importance attached to the teaching of the social functions of language should not obscure the crucial role of the grammatical system to the successful communication of ideas and intentions. It follows from this that the shift in emphasis in language teaching programmes has neither eliminated nor even reduced the need for teachers to assess their students' grasp of structural items of the target language. The requirement to assess grammatical competence is as necessary today as it ever was. However, the different views that we now hold of language, in particular the role of grammar in terms of its function within a semantic and pragmatic framework, do have implications for the way in which grammar will be assessed. The rest of this paper will examine the changes in the approach to test syllabus specification, the method, and the format of tests which are a direct result of the current trends in language teaching and learning programmes.

Hitherto, specifications for a grammar test have been in the form of an inventory of different aspects of English grammar. Such a list would include determiners, such as 'some', 'any', 'much', 'little', and verb forms such as 'present', 'imperative', 'modals'. Typically, test items to match these areas would be similar to those shown in Table 1 on the next page.

43

DETERMINERS	IMPERATIVE
We haven't got _____ tomatoes at all.	Q. '_____ a cigarette?' A. 'No thanks'
1. some 2. much 3. a few 4. any	1. Do you have 2. Have 3. You have 4. Have you got
PRESENT	MODALS
He often _____ in the bath.	Q. 'Must I do it this evening?' A. 'No, you _____'
1. is singing 2. to sing 3. sings 4. singing	1. mustn't 2. can't 3. needn't 4. won't

Table 1: Conventional multiple-choice grammar test items

Implicit in a specification of this kind is the belief that 'knowing a language' corresponds to accurate manipulation of the grammatical forms of that language, and test items have tended to re-inforce this belief by tapping knowledge of the (formal) rules of the language (usage). Thus, they account for only one of the two abilities involved in communicative competence. Given current concerns to develop communicative language proficiency, any test specification and any test item should

sample test specification which relates grammatical and communicative categories appears in Table 2 below.

The second inadequacy of existing grammar tests is associated with the method of testing used. The isolated sentences format illustrated in Table 1 is not valid within a communicative framework. It is obvious that a test method which excludes the total context in which the grammatical and lexical system of a language operates cannot claim to be

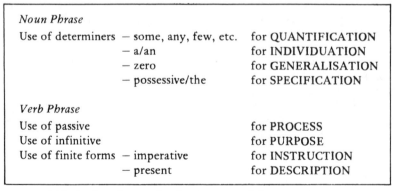

Table 2: Sample communicative test syllabus

also account for the second ability mentioned earlier, namely the appropriacy of language use. In other words, they should not only list and assess the grammatical functions basic to communicative activities but they should also assess the *application* of the rules of language use. A

assessing the appropriate use of grammatical structures and forms. There are three related difficulties which make the conventional methods incompatible within the framework of the communicative competence model.

1. Inadequate coverage and imbalanced item distribution

This is the inevitable consequence of testing grammar and vocabulary in discrete sentences. For example, there are some items which are very easy to test, such as adverb-tense collocation (perfect + just/never/ever/ + neg + yet/etc.) and question tags (isn't it/shouldn't we/didn't we/etc.). Thus we often find an overabundance of items of this type included in grammar tests. On the other hand, there are aspects which are more difficult to assess and are thus often excluded. These include areas such as the passive verb group, and modals.

2. Limited demands on students from test items themselves

Normally, test items are heavily weighted towards recognition-type tasks and rarely assess control (i.e. production) of appropriate linguistic forms. Students may be very used to manipulating grammatical forms transforming, for example, the present into the past tense, or direct into indirect speech. There is therefore a strong possibility that students produce correct answers on traditional multiple-choice test formats mechanically, and do not demonstrate an ability to use the appropriate forms as the 'real-life' context requires.

3. Lack of authenticity

The isolated sentences format is inadequate as there are a large number of items which cannot be adequately assessed without reference to the context in which they are normally found. In actual communication, an appropriate linguistic form is selected for its function within a text, which also involves decisions about the overall function of the text itself.

Having outlined above the invalidity of the uncontextualised method of assessing grammatical competence, the final part of this paper will make suggestions for an alternative approach. The test items which are illustrated below are designed as a more valid means of testing grammar. Additionally, these items permit the objective marking of questions, thus satisfying the criterion of practicability which is an overriding consideration when large numbers of students are involved in the testing process. The discussion is restricted to the communicative function area of 'description', and takes as a specific example the case of students whose purpose for learning English is to facilitate further studies through the medium of English.

Given this information, we are in a position to determine that these students may be required to use English, for example, to describe and relate historical facts, to explain physical and scientific phenomena, to compare and contrast events and processes, or to report on an experiment. Because a test syllabus is expected to reflect the relationship between linguistic forms and communicative functions, we become aware of the importance of, for example, finite verb forms — present and past — for 'description', of the passive verb group for 'process', the perfect verb group for 'development', use of the modal group for 'ability', 'possibility', and so on. The next step, once the syllabus has been detailed, is to select topics which are relevant to the purposes for which your students are learning the language. These should be sufficiently general and accessible to all students, and varied so as not to favour any particular group. After this comes the selection of a suitable text, followed by the design of the test items.

Example 1 is an illustration of the way in which, within the context of a report on an experiment, the ability to produce grammatically correct and appropriate verb forms can be evaluated. It mainly involves the selection between contrasting verb forms of the past active and the past passive.

Example 1

READ THROUGH the instructions for this experiment.

Pour the water into a displacement vessel until it overflows through the pipe into a measuring jar. Read the level of the water surface in the measuring jar. Then lower the solid into the vessel until it is completely covered by the water. . . . . .

YOUR REPORT

Water 1) . . . . . into a displacement vessel until it 2) . . . . . through the pipe into the measuring jar. The level of the water in the measuring jar 3) . . . . . . Then the solid 4) . . . . . into the vessel until it 5) . . . . . by the water. . . . . .

Pauline M Rea

Contextualisation of items in this manner allows the realistic assessment of mastery of individual grammatical elements appropriate to, in this case, the genre of sub-technical report writing. Depending on the level of students, we may require the recognition or the (cued or uncued) production of the required answer. Two further examples, assessing grammatical competence at the level of the verb phrase, focus on appropriate tense selection and accurate verb formation within the communicative category of description are given below. In the first example, students are expected to insert the most suitable word for each space in the passage.

Example 2

PORTUGUESE EXPLORATION OF THE COAST OF WEST AFRICA

The progress of Portuguese exploration 6) . . . . . slow at first. Madeira 7) . . . . . discovered in 1418, but Portuguese ships 8) . . . . . not pass Cape Bajador until 1434. The Azores 9) . . . . . first sighted in 1439 and in 1441 Cape Blanco 10) . . . . . rounded, and Arguin just to the south of it 11) . . . . . discovered in 1443 by Dias and Tristao. . . . . .

The next illustrates a cued production task in which the verbs to be used are provided in brackets. Students are instructed to put these verbs into the most suitable form so that they make sense within the passage.

Example 3

KINGDOMS OF THE SAVANNA

In the savanna region of the Congo there 12) (rise) . . . . . powerful kingdoms and empires whose beginnings can be 13) (trace) . . . . . to as far back as the fifteenth century. Long before this time, the area must have 14) (inhabit) . . . . . by Bantu speaking people who by A.D. 800 15) (live) . . . . . in organised agricultural communities, and in some places had already 16) (make) . . . . . long distance trade contacts with the east coast. Little was 17) (know) . . . . . about the history of these states until Jan Varsina's book, *Kingdoms of the Savanna*, 18) (appear) . . . . . in 1966. The account which 19) (follow) . . . . . 20) (come) . . . . . mainly from this book.

The final example is designed to assess word order, especially at the level of the adverb phrase (with adverbs used as modifiers), and noun phrase (adjective placement). Students are instructed that one word has been omitted from each line and that this word is listed on the right of each line. They have to choose the place (a, b, or c) where the word should be written.

Example 4

	OMITTED WORDS
(20) A^a/ walk through any^b/ of the^c/ slums	city
(21) in the^a/ world^b/ is an^c/ experience.	unpleasant
(22) They^a/ start just^b/ outside the city^c/	frequently
(23) limits.^{a}/ As^b/ they are^c/ peopled by	usually

---

The final, important stage in the process is the check on the adequacy of our testing procedures. We may do this by asking four main questions:

1. What is the test measuring?   CONTENT
2. How does it match the test syllabus?   COVERAGE
3. Which approach is used?   METHOD
4. Which item-types are used?   FORMAT

Our answers to these questions should indicate the extent of the test's potential validity, which operates at three distinct levels:

i) syllabus   — content and coverage

ii) method   — contextualised language samples from the appropriate field of discourse

iii) format — authentic item-types defined by their function within the selected text.

It should be clear from the preceeding examples that the selection and production of the required structure and grammatical form is determined not only on grounds of grammatical correctness, but also by its overall function within a given communicative area. These examples have been used to illustrate one alternative way in which linguistic competence may be evaluated within a communicative model of language teaching, learning, and testing. Although emphasis in the test items reflects a concern for appraising a large number of grammatical items, the method and format used is such that individuals are required to integrate their linguistic knowledge in a way similar to the normal use of language for communicative purposes. Users of language have to produce grammatical elements which are determined by their overall function within sequences of linguistic events; this requires an analysis and synthesis of these events rather than what might be simply the result of fortuitous recall of an item, or a mechanical response.

References

Cummins, J., 'Psychological Assessment of Immigrant Children: Logic or Intuition?', in *Journal of Multilingual and Multicultural Development*, Vol. 1, No. 2, 1980, pp. 97–111.

Halliday, M.A.K., 'Language Structure and Language Function', in *New Horizons in Linguistics*, Lyons, J. (Ed.), Penguin Books, 1970, pp. 140–65.

Leech, G & Svartvik, J., *A Communicative Grammar of English*, Longman, 1975.

Wilkins, D.A., *Notional Syllabuses*, Oxford University Press, 1976.

S F Whitaker

Dictation as a testing device

No doubt there are fashions in testing procedures, as there are in clothing and cars. Dictation, essay, précis, and transformation exercises are 'out', like mini-skirts and spats, but multiple choice and Cloze are 'in'. Yet rational currents are discernible: a search for economy, simplicity, speed on the one hand, and for validity, or something approaching natural language use, on the other. If a case is to be made for the use of dictation for testing purposes (and also for teaching purposes), we must consider in turn (1) the language skills that are involved, and therefore (2) the system of scoring results so as to measure these skills; (3) the sorts of texts which might be chosen, and (4) the practical procedure of dictating: speed of delivery, length of utterance (or frequency of pauses, the length of pauses, the number of repetitions (if any).

Reasons for unpopularity of dictation

(*i*) Dictation does not lend itself to mechanized scoring. A vital feature of it is that it allows scope for the learner's processing of aural input, and this processing yields a remarkable variety of products. Only the use of a standardized typewriter, or of an electronic word-processor, might permit mechanical scoring of the individual student's output — if he is a competent typist!

(*ii*) Dictation does not have an obvious face-validity, since not many normal language-users spend time writing down what they hear read out to them. It may also be out of fashion if it is regarded as a purely 'passive' skill, in which only the oral source, whether man or machine, is active, and dominant. It has a relish of another age, when classic tasks (like producing a précis, one-third of the original length) were meekly performed by students, and duly inflicted, by those who became teachers, on the next generation.

The flexibility of dictation

But when we consider the various possible treatments of a dictation (from noting a telephone message down correctly, through taking down a letter in shorthand, or writing minutes, to reproducing faithfully each graphic feature of a text which is already perfectly written down), and when we reflect upon the language competence required to process a stream of speech at natural speed, and to transform it into the conventional written record, we must see that dictation has more relevance to measuring linguistic ability than is generally recognized. Add to this theorizing the remarkably close correlation found in practice between results on tests in dictation and those on the best alternative tests devised, and we cannot ignore its claims. (See the work referred to in Oller, 1979, and in Carroll, B., 1980.) In order to use dictation to advantage, we must decide what it is we want to test, and then try to conduct the task, and score the results, in such a way that we give credit where we consider it is due. This clearly does not mean unthinkingly dictating in such a way, at such a speed, and with so many repetitions, that no student feels stretched or unsure, and then scoring only according to success in spelling, including punctuation — unless we have decided that that is all we want to test.

The language skills involved

The major skill, in taking dictation, is aural comprehension (with all that involves). The writing down of the text provides evidence of that comprehension. Filling in charts, tables of figures, completing diagrams, in accordance with dictated instructions, are non-verbal alternatives which may have their value. Since we rightly emphasize realism and naturalism in language learning designed to promote communicative ability, we can select texts, and contexts, in which messages are delivered orally, and typically in monologue (*one*-way communication, because in a test, at least, a class of students cannot all be given a chance to put individual questions).

Aural comprehension involves a much deeper level of processing sounds than is generally realised by the competent speaker. A parrot, even a cliff-face, may repeat a stream of speech — with some sort of neuro-muscular 'processing' in the case of the bird. But to identify units of meaning, in that stream of sound, calls upon powers of analysis, matching, recognition, and synthesis, of a high order. It is well known how misunderstandings between native speakers can arise through wrongly 'perceiving' one sound, or misinterpreting a homophone, with the re-casting of the whole utterance which that entails. Most examples are significant only in the circumstances in which they occur, and become trivial if quoted, but some have become classics. (Sadly my cross-*eyed bear*; Send *three-and* four*pence*; She left him with three hun*dred* children.) We need only look at the efforts of students attempting a suitably difficult dictation to see how fundamentally *constructive* their processing of aural data is: words that they know, or that seem plausible, will be written — because they have been 'heard' — instead of the original. (See examples by H.V. George, in Oller & Richards, 1973; and in Oller, 1979, pp. 276–285.) 'A *brought* taste in music', instead of 'a *broad* taste' (phonologically explicable, and 'heard' by an Armenian as well as by a Chinese); 'settlements', for 'sentiments' (U.S. pronunciation); the production of one preposition when another was dictated: *of* instead of *for, for* instead of *with, of* instead of *on* or *at*. We remember that these prepositions will be in their weak phonetic forms, and all these errors demonstrate the operation of a 'transitional competence', of a 'grammar of expectancy'. Even the words are not 'given' (as Lado alleged): they have to be inferred or constructed through linguistic ability, from various kinds of evidence arising from aural stimuli.

Further study and analysis of students' performance will demonstrate even more forcefully how the taking of dictation calls on an 'integrative' language competence, which combines elements of phonetic discrimination, availability of vocabulary, understanding of structure at the phrase, clause, sentence levels and above, together with overall textual comprehension. It is true that it involves a large number of different language features: this makes it difficult to offer specific remediation for errors committed, but it is precisely what gives dictations, even more than Cloze tests, their pragmatic validity, as approximating to natural language use.

Recognising the relevance of dictation

A number of practical decisions will have to be taken, once the principle has been agreed. But it is the conviction of its validity which will govern these decisions. It is also important that this conviction should be shared by the students carrying out the task. They must accept that the task of grasping the full content of (for example) an announcement, a broadcast, while difficult, is a desirable skill, and that it must be practised when it is difficult rather than when it offers no challenge. It is of a nature which must exclude any individual plea for external assistance when it is being trained, and of course when it is being tested. (I.e. Face the challenge with your own resources, instead of asking to have 'the answer' handed to you.) In that respect, it is individualised instruction,

focusing on the learner. Without the necessary rigour in its presentation, dictation would be useless, and students' acceptance of this rigour must be obtained, or they may feel frustrated, and fail to cooperate — to their own disadvantage.

Alternative texts

The more plausible and realistic the context for dictation, the easier this acceptance should be. What is plausible and realistic will depend on the learner's situation, his interests, his imagination. (A little make-believe is often appropriate and enjoyed.) Recorded information and announcements offer possible material, as do songs if one is anxious to get the words down. There is a built-in incentive. Ringing travel enquiries might yield something that would be written down like this (if time allowed):

'To get to Birmingham by 23.00, you should take the 19.37 from Grantham, arriving at Peterborough at 20.03, and change at Peterborough, departing at 20.23, and arriving at Birmingham at 22.52.'

This involves 'comprehending': (a) *times* (given in time-table form, probably), (b) *key verbs* (get, take, change, depart), and (c) *place-names*, a special area of lexis, helped by the possession of as much geographical knowledge and previous experience of characteristic English place-names as possible.

Of course this, like much information 'dictated' in this way, would normally be taken down in note form. Notes imply intelligibility to the writer, and may be in his own code; but he must be able to reconstruct the message from the notes, and it is not unrealistic to suppose that he might write it so that it would be intelligible to someone else. The minimum written version might then be: *To get to Birmingham by 23.00 take the* (Note that 'train' is understood from this use of the definite article with a time) *19.37 from Grantham, arrive* (or *arriving*) *Peterborough 20.03, change Peterborough, depart(ing) 20.23, arrive Birmingham 22.52.* In assessing and scoring such a dictation, one might decide that there are 18 essential bits of information to be intelligibly recorded in writing, and these have been underlined. It is not the spelling (eg of Peterborough) that is the criterion, but the recognizability of each bit of essential information in the written version. This may sometimes require some discretion (and the spelling of some place-names is unguessable), but the criterion is a relevant one.

Writing down a 'telephone' description of lost property would provide another plausible task, in which the criterion of success would be the number of specific bits of information.

E.g. 'It is a small, black, plastic bag, with a metal clasp, gold-plated, and my initials, DJB, in small silver letters on one side. There is a narrow strap for holding it, which has become rather worn and frayed in the middle . . . . .'

Students might enjoy getting a good story written down accurately, so that they could later memorize and re-tell it. Here notes would not suffice: fully articulated sentences would be required. But though spelling is certainly not unimportant, it would not have enough significance, in relation to the task, to justify spelling errors being scored on the same basis as others. (Oller, 1979, p. 281, showed that performance in spelling did not correlate at all with overall proficiency.) A text that is to be dictated, like one used for Cloze procedure, should be worthy of the attention it will receive, either because it fits well enough the lowly purpose or level it serves — at an elementary or intermediate stage — or because it is satisfyingly worded and expresses some memorable thought — at a suitably advanced stage. It should be well written.

Length of sections between pauses
It may be agreed without argument that dictation should be at a speed close to 'normal', with longer pauses for writing, rather than at an unnaturally slow speed, with words separated, and shorter pauses. For a standardized examination, a tape will be provided, or precise instructions given regarding timing and repetition. The teacher working on his own will be guided by experience and reflection. While it is obvious that *sense-groups* must form the basis for deciding where pauses should be made in the dictation, the border-line cannot always be clear-cut. In fact, noun phrases are likely to be cut off from verb phrases, head-words from defining relative clauses, and verbs from their complements. Some texts will have to be rejected as unsuitable for intelligible division into suitable short portions for dictation at a given level. Texts will always need to be carefully prepared, and pauses studied and marked, with particular attention to intonation, respecting the natural tunes of speech-that-has-been-exploded, rather than adopting the 'listing' intonation. During practice it may be better to err towards dictating *longer* bursts, stretching the short term memory span, thus providing enough data for successful processing, rather than uttering short fragments that need to be re-interpreted as the co-text is added. This may well

justify the repetition of each burst, but once only, in order not to approach the frustration threshold too closely. Readers may like to experiment with the division and delivery of a short narrative extract, from William Trevor:

> 'Without in any way sounding boastful, Edwin told her of episodes in his childhood, of risks taken at school. Once he'd dismantled the elderly music master's bed, (*rising or falling intonation?*) causing it to collapse when the music master later lay down on it. He'd removed the carburettor from some other master's car, he'd stolen an egg-beater from an ironmonger's shop. All of them were dares, and by the end of his schooldays he had acquired the reputation of being fearless: there was nothing, people said, he wouldn't do.'

The dictation of punctuation
There is no clear reason why a text, spoken at something like the normal speed and in something like the normal manner, should solemnly include the announcement of 'comma', 'speech marks', 'full stop'. These are not part of the spoken language, which has another signalling system. If knowledge of certain conventions of the written system is being tested at the same time, that knowledge can be displayed better by the student supplying the punctuation he judges necessary, as in straight composition, rather than by his showing that he recognizes the words 'full stop', and succeeding in making a dot on the line. In this way the learner will be actively producing even more for himself, in the act of taking dictation. Scoring will again require the exercising of a little discretion.

Conclusion
Inevitably, there are some difficulties in the preparation, execution and scoring of a dictation, but these are not as great as the difficulties, and expense, of compiling really satisfactory multiple-choice tests. Even more important, the validity of dictations, when it has been measured rigorously, appears to be much higher. (Oller, 1979, p. 267.) 'Dictation and closely related procedures probably work well precisely because they are members of the class of language processing tasks that faithfully reflect what people do when they use language for communicative purposes in real life contexts.' It is not suggested that dictation should be adopted as a predetermined package, but approached and developed according to a pragmatic view of language teaching.

Summary of suggestions

i. Reflect upon the validity of dictation for yourself, so that you can use it in a way that exploits its useful features.

ii. Convince students of its value, through the relevance of your procedure and the satisfaction and enlightenment that reasonable success at it can bring.

iii. Select and prepare your text judiciously; present it strictly in line with principles agreed upon. Each occasion is a real linguistic encounter, even though only 'one-way', in the oral-aural mode.

iv. Score the performance in a way that is consonant with your priorities in teaching.

References

Carroll, Brendan, *Testing Communicative Performance*, Pergamon, 1980, p. 99.
Oller, J.W., *Language Tests at School*, Longman, 1979.
Oller, J.W. & Richards, J.C. (Eds.), *Focus on the Learner: pragmatic perspectives for the language teacher*, Rowley, 1973.

Penny Frantzis

Listening comprehension

Listening to and understanding spoken English involves the student in a range of skills: for example, the ability to identify individual words from a blur of speech, recognizing the significance of stress, intonation and syntactic patterns, and retaining what is heard long enough for the message to be understood in its entirety. Along with these skills is the ability to anticipate or predict what is likely to be heard in a given situation, using clues drawn from the cultural context in which the speech is heard and from the observation of such features as the speaker's facial expression, speed or loudness of voice.

Comparing examples of students' transcriptions of spoken discourse in the form of a news broadcast from a tape with the original text, one finds some indications of the complexity of the listening task.

ject 'studio commentator' or on the verb form itself, such a lapse being at variance with this particular student's usual grammatical performance.

What seems to be restricting the students' accurate decoding of the message is their limited experience of the range of phonological realizations that words or strings of words can possess. Furthermore, this limitation seems to override any semantic or syntactic knowledge the student could usefully bring to bear on the listening comprehension process, and is characterized by the common complaint that the English the overseas student hears in Britain in no way corresponds to the English he has been exposed to in his own country.

The following description is of an attempt to tackle this problem. The primary consideration was to make the student aware that full and explicit articulation of each word is not a feature

Original text	Student transcription
1. as a result of	as result of
2. planning a holiday	planning holiday
3. in favour of granting	in favour granting
4. due to land in this country	due to London this country
5. the studio commentator read the rest, giving rise to	and studio come into the reverence giving rise to/the studio commentator never rest giving rise to
6. to wear their own clothes	weather and clothes

In transcribing, any visual clues are absent, the acoustic signal is paramount and the listener's internalized knowledge of syntactic, semantic and phonological rules are what he must refer to in order to decode the message on the tape. Although in the first three fragments above, the students' comprehension is not in question, what is surprising is that the students were aware of the use of articles and familiar with such strings as 'in favour of', and 'as a result of', yet they failed to use this knowledge to modify what they heard, whereas the native speaker would automatically have cued in the missing words. Similarly, in example 5, the listener codes 'rest' as a verb but fails to provide any compatible number marker either on the sub-

of normal speech and thence to enable him to identify words from the blur of elided, assimilated, stressed and unstressed vowels and consonants that make up the acoustic signal he receives.

At the same time, however, it was recognized that close attention to spoken discourse at the phoneme level results in the loss of overall comprehension of the text. A combination of exercises, tasks or tests had therefore to be devised to ensure that predictive skills were encouraged, overall comprehension was not lost and that phoneme discrimination was developed — in other words that the students' awareness of the phonological potentiality of the language was extended.

The material chosen for presentation at a weekly

one-hour session was a two-minute news bulletin from Radio 4, recorded the day before the class to allow time for a transcription and preparation of exercises to be made. The language of a news bulletin is, of course, distinct from the spontaneous spoken discourse of conversation in that the language heard is being read from a prepared text and is thus devoid of such verbal redundancies as hesitation, re-phrasings and false starts. Furthermore, as the maximum amount of news has to be condensed into a given time, the information content of a news bulletin is extremely high, the choice of syntactic structure is correspondingly economic, delivery is rapid and the articulation is not always explicit. To counter objections that this is a very restricted diet of spoken discourse, it should be mentioned that tapes of conversations, interviews and lectures are presented for study in other classes. The rationale behind the choice of a news bulletin, however, was based on several factors. Firstly, it was felt that its content was of general interest and relevance to the student, informing him of the current issues in Britain and providing him with topics and the necessary structure and vocabulary to initiate or join in English conversation outside the classroom. It appears also that the ability to understand news broadcasts can serve to combat feelings of loneliness; one student remarked that he spent a great deal of time studying in his room, with the radio providing background music, and had very little contact with the 'outside world'. Subsequently having attended the class, he actively listens to the news coverage instead of allowing a stream of sound to wash over him and feels much less isolated from the community in general.

Secondly, given the repetitive nature of news bulletins in Britain, i.e. strikes, earthquakes, hijacks, riots and the Financial Times Share Index, lexical items as well as structural features are frequently recycled in slightly altered contexts, allowing the student the opportunity to consolidate his previous learning. Reinforcement of the material presented is, of course, also available outside the class in the form of newspaper articles, TV and radio news coverage.

Moreover, unlike spontaneous discourse, in a news bulletin there are no changes of register or significant differences in the accents of the news readers and thus a measure of continuity can be guaranteed each week. These constant factors have the advantage of enabling both teacher and student to become more clearly aware of the progress made from week to week, thus quickly generating confidence in listening to radio broadcasts. At the same time, however, two of the problematic features of spontaneous discourse are still very much in evidence in the material chosen: rapid delivery and incomplete articulation.

The presentation of the material falls into three sections. The first section deals with overall comprehension. The two-minute news bulletin is played and the students are instructed to identify the number of news items (usually between six and seven items). After students' answers have been compared and a consensus has been reached, the tape is played again. This involves a writing task: jotting down keywords or notes to identify the gist of each news item. Students then pool their information in pairs or in groups, and are invited to give the main content of each item, thus eventually arriving at a general outline.

An alternative presentation involving reading can be used for testing purposes. Students are given a sheet containing a list of ten possible headlines and asked to pick out those they expect to be included in the news bulletin before it is actually heard. While listening to the tape, they are instructed to number the headlines in the order in which they occur.

During the next re-play, the tape is stopped at intervals to allow more precise questioning and to identify any vocabulary problems. Names of people or places unlikely to be known are written on the blackboard or on a handout, and any cultural information crucial to general understanding is provided either by the teacher or students. Throughout this stage, it has frequently been observed that students in their replies to questions do not use the vocabulary of the actual news bulletin but provide a synonym, the inference being that the word heard (although understood) may not yet be in their active vocabulary: e.g. 'strike' is used instead of 'industrial action' or 'stoppage'; 'wind' instead of 'gales'; 'snowstorms' instead of 'blizzards', etc.

A technique which can be used at the more detailed questioning stage is a series of oral statements constructed so as not to include sections from the text, requiring 'true or false' judgements. Students reply by saying or writing T or F to each statement. Written replies can be checked by means of self-monitoring, pair work or group work.

The amount of material listened to before the tape is stopped and questions are asked can vary in length depending on the density of the information carried. During a whole course on listening comprehension it is noticeable how students' auditory memory develops and retains increasingly more information. Even when the material has not been totally understood, the student's echoic memory (i.e. of the sound signal) is frequently long enough to enable him to arrive at the sense of the stream of sound, especially if prompted by a searching question. This whole section could be presented in the form of a series of short multiple-choice questions, but this, as I will amplify later, is

more suited to a self-study mode in the language laboratory than to a class presentation.

The second stage of the presentation dealing with phonemic discrimination more obviously involves testing techniques. Students are given a sheet containing gap-filling tasks.

Text A

Every fifth word has been omitted in the text below. Listen to the item and fill in the gap.

The Civil Service campaign . . . support of wage increase . . . . brought two of Scotland's . . . . . airports to a complete . . . .
Air traffic controllers at . . . . and Edinburgh walked out . . . . . . after 7 o'clock this . . . .
and they're not expected . . resume work until this . . . .

Transcription

The Civil Service campaign [in] support of wage increase [has] brought two of Scotland's [major] airports to a complete [standstill.]
Air traffic controllers at [Prestwick] and Edinburgh walked out [shortly] after 7 o'clock this [morning] and they're not expected [to] resume work until this [afternoon.]

Text B

Listen to the news item and fill in the gaps in the transcript below. Each dash represents one letter.

The employers' organisation --- --- says the recession -- ----- deepening but -- ---
--------- report -- ---- there are some signs ---- -- -- levelling out. The report predicts - ------- small decline ------ --- next 4 months and cautions ------- undue optimism.
The report ---- that encouraging signs ------
--- distract attention ---- --- ---- that manufacturing output is ---- 12% ----- its 1975 level.

Transcription

The employers' organisation [the CBI] says the recession [is still] deepening but [in its] [quarterly] report [it says] there are some signs [that it is] levelling out. The report predicts [a further] small decline [during the] next 4 months and cautions [against] undue optimism.
The report [says] that encouraging signs [should] [not] distract attention [from the fact] that manufacturing output is [over] 12% [below] its 1975 level.

Text C

Words have been missed out from the transcript below. Indicate with a '/' where the words should be and write in the margin the words you hear. The number in brackets indicates how many words are missing in each line.

Many in Lincolnshire and Oxfordshire are without   (2)
electricity after the blizzards, and supplies may be   (3)
restored until tomorrow. Extra teams have brought   (4)
in from as far as Cumbria to help restore power to   (1)
three homes in Lincolnshire and people in Oxfordshire.(4)

Transcription

Many [people] in Lincolnshire and Oxfordshire are [still] without electricity after the [weekend] blizzards, and [full] supplies may [not] be restored until [late] tomorrow. Extra teams **of** [engineers] have [been] brought in from as far [afield] as Cumbria to help restore power to three [thousand] homes in Lincolnshire and [about two thousand] people in Oxfordshire.

Text D

Complete the following gaps with numbers after listening to the news item.

All . . . . were arrested . . . years ago and are accused of handing out . . . . . . rifles, . . . artillery pieces and more than . . . . rounds of ammunition to their militia.

Transcription

All 4 were arrested 10 years ago and are accused of handing out 74,000 rifles, 300 artillery pieces and more than 10,000,000 rounds of ammunition to their militia.

The first exercise (*Text A*) is a cloze exercise and generally causes few problems after the first comprehension section has been dealt with. However, it is a useful indicator of inaccurate comprehension and alerts the teacher to the problem. An alternative exercise might be such as described by H. Templeton (*ELTJ XXXI*, 4, 1977) in 'A new technique for measuring listening comprehension' – a cloze exercise specially designed for listening, where no reading is involved and where the sound is bleeped out of the text at given intervals.

Text B enables the teacher to concentrate on words or strings of words which in their unstressed or elided forms are likely to cause problems of discrimination for the student. The tape should be played in small sections and repeated as often as necessary, allowing the student time to read the text and write in the words.

Similarly, *Text C* allows the teacher to remove from the text such grammatical features as articles, prepositions, and weak verb forms, which require acute phonological discrimination and syntactical awareness. By systematically drawing attention to these forms in this way, the teacher can discover the problem areas of the students and can also sensitize the students to these difficulties.

Text D concentrates on the understanding of numbers, a special skill which can be developed separately by a similar gap-filling exercise with recorded time-tables, the Financial Times Index or even football results. Interesting intonation patterns can also be observed in the latter, and students have fun predicting draws, wins or losses depending on the intonation of the broadcaster!

The final section of the presentation involves the student being given a full transcription of the news bulletin. This time the text is followed while listening to the tape. Exercises requiring students to mark in tone unit boundaries, stressed words and stressed syllables, and to check for contrastive stress are of great help in developing listening ability. The significance of the position of the stress in the following sentence, for example, falling on a word usually unstressed needs an explanation:

'It's understood that Mrs. Thatcher WILL now make a statement in the House of Commons about her talks with President Reagan.'

WILL is clearly being contrasted with WILL NOT, although no explicit reference is made to a change of mind.

During the course of the lesson, the student will hear the entire news bulletin five or six times, for the most part concentrating on different listening skills each time, the phonological properties of the language having been explored at the same time as the meaning of the text has been unravelled and sound and syntactic patterns have been registered. This material can, of course, be used on a self-access basis in the language laboratory. The selecting and ordering of a list of headlines, a set of multiple-choice questions and true/false statements would cover the initial comprehension stage. Testing and developing phoneme discrimination would be covered in the second section with gap-filling exercises as illustrated for some of the news items. These tests could all be checked by the student himself against a full transcription.

The transcription exercise, a sophisticated form of dictation where the sounds, however, are not distorted by segmenting, is particularly useful for the teacher and the student in diagnosing problem areas and also in making the teacher aware of the complexity of the listening task the student is confronted with. E.g. The phrase 'in and out of' was transcribed as 'in doubt of' by a number of students, so reduced was the 'and' acoustically that a strong conviction about the meaning of the text was required for the student not to believe his own ears!

One final comment about this particular self-access format. I have used it for some time as a listening comprehension progress test administered to a group of students at the beginning of their general language course and at the end of the course. The first test is not administered until the students have become familiar with all the types of test during two or three class sessions, and the final test results correlate well with the teacher's subjective impression of the students' progress and with their performance in general language proficiency tests. Furthermore, the student is immediately made aware of his progress by the degree of ease with which he feels he has understood the news broadcast.

Keith Morrow

Testing spoken language

There is general agreement among language teachers that testing students' command of the spoken language is one of the most important aspects of an overall evaluation of their language performance; at the same time, it is widely recognised that most public or institutional examinations, if they have an oral component at all, often attach far less weight to it than they do to written papers. And, furthermore, most teachers, if they wish to devise their own informal oral tests, find the job an extremely daunting one. So we have a situation of generally recognised need and pitifully inadequate supply. Why should this be?

The first and most obvious answer is that testing command of the spoken language in any systematic or realistic way is extremely difficult. Some of the reasons why it is so difficult are discussed in the next section, but there is another reason which it is worth mentioning briefly. In many countries, the educational system as a whole values the written word above the spoken. The study of literature has prestige, while the ability to use the language for everyday communication, especially in speaking, is less acceptable as proof of academic or intellectual worth. Interestingly enough, many language teachers now see their job very much in communicative terms, so there is often a mis-match between the requirements of official examinations and the sort of language which teachers want to teach. There are many casualties in this battle, but the most likely sufferer is the spoken language.

SOME PROBLEMS

But what are the problems which a teacher wishing to devise some end-of-term or end-of-course oral tests is going to face?

1 Oral testing is very time-consuming. If you have 30 pupils in your class and you want to spend even 5 minutes with each one, it will take at *least* 2½ hours, and probably a lot longer. Furthermore, it is 2½ hours when you must be there at the same time as the pupils, whereas a written paper can be marked in your spare time. An additional problem is relativities. If you devote only 5 minutes to an oral test, and say 1 hour to a written test, it is clear which the pupils will perceive as being more important, even though this may be the exact opposite of what you intend.

2 It is very difficult to get the pupils to say anything interesting. I don't mean, of course, that we should expect pupils to entertain us with witty anecdotes or brilliant conversation, but for a pupil's spoken language to be 'interesting' for testing purposes, he/she must be able to do a number of things.

   a. He must have the chance to show that he can *use* the language for a variety of purposes. These will include both the language of 'reporting' (e.g. describing, narrating) and the language of 'doing' (e.g. apologising, warning).

   b. He must have the chance to show that he can take part in a spontaneous conversation, responding appropriately to what is said to him by another speaker and making relevant contributions.

   c. He must have the chance to show how he can perform linguistically in a variety of situations, adopting different roles and talking about different topics.

Needless to say, it is difficult to devise testing procedures that meet even one of these criteria, let alone all three.

3 Assessing what the pupils actually say is very difficult. What sort of scale can we use? How reliably can we indicate one pupil's performance compared to that of another? How reliably can we indicate a pupil's performance now compared to the same pupil's performance six months ago?

SOME SUGGESTIONS

These are suggestions rather than solutions, because I don't want to claim that they answer all the problems. But they might encourage experimentation.

1 Tasks

My plea is that all evaluation of spoken language should be based on a task or activity which the pupil performs through using the language. Furthermore, the task should as far as possible be one which the pupil might recognise as being the sort of thing that real people in the real world really do. So, for example, the traditional oral test where pupils are asked to read aloud a passage in the foreign language and then answer a series of questions on it would not meet this criterion of 'reality'. Exactly what sort of task you ask your pupils to perform will depend very largely on the syllabus they have been following, but if they are familiar with role-play exercises, these are an obvious possibility. Of course, even role-plays are not 'real', but the classroom can never re-create all aspects of the world outside. The question is whether it is worth incorporating as much as we can, and for me there is no doubt about the answer.

2 Groupwork

Setting tasks to groups of students for evaluation purposes may have at least two important advantages. Firstly, it may help with the problems of time outlined above, in that a number of students can be evaluated simultaneously. Equally importantly in terms of time, it will allow tasks to be set which will take long enough to complete for the pupil to feel that what is being done is significant and worthwhile. A second advantage is that taking part in a group task gives the pupil the chance to use language in some of the ways described above, i.e. spontaneous conversation involving a variety of functions.

3 Assessment

The most important pre-requisite here is that the teacher has to have a clear idea of what is being looked for in a particular test at a particular time. A number of criteria have been suggested for evaluating spoken language, but not all of these may be equally relevant to all pupils at all times, and of course there may be other criteria which particular situations may demand. As a point of departure, though, it may be useful to think in these terms:

ACCURACY: What level of accuracy in grammatical and pronunciation terms are you looking for? Is less than total accuracy acceptable at a given time?

APPROPRIACY: Are you looking for a simple or sophisticated degree of relationship between the forms of the language used by the pupils and that particular message they wish to convey. For example, does it matter in a given test if a pupil who does not understand what is said by another says:

'Repeat' or 'Please repeat' or 'Could you repeat that please'?

FLUENCY: How do you equate a pupil who says very little, all of which is totally correct, with one who contributes well to the task but whose language may have some mistakes. Clearly, there is no point in being totally accurate if you never say anything: equally clearly, we do not want to encourage the idea that anything goes.

Finding the right balance between these aspects of production is an extremely difficult and controversial area, and it may well be that different things should be stressed at different times in the learning process. However, the main advantage of using labels like these as a basis of evaluation is that you can describe the type of language production you are looking for in terms of what the pupil can do. It might be interesting to look at a concrete example of a specification in these terms based on the Royal Society of Arts 'Examination in the Communicative Use of English as a Foreign Language', basic level. (i)

ACCURACY: Pronunciation may be heavily influenced by native language but should be generally intelligible. No confusing errors of grammar or vocabulary.

APPROPRIACY: Use of language broadly appropriate to what the speaker means to say, though no subtlety should be expected. The intention of the speaker is generally clear.

FLUENCY: The speaker may often have to search for a way to say what he wants to say. Contributions may be limited to one or two simple utterances.

Scoring can be on a scale of 1–5. Performance which is of the level specified scores 3, while 4–5 and 1–2 are awarded for performance above or below the criteria.

This is a specification designed for a particular examination at a particular level, and it is clearly not applicable to every classroom. But the important point to note is that performance which is clearly not perfect in absolute terms is defined as being acceptable at the particular time.

Using criteria of this sort, and describing what is expected from pupils in these terms, provides a framework which can be used by teachers in many different situations.

(i) Further details of this examination can be obtained from Miss H. Orchard, RSA, 18 Adam Street, London WC2N 6EZ.

Robert K Johnson

Questioning some assumptions about cloze testing

Cloze testing is used in this paper to provide a familiar point of focus for questions which are applicable to language testing as a whole; not because cloze tests are poor tests — on the contrary, they have been shown to be more effective than most — nor because they are more vulnerable than other tests to the kinds of questions asked.

'Objectivity' and the Statistical Validity of Cloze Tests

There are a number of myths quite widely held about cloze testing, which have arisen perhaps out of wish-fulfilment rather than the literature itself, and are based on the false premise that cloze is 'an automatically valid procedure which results in universally valid tests of language and reading' (Alderson, 1979: 220).

Those who adhere to this belief in its strongest form stress the 'objectivity' of cloze procedures. At some point, the words 'statistically valid' or worse 'proved statistically' are likely to be used as the ultimate knock-down argument. This position, named by Strauch 'quantificationism', and by Polanyi 'objectivism' (House, 1977: 14/15), results from the desire to find objective procedures which will relieve the investigator of any responsibility for the results. Given the pressure that is placed upon those who set tests and examinations, this is an understandable aim, but the conclusion that cloze procedures fulfil this requirement cannot be sustained (1) because the claims regarding the objectivity and automatic validity of cloze tests are largely false, and (2) because statistics are data and not arguments, and valid conclusions can only be reached by processes of argument. (Statistics provide a basis for argument.) The first point has been demonstrated by research findings and can be amply supported by appeal to common sense; the second is taken up in the later sections of this paper.

Alderson (1979) focuses upon three factors which are critically important for claims that effective cloze tests can be constructed by objective procedures which are independent of the intuitions and judgements of the person constructing the test, and give results which are valid and reliable.

The three factors are: (1) choice of text, (2) the scoring procedure, and (3) the deletion rate.

Alderson's findings are that 'individual cloze tests vary greatly as measures of EFL proficiency . . . . . changing the deletion frequency of the test produces a different test, which appears to measure different abilities, unpredictably. Similarly, changing the text used, results in a different measure of EFL proficiency . . . . . (and) changes in scoring procedures also result in different validities of the cloze test, but the best validity correlations are achieved by the semantically acceptable procedure.' (Ibid., p. 225)

Alderson concludes: 'Testers should above all be aware that changing the deletion rate, or the scoring procedure, or using a different text may well result in a radically different test, not giving them the measure that they expect.' (Ibid., p. 226)

Other investigators have of course obtained different results, e.g., Stubbs and Tucker (1974), replicating correlations obtained by Oller and others, showed significant positive correlations between exact and contextually appropriate responses (r = 0.97; p < 0.01). However, there is no necessary conflict between the results obtained by Stubbs and Tucker and Alderson, which suggest the eminently reasonable conclusion that the effect of changes in deletion rate will vary, depending upon the characteristics of text and subject. These and related factors are discussed further below. It may be worthwhile at this point to make two further points about statistical data and the conclusions that can be based upon them. Firstly, a statistically significant difference is not necessarily an important difference and an important difference may not be statistically significant (Carver, 1978); secondly, tests which are statistically identical in relation to a particular population may yield very different outcomes when used with a different population (Farhady, 1979).

The Selection of Cloze Texts

Having dealt with the question of automatic validity, there remains the question of objective procedures. Cloze tests do not satisfy the basic prerequisites for a claim to objectivity, and seem typical of that class of instrument discussed by House which has 'replicable procedures', but is 'infected by biases and hence . . . . . qualitively subjective' (House, 1977: 41).

To quote from Moser and Kalton, bias arises when

(1) the selection is consciously or unconsciously influenced by human choice
(2) the sampling frame which serves as the basis for selection does not cover the population adequately, completely or accurately (Moser and Kalton, 1971)

'To ensure true randomness, the method of selection must be independent of human judgement.' (Ibid., p. 82)

Consider at least some of the major acts of human choice based on judgements which go into the selection of a suitable cloze text for a particular group of language learners:

(a) intellectual content,
(b) cultural content,
(c) linguistic difficulty,
(d) register,
(e) level of formality, and
(f) idiosyncracies of style, e.g., lists of items and a high proportion of idioms, proper names, and numbers.

Consider too the adequacy of a cloze passage, usually 250–300 words in length, as a sample. Clearly, it does not cover the population (everything ever written in the English language?) adequately, completely or accurately, and any attempt to do so would be ludicrous because of its insensitivity to the requirements of the testers and the purposes and abilities of the learners.

Given that these requirements regarding the selection of a suitable passage are met through processes of rational argument, intuition, and common sense by people with the necessary knowledge and experience to support their judgements, a number of conclusions seem likely to follow, e.g. that the results from a cloze test based on a carefully selected passage would correlate less highly and discriminate less well. It also seems likely that, given a highly selected passage, variation of the deletion rate might not affect the results to a statistically significant degree, while this would be less likely if a passage were selected at random.

I would argue then that the high levels of correlation achieved in a number of studies involving cloze tests may be regarded as resulting from, and providing supporting evidence of, the reliability and validity of the judgement of the person who selected or prepared the texts rather as evidence bearing upon cloze procedures *per se*.

It should be clear from the above that the exercise of judgement in the selection of passages necessarily causes cloze tests to be 'infected by bias', and it is eminently sensible and desirable that this should be so. Subjectivity in the form of the legitimate exercise of informed judgement is not and should not be regarded as harmful. To quote House once again:

> The evaluator must be seen as caring, as interested. as responsive to the relevant arguments. He must be impartial rather than simply objective. (House, 1977: 46)

Deletion Rate

Most studies which have focused upon deletion rate have shown that there is a high level of correlation in the results achieved if the rate is every fifth word or above, and that going beyond every fourteenth word is uneconomical and unnecessary.

It is not valid to conclude from these studies that it makes no difference whether every fifth, seventh, ninth etc., word is deleted, and evidence exists that deletion rate does make a difference in some cases (see Alderson above). A more valid and obvious conclusion would seem to be that two very similar cloze passages, tested with identical populations, will give very similar results. As a corollary we might note that changing the gapping procedure for a passage may provide two tests which are practically identical, and that this has been shown to be the case in a number of studies, though not in all.

There is nothing magical about a randomizing process for gapping a cloze passage. Given the subjectivity of the judgements that normally contribute to the selection of the passage there can be no subsequent claim to objectivity. Alderson offers a revealing analogy, and draws what seems to me to be the appropriate conclusion:

> The (deletion rate) procedure is in fact merely a technique for producing tests, like any other technique, for example the multiple-choice technique, and is not an automatically valid procedure. Each test produced by the technique needs to be validated in its own right and modified accordingly. (Alderson, 1979: 226)

We are all accustomed to the notion of a bad multiple-choice item, yet the notion of a 'bad' item in a cloze test seems alien. It should not be. Each gap is an item and capable of being validated in the same way that other items are validated.

1. *Rational justification.* It seems to test the kind of thing we think should be tested; which ideally

would require a theoretical framework including a theory of language, of reading (or listening), of the relationship between reading and cloze, and a full statement of the learners' aims.

The fact that we do not have such a theoretical framework at present does not mean that we should abandon rational justification, which as has been stated, is the basis for the selection of the passage in the first place. There are theoretical models available and these can and should be used. There are also insights based on experience which can be brought to bear.

2. *Statistical justification.* Does this item adequately discriminate amongst the subjects in relation to their known abilities and/or in relation to their abilities as shown in the overall test results? If not, then the item should be changed.

Let us consider a specific example. The passage selected contains the following sentences:

A. Inspector McTavish mused upon the inadequacy of the clues. On the first day, (*John*) was interviewed by a (*person*) introduced to him as (*Smith*). On the second day (*his*) body was recovered from the river. Inspector McTavish sighed and turned his mind to more promising areas of investigation. (No further mention is made of 'John' or a 'person' named 'Smith'.)

Anyone trying to fill the gaps indicated would certainly sympathise with Inspector McTavish over the lack of clues. It would hardly be necessary to pre-test in order to be certain that the deleted items would fail to discriminate, even though the passage as a whole may work well. Various satisfactory solutions might be proposed, but retaining such items on the grounds that they were arrived at objectively is not one of them. Alderson suggests that the principle of randomness might be abandoned in favour of the rational selection of deletions, based on a theory of the nature of language and language processing (Alderson, 1979: 226).

Exact and Acceptable Items as Gap-fillers
Selection of the cloze passage and of cloze items has already been identified as an aspect of cloze testing in which judgement should be exercised and decisions defended by reasoned argument. These same arguments apply to methods of scoring, and will be taken further in the next section of the paper, which deals with the influence of historical factors on attitudes to random versus non-random deletion and exact items versus acceptable items as gap-fillers.

Before looking at these factors in some detail, it may be desirable to clarify the situation with regard to claims that exact scoring solves the problem of marker subjectivity. If the examiner is in a situation where the markers cannot be trusted or adequately supervised, exact scoring is a useful expedient, no more and no less. The subjectivity of judgement has simply been transferred from the marker, who is in a position to know what he is doing and why he is doing it, to the author, who, unless the passage was specially prepared, had no idea that his work would be used in this way.

The Historical Provenance of Cloze Tests

From Readability to Reader-Ability
The cloze procedure was developed, as is well known, as a test of the readability of a particular text in relation to a particular population of readers. The assumptions underlying the use of the procedure for this purpose were given clearly by Taylor in 1953, and though the behaviourist model of language on which his approach was based is no longer generally accepted, the basic premise

> (that) a cloze score appears to be a measure of the aggregate influences of all factors which interact to affect the degree of correspondence between the language patterns of transmitter and receiver (Taylor, 1953: 432)

has not been challenged and is not challenged here.

It is important, however, to emphasize that as a measure of readability, there was and could be no suggestion of a value judgement, only of the degree of match between texts and readers. Random deletion and exact replacement are in this context, to use Taylor's words, 'not only defensible but rationally inescapable'. No judgement was implied regarding the writer or the reader, and any question as to whether a non-exact replacement was acceptable or not must be irrelevant. The point of focus is the text, and acceptance of a non-exact replacement involves accepting a different text.

One of the great advantages of cloze procedure as a readability measure is that it takes some account of such factors as literary genius and idiolectal eccentricity. To give one example, the passage Taylor used from *Finnegan's Wake* gained a low readability score. To provide an equally extreme counter example, the writings of a semi-literate speaker of West African pidgin would also receive a low readability score. Both use the English language in highly unpredictable ways. There the comparison ends. Above all, no judgement can be made or is required as to whether non-exact replacements are in some sense worse than, or better than, the original.

Once the focus changes from the passage to the reader, the purpose from establishing degrees of compatability of text and reader to determining absolute levels of attainment by the reader, and conclusions from value free to value loaded, then the premises underlying the use of cloze procedures must be re-examined very closely indeed in order to justify their continued use. In particular the wording of the passage is no longer unchallengeable. There is no reason for example why a non-exact replacement should not be 'better' in some sense, e.g., more precise, more expressive, less ambiguous, etc., than the original. Similarly, the rationale for random deletion is no longer obvious once the purpose is the comparison of readers and not of passages. The justification for cloze procedures which provide a means for comparing passages becomes irrelevant.

There are a number of problems relating to the shift from readability to reader ability where the reader is a native speaker of the language, e.g., variations of dialect, idiolect, control of the 'elaborated' variety, etc., but these are not considered here, and can be implied from the arguments regarding the next change in the function of cloze: from the assessment of native speaker reading ability to the assessment of second language speaker reading ability.

From Native Speaker to Second Language Speaker Evaluation

The use of procedures with second language speakers which were considered appropriate for testing the language skills of native speakers involves a number of assumptions. The first assumption that has to be challenged is that the constraints under which a second language speaker operates are the same as those of a first language speaker. The second assumption is that the second language is acquired for the same purposes as the first language.

Carroll has stated the position very clearly in laying down principles for dealing with educational issues in relation to native speakers and non-native speakers of languages as well as non-standard dialects:

(1) Language is a complex human phenomenon that takes the same general form wherever it is found. It permits the expression of a certain very wide range of information, experiences,

feelings, and thoughts, and it does so in somewhat the same way regardless of the particular form of the language or the culture of the user, as long as the language is a so-called natural language that is used from childhood on as a native language by its users. (Carroll, 1971: 177)

It is not possible therefore to assume that the second language speaker uses that language in ways which are directly comparable to the first language speaker. The experience of learning a language primarily in the classroom (and this discussion relates only to such learners) is totally different from the experience of learning a language 'naturally' as part of the general process of socialization and maturation. It is not to be expected that the range of information, experience, feelings, and thoughts will be as wide, nor will the language usage be particularly closely attuned to the native speaker culture. The imposition of a native speaker equivalence as the performance standard by which the second language speaker should be measured is therefore impractical. It is also undesirable in that the aim is set far beyond the rather limited requirements and purposes of most second language learners and second language teaching programmes.

It cannot be assumed, therefore, that testing procedures which are valid for native speakers can be applied automatically to second language speakers. In the case of cloze procedures there are many reasons for concluding that such an assumption would be false.

Text type is one factor which is revealing. One part of native speaker competence seems to be the ability to identify different registers and styles to the extent that text type is not normally a source of variation in native speaker cloze scores. Research has shown however that for second language learners, text type is an important source of variation (Freeland, 1979). Freeland concludes (p. 6) that

certain assumptions about cloze tests need reexamining . . . . . And the practice of expressing learners' scores as a ratio of native speakers' is suspect, since the relationship between native and non-native scores can fluctuate in unknown ways.

Oller came to a similar conclusion:

There is little if any reason to assume that conclusions from research with native speakers can validly be generalised to the case of non-native speakers (Oller, 1973: 107).

On the question of exact versus acceptable scoring, Oller states: 'Clearly, when dealing with non-native speakers there is something counter-intuitive about requiring the exact word' and data from tests reported by Oller (1973: 109)

> supported the conclusion that with non-native speakers the method of allowing any contextually acceptable response is significantly superior to the exact word scoring technique.

Elsewhere, Oller discusses the problem further, noting (1) that exact word replacement makes tests extremely difficult for L2 speakers, and (2) that exact word replacement often requires insights which may not be regarded as language skills (Oller, 1972).

Thus there is evidence of the need for principled judgements to be made in the development of cloze tests in relation to the selection (or development) of suitable texts, decisions regarding the elements to be deleted, and regarding degrees of acceptability under a system of non-exact scoring.

The Selection of Cloze Passages

Intellectual Bias

The relevance of intellectual knowledge is well illustrated by a short cloze passage taken from Anderson (1971).

> B. The idea that the (1) _____ of a language, unlike (2) _____ words, are probably infinite (3) _____ number, so that they (4) _____ be listed, is no (5) _____ one, however familiar it (6) _____ recently have become through (7) _____ writings of Chomsky and (8) _____ followers.

Some readers may be 'tuned in' by the word 'infinite' as a cue for 'sentences' as gap-filler for (1). (Though why not 'sounds' or 'phrases', 'messages' or 'meanings'?) The real clue is 'Chomsky', whose often quoted position on the generative power of language is invariably expressed in terms of 'sentences', no doubt because transformational generative grammar was until recently essentially a sentence grammar. In other words, if the cloze reader does not have an intellectual grounding in the transformational generative orthodoxy as propounded by Chomsky and his followers, he will not be able to fill gap (1) and possibly gap (5). If failure to understand results in carelessness in the use of clues which are available, the learner may fail to fill gap (4) satisfactorily. The other gaps will probably be filled satisfactorily by most native speakers even though they have no knowledge of linguistics, and little if any understanding of the passage.

Two points are at issue here: the largely self-evident one that the intellectual content of a passage will affect the scores, and is a potential source of bias; and the less obvious point, which for that reason may be more important, that it is possible to complete items satisfactorily in the absence of any global understanding of the meaning of the text.

The test setter therefore has to make decisions regarding the intellectual neutrality of the passage content in order to avoid criticisms that the text favours some learners and disadvantages others. It may be desirable to bias the content of a passage to reflect the purposes of a particular course (English for nurses; English for engineers, etc.) but the question still remains whether the content should be truly neutral, i.e., intellectually familiar to all learners so that the gap-filling exercise tests primarily language ability, or whether the content of the passage is regarded as part of the challenge to the learner in reconstructing a genuine piece of communication. The latter will bring into play powers of deduction and other analytical skills as well as memory, which will not be required by the less intellectually demanding passage.

Cultural Bias

The problems of cultural bias can be illustrated very obviously by the following:

> C. _____ blind _____ . Three _____ mice. _____
> how _____ run. _____ how _____ run. _____ all
> _____ after _____ farmer's _____ who _____
> off _____ tails _____ a _____ knife. _____ you
> _____ see _____ a _____ in _____ life _____
> three _____ mice.

Those who have had at some time or another an intimate experience of certain aspects of the child-rearing practices of native speakers of English will be able to complete this cloze passage without difficulty. Of those who lack this experience, only those who have studied eighteenth century British political history are likely to have come across the passage in its original role as political satire.

It is obvious that such a passage would not be selected because of its idiosyncratic style and the fact that some learners at least may have memorized it. Yet the same reasoning applies to expressions such as:

> D. Birds of a _____ flock together.

Such idioms are 'known' in very much the same way as nursery rhymes are known and for the same reason. Success in filling the gap is directly related to the extent to which this particular string of words has been committed to memory. Anyone who has not committed the string to memory will insert, for example, 'kind' or 'species'.

The step from so-called common sayings such as the above, to clichés, which are in fact far more common, is a short one, and objections to 'birds of a feather', etc., apply equally to surviving archaisms such as

E. The situation was _____ with danger

where 'fraught' is the past participle and only surviving form of a now obsolete verb. Those whose reading has included at some time or another a certain type of adventure story will be (all too) familiar with 'fraught'. Others have probably never encountered the word.

The following is an even more extreme example of a particular genre:

F. The traitorous Lord Fred was arraigned at Westminster before the King, condemned, carried thence and _____ into the foulest darkest _____ in the Tower of _____.

Those who know something of English history might identify the Tower of London; those who read or have read a certain genre of historical novel will probably identify a 'dungeon' as the appropriate place for traitorous villains, and will know that traitors are not 'put' or 'placed' or 'locked up' in a dungeon, they are 'cast' into them. On second thoughts they might be 'flung', but I would vote for 'cast'. One more example:

G. The posse rode unsuspecting into the ambush and was met by a _____ of bullets from the outlaw guns.

Those of us who have read our Westerns, not to mention war stories and detective stories, are sufficiently habituated to the notion of a 'hail of bullets' not to notice how extraordinary the metaphor, which presumably preceded the cliché, really is. In this context 'hail' is almost a collective noun, to be included with a 'pride of lions' and a 'gaggle of geese'. The meaning is linked to the base meaning in the sense of a large number of small, hard, punishing objects travelling at speed and in close order; yet 'hail' operates on a more or less vertical axis, while bullets, generally, do not. You can have a 'hail storm' or a 'hail stone', but you cannot have 'a hail' any more than you can have 'a rain' or 'a snow'. Perhaps the cliché is very venerable indeed and goes back to the days when archers deliberately fired high so that arrows fell almost vertically on the enemy with a sound very much like a hail storm, no doubt, as a roof of shields was hastily erected as protection. The weapons may change, but the clichés live on.

There are no easy dividing-lines to be drawn. When does a metaphor become a cliché? How do we differentiate between a cliché and a string which has a high level of sequential or collocational probability (Beattie and Butterworth, 1979: 210)? It is no more possible to have a piece of discourse which has no cultural content than it is to have one which has no intellectual content, but as in the latter case it is necessary to make judgements about the nature of the cultural content and its acceptability. As in the case of intellectual content, the test may be deliberately biased in a particular direction, e.g., it may be desirable for certain purposes to place a premium upon knowledge of the British cultural heritage and of contemporary life in Britain. However, in most countries where English is taught as a second language, or for international purposes, it would be necessary to select passages in which the cultural content is neutral with regard to those taking the test, and very careful consideration is needed to ensure that this is achieved.

It might be argued that the modern economic and technological world is culturally neutral in the sense that there is nothing specifically British about it, that access to this world is the main purpose of learning English as a second language and any bias that results from a choice of passages relating to this world is therefore fully justified. The argument is sound in international terms, but in relation to a national education system for example it may be said to introduce an unacceptable level of discrimination in favour of the socially and economically advantaged sections of the community, who have access to that world, and against the socially and economically disadvantaged, who have spent their lives in villages or urban slums.

As Oller (1973) has observed, you cannot and should not try to separate language skill from knowledge of the world in the measurement of performance, but it is necessary to consider precisely what knowledge of the world can reasonably be expected of particular learners given the constraints under which the learning has taken place. If such factors are not taken into consideration the cloze test may become an instrument for social and economic discrimination, or might be seen as such by those who consider themselves to have been disadvantaged.

Linguistic Bias

In addition to the judgements that have to be made regarding intellectual and cultural content, there is linguistic content. (It is not suggested of course that these are discrete categories; they are merely convenient points of focus.)

R.E. Johnson has noted the high level of correlation between cloze scores, and measures of redundancy (Johnson, 1975: 435) and raises several points which are relevant to the selection of texts, and other issues (marking and what it is that cloze tests measure) which are discussed further at a later stage.

1. Johnson notes that missing words may be inserted without an understanding of the passage as a whole, or even, in some instances, of the particular linguistic string in which a gap occurs.

   It may therefore be questioned whether the purpose of the cloze test is in fact the recovery of the original message. It seems rather to be the recovery of the original text.

2. He suggests that passages may prove effective for cloze testing because they are highly redundant and that such passages may be extremely boring in their unreduced original form.

   It is arguable then at least that texts selected for cloze tests are by normally accepted standards poorly written, a strong argument against accepting only exact replacements.

On the first point, it is easy to demonstrate that cloze passages may test something other than the ability of the reader to reconstruct the original message. The following passage was constructed by Bransford and McCarrell in such a way as to ensure that the reader finds it totally incomprehensible regardless of the fact that there are no linguistic difficulties. The fact that the writer's overall meaning remains totally obscure does not materially affect the use of this passage as a cloze test, which gives support to the argument that cloze tests focus on relatively low order language skills relating to 'core proficiency' rather than higher order language skills like reading comprehension (Alderson, 1979: 225).

Clearly, the following passage tests core proficiency in some limited sense and little else.

H. If the balloons popped _____ sound wouldn't be _____ to carry since everything _____ be too far away _____ the correct floor. A _____ window would also prevent _____ sound from carrying, since _____ buildings tend to be _____ insulated. Since the whole _____ depends upon a steady _____ of electricity a break _____ the middle of the _____ would also cause problems. _____ course, the fellow could _____, but the human voice _____ not loud enough to _____ that far. An additional _____ is that a string _____ break on the instrument. _____ there could be no _____ to the message. It _____ clear that the best _____ would involve less distance. _____ there would be fewer _____ problems. With face to _____ contact, the least number _____ things could go wrong.*

In making judgements regarding the linguistic features of a text, then, it is necessary to decide the extent to which the gaps in a given passage can be filled regardless of an understanding of the passage as a whole, and to determine whether or not this is acceptable in view of the purposes for which the test is being set.

Before advancing any further it is obviously necessary to attempt to come to terms more closely with what it is that cloze tests actually measure.

A Transfer Feature Theory of Cloze Items

Reading has been described by Goodman as 'a psycholinguistic guessing game', a characterization which many people have found intuitively satisfying. The objective of the game is to achieve understanding, and it is generally accepted that the meaning of a linguistic string is not the arithmetical product of the elements in that string, nor is the meaning of a passage the arithmetical product of the meanings of all its sentences. On the contrary, the global meanings which result from the processing of linguistic strings in the short-term memory are achieved partly in terms of the constraints exercised by the linguistic items in the string, and partly by means of the non-linguistic information that the receiver brings to the task of comprehension. Smith (1971) and others have suggested that what the receiver brings to the task of decoding is of far greater importance to eventual comprehension than the linguistic items on the page. This extra-linguistic data was categorized by Uhlenbeck (1963) as follows: (1) the situation in which the sentence is spoken, (2) the preceding sentences, if any, (3) the hearer's knowledge of the speaker and the topics which might be discussed with him.

These extra-linguistic factors will be referred to here as the 'presuppositional base'. It will be clear

*See Appendix on page 71

that the failure of the reader to understand the passage quoted earlier from Bransford and McCarrell, even to its fully restored form, results from the lack of an adequate presuppositional base.

A recent discussion of cloze procedure by Finn (1977) provides a useful means for relating the general model of decoding characterized above to the specific case of completing a gap in a cloze passage. Finn proposes a 'transfer feature theory' of processing in reading, which combines Shannon and Weaver's (1949) contribution to communication theory and Weinreich's (1966) semantic theory.

Finn defines the 'cloze easiness' of a word in terms of the percentage of subjects supplying the exact word in a cloze task, and argues that cloze easiness is a measure of the information carried by the word in the passage (Finn, 1977: 512).

Cloze easiness is affected by word frequency, the difficulty of the passage, and the number of times a word occurs in the passage.

The Shannon and Weaver theory of communication is based upon the relationship between 'information' and doubt, i.e., where the occurrence of a word is totally predictable there is no information. Thus the greater the doubt (the lower the cloze easiness score) the more information is said to be carried by a particular item. (It will be obvious from such examples as a function word with a low easiness score, that 'information' here is used quite differently from 'meaning' and is in fact determined without reference to meaning.)

Finn uses the term 'transfer features' to describe those grammatical and semantic markers and 'distinguishers' which supply redundancy or which generate expectancy. The term is taken from Weinreich and relates to the fact that the inclusion of a particular word in a discourse can dictate some lexical features for other words in the discourse, and Finn defines 'information in a word' as 'a function of the number of features not supplied by transfer features in discourse' (Finn, 1977: 520).

In a theory of processing in reading, I find the distinction between information and meaning inappropriate and unhelpful since the objective of the processor is to arrive at meaning and not 'information'. In cloze testing, however, the processor actively seeks transfer features in order to achieve a high level of expectancy regarding the identity of a particular linguistic item. In this context, and for my purposes (unlike the Weinreich model), transfer features are seen as being derived from the non-linguistic aspects of the presuppositional base as well as from the text.

Selection of items

It is now possible to return to the consideration of some types of judgement that might be made in selecting items for gapping.

It has been suggested that one reason for using objective procedures in gapping a cloze passage is that no adequate theoretical base exists for making decisions affecting which linguistic items should or should not be gapped. As the previous section shows, we may not have all the answers, and may never have them, but we do have a basis for approaching the task in terms of transfer features, and in particular in terms of the analysis of the sources of the transfer features, e.g.,

(1) Are there transfer features which would cue successful completion? If not, as in the case of proper names or numbers in certain contexts, the item should not be used.

(2) If transfer features exist, are they drawn primarily from the text or from presuppositional sources other than the text?

 a. If the latter, is it acceptable within the context of this test to use items which are dependent upon intellectual or cultural knowledge? It should be noted that no comprehension question would be acceptable if it tested knowledge derived from sources other than the text, and the only grounds for accepting such an item in a cloze test would be that the non-textual knowledge forms an integral part of the learning programme and/or the inclusion of this presuppositional element provides a desirable bias in view of the aims of the test (a decision which most public examiners might find it hard to defend) or that the information in question is neutral in that it is readily and equally accessible to all candidates.

 If the presuppositional requirements for the items cannot be justified in these terms, the item should not be used.

 b. If the transfer features are drawn from the text, do they relate to meaning or form? Do the transfer features arise out of an understanding of the passage as a whole, are they dependent upon understanding the immediate context only, or do they depend primarily upon collocation or other primarily linguistic features? It seems reasonable to suggest that cloze tests can only claim to test communicative skills if items which depend on recovery of the theme and reasonably precise grasp of the meaning of local contexts are emphasised, while those which require a purely linguistic response are restricted in number if not eliminated. This does not imply an emphasis on content words at the expense of function words. It means the selection of items which exercise a positive constraint on the meaning of the passage and which carry sufficient transfer features from other aspects of the text to make that constraint readily apparent to those who have achieved the level of language ability which the test is designed to evaluate. An example may be helpful at this stage to illustrate the notion of constraint exercised by an item on the meaning of a passage; a function word is used in the example because the notion of constraint on meaning is comparatively obvious in the case of content words. Articles have been chosen because automatic deletion procedures tend to provide a large number of such items.

I. Yesterday as I was crossing (1)_____ road, dodging cars and bicycles to catch (2)_____ bus that passes near RELC, (3)_____ driver swore at me in English, (4)_____ first time this has ever happened to me in Singapore.

Let us assume that I intend to include at least one item in my cloze passage which tests control of the distinction between the definite and indefinite articles, and I have to consider the merits of (1)–(4) above for this purpose.

(1) Neither 'a' nor 'the' exercises a constraint on the meaning of the passage. 'some' or 'my' would be acceptable alternatives, and I would not really want to reject 'Orchard' or any other road name: (1) requires some grasp of English noun phrase structure, i.e., that a gap-filler is required, but this is obvious anyway, and on the whole (1) is a poor item.

(2) 'a' is possible and exercises some degree of constraint on the meaning, i.e., one of the many buses which travel to RELC. 'the' is also possible and exercises a constraint on the meaning, e.g., that particular category of bus which serves RELC and no other. Again the two are broadly synonymous and interchangeable in this context and the item merely tests an elementary grasp of the noun phrase structure of English.

(3) 'the' exercises a strong constraint on the meaning since it identifies the 'swearer' as the driver of the bus. 'a' also exercises a strong constraint in that it eliminates the driver of the bus and indicates some other driver.

(4) 'a' is unacceptable, eliminated by transfer features from 'first' and exemplifies a collocational pattern which should be familiar, e.g., the / first, last, only / time, chance, etc. The meaning constraint is extremely localized; however, the item is suitable and could be pre-tested.

A subsequent part of the (reconstructed) cloze passage reads as follows:

As I got off the bus, I heard the driver call out: 'Mind the traffic this time!'

It is now clear from transfer features based on evidence internal to the text that gap (3) should be filled by 'the'. It is considered to be an excellent item in that it tests understanding of the text as a whole and should be included in the pre-testing.

The example given above illustrates another point very clearly. It is not the case that we do not know what is being tested in a cloze passage. It seems to me that we can state rather precisely what it is that each item is testing, and to this extent it could be claimed that cloze tests are not integrative, but a means of providing discrete point items which have a somewhat enhanced presuppositional base. However, the distinction (discrete point/integrative) is not one which can usefully be applied to the nature of the learner's task (e.g., a comprehension question: free choice, multiple-choice, or true/false might be set regarding the identity of the 'swearer' in the example just given and would thus be essentially a discrete point question. Another question might address itself to the 'best' summarizing statement. It is possible to imagine a cloze item requiring a similarly global strategy in gathering and evaluating a range of transfer features, though again it should normally be possible to give a reasonably precise account of these features and their origins, and to estimate the potential value of the item accordingly).

One result of randomising procedures in item selection has been, in my experience, the development of tests which tend to be too difficult. Pass marks are set fairly low (30%–40%) and many candidates achieve the pass mark giving little evidence that they have understood more than occasional sentences and phrases, and much evidence that they have not. Their correct answers are achieved primarily through linguistic transfer features. Rational justification for the selection of items and a requirement that the pass mark must be in the 60%–70% range would greatly improve the quality of cloze tests and cause them to bear more closely upon the aims of the teaching programme they are used to evaluate as well as promoting more constructive classroom practices.

Scoring

Once it is accepted that it is quite possible to have exact word replacement with little or no understanding of the text, that the exact word need not necessarily be the 'best' word in terms of precision, expressiveness, etc., or the only suitable word, and that the requirement of exact word replacement may introduce bias into the test in favour of those whose socio-economic position gives them greater access to western culture in general, or native speakers of English in particular, the arguments for acceptable word scoring become very strong indeed. However, a number of issues then arise, and in particular a number of studies (Bowen, 1969; Oller *et al.*, 1972; Clarke and Burdell, 1977) have shown the difficulty, perhaps the impossibility of setting up objective criteria for determining degrees of acceptability.

Clarke and Burdell write (to give one example):

Judgements of synonymity of 'non-nativeness' are almost entirely idiosyncratic and heavily influenced by one's dialect (Clarke and Burdell, 1977: 140).

A judgement amply confirmed by the following data, which is cited as totally acceptable to Clarke and Burdell but would be judged marginally acceptable or unacceptable by most speakers of my dialect.

J. I just wrote a *hotel* (letter) asking for a room in August. (Where 'letter' was the original, and 'hotel' the non-exact replacement.)

The first step, it seems to me, might be to abandon the notion of acceptability to a native speaker in favour of acceptability to an (idealized) speaker of international English.

The second would be to attempt to establish principles on which judgements of acceptability could be made in terms of degrees of meaningfulness and deviation from forms which would be acceptable for the purposes of international English.

Whatever guidelines are adopted by markers, they should be sufficiently flexible to ensure a very high mark indeed for an (imaginary) candidate who produced the following in response to the cloze test on *Three Blind Mice* that was considered earlier.

K. Ignoring blind alleys. Three investigated mice, analysed how they run, studied how farms run. Three all sought after rich farmers. One, who casts off his tails to a deserving knife grinder you often see, became a millionaire in his life time. Three studied mice.

Note that the deletion of every other word increases the difficulty of the cloze task but also (dangerously) increases the reader's freedom to head off in directions of his own.

(K) is of course an extreme, and highly unrealistic example, yet the point it raises is a valid one. By 'acceptable alternative', do we judge degree of synonymity or degree of functional equivalent to the original text? If acceptability is given this narrow interpretation (as it usually is), the candidate whose virtuoso performance is presented above would receive no marks, and a gross injustice would have been done, particularly when, as was noted above, many candidates achieve pass marks having offered as a reconstruction of the original a text which has no theme, and is in fact gibberish, though admittedly English gibberish. How can we place a premium on the ability of the candidate to make sense out of the cues available to him and construct a message of some kind out of these cues, even if it diverges somewhat from the original message? If we cannot do this, then we must accept that many cloze tests are tests of a very low order of language ability indeed.

One solution, which was suggested above, is to ensure through pre-testing that passages are not so difficult that the pass mark has to be lowered to a point where comprehension is hardly required in order to reach the necessary score. Easier passages admittedly will tend not to discriminate amongst the candidates as effectively as the more difficult passages, even though what is being tested is more rationally defensible, but it should not be impossible to identify texts which, perhaps with suitable modification, can satisfy both requirements.

One further point should be made if acceptable alternatives are permitted. The use of expressions such as 'mutilation of the text' to describe the gapping procedure suggests that, for some people at least, a text has a certain inviolability and exact word replacement is an act of restitution as well as restoration. I find this attitude irrational but understandable. It is much harder to sympathize with a desire to sustain the inviolability of the one word gap. Provided that the candidate performs those functions which have been identified as the aim of the particular test, are there really grounds for rejecting acceptable replacements which consist of two words or more, rather than one? Is there any reason why the gaps themselves should consist only of a single word? The gap could consist of a phrase, a sentence, or indeed of a complete paragraph.

The answers to such questions should be formulated in terms of the purposes of the tests and the constraints under which the examiners have to operate. Assertions that such tests would not be 'proper' cloze tests reflect the desire discussed earlier to elevate procedures to the level of principles.

What do Cloze Tests Test?

It has been shown above that it is possible to restore considerable parts of a cloze passage without understanding its overall meaning. The reverse is also possible, i.e., that the essential meaning may be understood while the candidate fails to produce an acceptable linguistic item as a slot-filler. What then does cloze test: receptive ability or productive ability, understanding or linguistic knowledge? The rather unsatisfactory answer seems to be almost any combination of these, but with a premium, at the lower levels of achievement, against communicative competence (i.e., the ability to gain understanding in spite of linguistic deficit) and in favour of linguistic competence (i.e., the ability to identify an acceptable slot-filler in spite of a communication deficit). A high level of achievement would normally reflect a balance of communicative and linguistic competencies, but, as has been noted, accepted achievement levels on cloze tests are frequently low.

Perhaps the best way in which to approach the question of what it is that cloze tests test is to look at what the candidate does. It is sometimes claimed that the gaps in a cloze passage are equivalent to unknown elements in a text, and that gap-filling samples a natural and normal reading activity. The claim is false on both grounds. Gaps do not reflect unknown elements in a text, which are normally low frequency content words. Gaps in cloze tests are rarely of this type and often consist of function words. Secondly, whatever the gapping rate (or average gapping rate if non-random selection is used) the proportion of unknown elements will be far higher than would be acceptable for any normal reading purpose.

Experience has shown that more than twenty five new words per thousand running words usually make a text unduly difficult. (Bright and McGregor, 1970: 20)

Difficult texts can be toiled painfully through . . . . . but the process is dreary, bears no resemblance to reading and is not conducive to the establishment of good learning habits. (Ibid., p. 19)

Even a revised claim, that cloze activities correspond to intensive reading with a difficult text, cannot be sustained; partly because of the type of item as previously stated, but more importantly perhaps because what cloze requires is entirely different from the normal and important language skill of inferring meaning from context.

As Rivers (1968) and others have pointed out, in reading it is common for a person to come across a word which is unknown. This requires the reader to infer a meaning from context, etc. Language teachers are frequently urged to help learners to develop confidence in their ability to do this, e.g.,

The new vocabulary should not co-occur with difficult structures and a certain amount of vagueness in guessing the meaning of words must be accepted. The teacher should not expect students to come up with exact meanings while guessing in this manner. (Kruse, 1979: 209)

This is a very different, and much less precise requirement than that of filling a cloze gap; it challenges the reader's communicative competence in the broadest possible terms, while the cloze item challenges the linguistic competence in very precise terms indeed.

Can Cloze Technique Be Taught?

One aspect of test construction which is rarely considered as seriously as it should be is the effect that tests have upon the classroom teaching and learning situation. A great deal has been written and said in the last twenty years about accountability and the 'contract' between teacher and learner. It is often assumed that the primary contract between the English language teacher and learner involves the acquisition by the learner of a certain competency in the English language. In these terms, the relevant function of the examiner is to devise a test which samples the knowledge and skills of the learner in such a way as to determine whether or not a satisfactory level of language ability has been achieved. The examiner's task would be much simpler if this were true, and one major question regarding reliance on cloze tests could be eliminated. In fact the primary contract that teachers have with the learners is to get them through their examinations, which leads to the well-known practice of 'teaching to the exam'. It should be true that the best preparation for an examination which tests language ability would be the development of the learners' language ability, but this is generally not the case, partly perhaps because examiners are really concerned more with obtaining a satisfactory distribution of marks than with true accountability. As a result, teachers have to decide whether to develop their pupils' language abilities to the greatest possible extent, while accepting that for most of them this will mean failure in the examination, or abandon true communicative competence as a goal and aim instead at the appearance of such competence as demonstrated by the ability to carry out the tasks required by examiners at a level which will secure a pass.

No doubt, in seeking to acquire these examination skills, pupils' language abilities improve, but the examination is the goal and a pass is the motivation.

In these circumstances, it behoves any examiner to bear in mind the likely classroom repercussions of the selection of a particular testing technique.

The next claim that we might consider regarding cloze is that the technique for completing such tests cannot be taught and therefore the only way to prepare pupils is by improving their language ability. This seems doubtful in view of the differences already discussed between the activity of completing a cloze test and normal language activities such as reading, with which cloze bears the closest superficial correspondence. It seems much more likely that rather specialised skills can be brought to bear on the task, and that these skills can be taught.

One way of improving scores on a particular type of test is to give massive amounts of practice. If the test passages are typically so difficult that most learners will understand very little of what they read, then it will be necessary to practise with passages of a similar level of difficulty. Work with more suitable passages would have little transfer to the examination task, though it would be more likely to result in a genuine development of communicative ability.

It has been noted that 'good' readers tend to use the whole text in determining the appropriate gap-filler, while 'poorer' readers tended to make mistakes which showed that they paid attention only to preceding text, or to the immediate textual environment (Neville and Pugh, 1976). One way of improving performance on cloze tests, therefore, though not necessarily of reading ability, would be

to give poorer students intensive practice in obtaining transfer features from the gapped text which would assist in determining an appropriate replacement item.

As was noted above, varying proportions of the transfer features on each item are grammatical. The 'good' second language speaker shares the native speaker's ability to judge grammaticality to some extent at least; the poorer reader will be less able to make such judgements and this will be reflected in the cloze scores. Another approach then would be to develop an intensive basic programme in grammatical analysis. This might go some way towards compensating for the deficiency in the poorer reader, and repay time and effort as regards cloze score improvement rather better than a programme designed to develop overall language and reading ability.

Various writers have shown that very high levels of correlation can be obtained between cloze test results and a range of other tests and conclude that the cloze test can, under these circumstances, be substituted for the scores from a whole battery of tests with consequent saving in time and resources of examiner and learner alike. Perhaps the most important reason against such a step is the effect that this would have upon the language teaching programme. Even if it is true that cloze cannot be taught, teachers and learners will believe that it can.

Conclusion

The problem in language testing, as in linguistics, is that the chief result of increasing methodological rigour has been to show how little we actually understand what we are dealing with. This is true on the macro level and may always be true since the ultimate questions (what is language? How is it different from/related to intelligence, cognition, and the broader issues of communicative competence? etc.) may prove to be unanswerable. However, it is no solution to hope that safety from these imponderables lies in the rejection of judgements based on principled argument; nor is it true that at the micro level (the level of the construction of tests and test items for particular groups of learners following specific programmes for specifiable purposes), that we lack resources for making reasonable and reasoned judgements. By doing so, we can increase both the true validity of our tests and our understanding of what it is that we are testing, while minimising the dangers inherent in any situation where an examination rather than a syllabus or teaching programme may determine what happens in the classroom.

Appendix

The reconstructed text of H is as follows:

If the balloons popped the sound wouldn't be able to carry since everything would be too far away from the correct floor. A closed window would also prevent the sound from carrying, since most buildings tend to be well insulated. Since the whole operation depends upon a steady flow of electricity a break in the middle of the wire would also cause problems. Of course, the fellow could shout, but the human voice is not loud enough to carry that far. An additional problem is that a string could break on the instrument. Then there could be no accompaniment to the message. It is clear that the best situation would involve less distance. Then there would be fewer potential problems. With face-to-face contact, the least number of things could go wrong.

References

Alderson, J. Charles, 1979, 'The Cloze Procedure and Proficiency in English as a Foreign Language', *TESOL Quarterly* 13, no. 2, pp. 219–27.

Anderson, J. 1971, 'A Technique for Measuring Reading Comprehension and Readability', *English Language Teaching* 25, no. 2, pp. 178–82.

Beattie, Geoffrey W., and Butterworth, B.L., 1979, 'Contextual Probability and Word Frequency as Determinants of Pauses and Errors in Spontaneous Speech', *Language and Speech* 22, pt. 3, pp. 201–11.

Bowen, J.D., 1969, 'A Tentative Measure of the Relative Control of English and Amharic by 11th Grade Ethiopian Students', *UCLA Workpapers in Teaching English as a Second Language* 2, pp. 69–89.

Bransford, J.D., and McCarrell, N.S., 1974, 'A Sketch of Cognitive Approach to Comprehension'. In Weimer, W.B. and Palermo, D.S. (Eds.), *Cognition and the Symbolic Processes*, Hillsdale, N.J., Lawrence Erlbaum Assoc..

Bright, J.A. and McGregor, G.P., 1970, *Teaching English as a Second Language*, London, Longmans.

Cambourne, Brian, 1976, 'Getting to Goodman: An Analysis of the Goodman Model of Reading with Some Suggestions for Evaluation', *Reading Research Quarterly* 12, no. 4, pp. 605–36.

Carroll, John B., 1971, 'Language and Cognition: Current Perspectives from Linguistics and Psychology'. In Laffey, James F. and Shuy, Roger (Eds.), *Language Differences: Do They Interfere?*, Newark, Del., International Reading Association.

Carver, Ronald P., 1978, 'The Case Against Statistical Significance Testing', *Harvard Educational Review* 48, no. 3, pp. 378–99.

Clarke, Mark A. and Burdell, Linda, 1977, 'Shades of Meaning: Syntactic and Semantic Parameters of Cloze Test Responses'. In Douglas Brown, H. *et al.* (Eds.), *On TESOL '77 — Teaching and Learning English as a Second Language: Trends in Research and Practice*, Washington, D.C., TESOL.

Finn, Patrick J., 1977, 'Word Frequency, Information Theory and Cloze Performance: A Transfer Feature Theory of Processing in Reading', *Reading Research Quarterly* 13, pt. 4, pp. 508–37.

Farhady, Hossein, 1979, 'The Disjunctive Fallacy between Discrete Point and Integrative Tests', *TESOL Quarterly* 13, no. 3, pp. 347–57.

Freeland, Jane, 1979, 'Text Type as a Factor in the Cloze Testing of Foreign Languages', *BAAL Newsletter*, no. 8.

Green, Raphael, 1979, 'An Experiment with Cloze Testing', *English Language Teaching Journal* 33, no. 2, pp. 122–26.

Hildyard, Angela, and Olson, David R., 1978, 'Memory and Inference in the Comprehension of Oral and Written Discourse', *Discourse Processes* 1, pp. 91–117.

House, E.R., 1977, *The Logic of Evaluating Argument*, C.S.E. University of California Monograph Series in Education, no. 7.

Jongsma, E.R., 1971, *The Cloze Procedure: A Survey of the Research*, ERIC ED 058 015, Bloomington, Indiana University.

Johnson, Ronald E., 1975, 'Meaning in Complex Learning', *Review of Educational Research* 45, no. 3, pp. 425–59.

Kruse, Anna Fisher, 1979, 'Vocabulary in Context', *English Language Teaching Journal* 33, no. 3, pp. 207–17.

Littlewood, William T., 1979, 'Communicative Performance in Language Developmental Contexts', *IRAL*, 17, no. 2, pp. 123–38.

Mishler, Elliot G., 1979, 'Meaning in Context: Is There Any Other Kind?', *Harvard Educational Review* 49, no. 1, pp. 1–19.

Moser, C.A. and Kalton, G., 1971, *Survey Methods in Social Investigation*, 2nd ed., London, Heinemann.

Neville, Mary H. and Pugh, A.K., 1976, 'Context in Reading and Listening: Variations in Approach to Cloze Tasks', *Reading Research Quarterly* 12, no. 1, pp. 11–31.

Oakshott-Taylor, John, 1979, 'Cloze Procedure and Foreign Language Listening Skills', *IRAL* 17, no. 2, pp. 150–58.

Oller, J.W. Jr., 1972, 'Scoring Methods and Difficulty Levels for Cloze Tests of ESL Proficiency', *Modern Language Journal* 56, no. 3, pp. 151–58.

Oller, J.W., Jr., Bowen, D., Dien, T.T. and Mason, V.W., 1972, 'Cloze Tests in English, Thai, and Vietnamese: Native and Non-Native Performance', *Language Learning* 22, no. 1, pp. 1–16.

Oller, J.W., Jr., 1973, 'Cloze Tests of Second Language Proficiency and What They Measure', *Language Learning* 23, pp. 105–18.

Oller, J.W., Jr. and Perkins, Kyle (Eds.), 1978, *Language in Education: Testing the Tests*, Rowley, Mass., Newbury House.

Riley, Pamela M., 1973, *The Cloze Procedure: A Selected Annotated Bibliography*, Lae, Papua New Guinea University of Technology.

Rivers, Wilga M., 1968, *Teaching Foreign Language Skills*, Chicago, University of Chicago Press.

Robinson, Richard David, 1972, *An Introduction to the Cloze Procedure: An Annotated Bibliography*, Newark, Del., International Reading Association.

Strauch, R.E., 1976, 'A Critical Look at Quantitative Methodology', *Policy Analysis* 2, no. 1 (Quoted by House, 1977).

Streiff, Virginia, 1978, 'Relationships among Oral and Written Cloze Scores and Achievement Test Scores in a Bilingual Setting'. In Oller and Perkins, 1978.

Stubbs, Joseph Barstow and Tucker, G. Richard, 1974,

Robert K Johnson

'The Cloze Test as a Measure of English Proficiency', *Modern Language Journal* 58, nos. 5–6, pp. 239–42.

Taylor, Wilson L., 1953, 'Cloze Procedure: A New Tool for Measuring Readability', *Journalism Quarterly* 30, pp. 415–33.

Uhlenbeck, E.M., 1963, 'An Appraisal of Transformation Theory', *Lingua* 12, pp. 1–18.

Valette, Rebecca M., 1977, *Modern Language Testing*, 2nd ed., New York, Harcourt, Brace, Jovanovich.

Wainman, H., 1979, 'Cloze Testing of Second Language Learners', *English Language Teaching Journal* 33, no. 2, pp. 126–32.

Zurif, Edgar B., and Blumstein, Sheila E., 1978, 'Language and the Brain'. In Halle, Morris, Bresnan, Joan and Miller, George A. (Eds.), *Linguistic Theory and Psychological Reality*, Cambridge, Mass., MIT Press.

Getting information from advanced reading tests

Two kinds of tests

Here is a short reading text followed by two kinds of tests.

A major construction problem is the diversion of the river to enable the foundations for the dam to be excavated and the concrete placed. Since it would be uneconomical to construct diversion works and cofferdams to divert the full flood discharge of the river, the diversion has been divided into several distinct operations. The critical period will be during the low-water season, because, as the river falls,
5   the cofferdam on the left bank will be demolished where it crosses the diversion channel, allowing water to flow through the temporary openings in the dam wall. This having been done, a rockfill cofferdam will be constructed across the main river channel downstream of the main site. This will cause the water at the dam site to remain quiescent by preventing any flow in this part of the main river channel and directing water through the diversion tunnel.

(from Adamson & Lowe, 1971, pp. 106–107)

1   The diversion has been divided into several distinct operations because

   a. the full flood of the river must be diverted.
   b. the foundations have to be excavated.
   c. a complete diversion is too expensive.
   d. it occurs during a critical period.

2   The rockfill cofferdam
   a. will direct the flow through the diversion tunnel.
   b. is on the main site.
   c. will increase the flow at the dam site.
   d. is on the left bank.

3   *it* in line 5 refers to   in line

4   *This* in line 6 refers to   in line

5   *This* in line 7 refers to   in line

The multiple-choice test tells us how much information the reader got from the passage. We can use the results of this test to classify our learners into groups (Pass/Fail) or rank them on a scale (A, B, C . . . . .).

The reference word test, on the other hand, can provide us with several kinds of information. It can give us information about language learning in general. For example, in a class of 40 learners, 5 did not answer item 3 correctly. Twenty-two did not answer item 4 correctly. If we compare the two items, we find that *it* in item 3 refers to a noun group (*the cofferdam on the left bank*) whereas *This* in item 4 refers to a larger unit (*the cofferdam on the left bank will be demolished*).

The test shows that reference words referring to a noun group are easier than those referring to a clause.

The reference word test can also give us information about individual learners. If a learner does not answer item 4 and similar items correctly, we know that that learner needs help or extra practice with the reference words *this, that,* and *it* where they refer to a clause.

We can contrast the two kinds of tests by thinking of learning as a journey. The first kind of test, exemplified by the multiple-choice items, tells us how far the learners have come along the road. The second kind of test, exemplified by the reference word items, tells us what the road is like, what difficulties can be found on the journey, and how learners have coped with these difficulties.

There is another important difference between these two kinds of tests. Good multiple-choice items, comprehension questions, and true/false statements are not easy to make. Items like the reference word items however are easy to make because the items can follow a fixed formula like

   This in line 6 refers to   in line
or
   What does *This* in line 6 refer to?

The only difficulties involved in making such items are knowing what language features to test and finding examples of these features in the text. In the rest of this article we will look at useful features to test to gain information about reading, and we will look at possible types of items.

Types of test items: language features

Comprehension questions direct attention to the message of a text which is peculiar to that text. This makes it difficult for the teacher or the learners to get information about points that need further attention in order to make it easier to read other texts. The items described in this section, however, test language features that are important for the understanding of almost every text. Performance on these items can be used as a basis for planning further teaching.

1 Noun groups

Much of the complexity at the sentence level is caused by noun groups containing relative clauses or reduced relative clauses. Here are two sentences from an unsimplified text. The noun groups are in brackets. Notice how the relative clauses and reduced relative clauses complicate what is basically a simple sentence pattern.

(The advent of jet and rocket propulsion, and of nuclear reactors,) has shown that (the materials which previously served for constructional purposes) are no longer wholly satisfactory for (the manufacture of equipment on which the efficient functioning of these new sources of power depends.) (An industrial demand) has arisen for (entirely new metals which were merely laboratory curiosities a few years ago, or which, in the case of the transuranic elements produced by nuclear fission, never before existed within the history of Man.)

(Adamson & Lowe, 1971, p. 25)

There are various levels of difficulty of relative clauses, and test items will reveal these. Briefly, the most difficult relative clauses are those that interrupt the normal subject verb (object) pattern. So a relative clause which is attached to the subject of a sentence causes more difficulty for a reader than one attached to the object. In addition, relative clauses with the object of the relative clause replaced by the *wh-* word are more difficult than those with the subject of the relative clause replaced by the *wh-* word. That is, *The man who I saw . . . .* is more difficult than *The man who saw me . . . . .*

Understanding of complex noun groups can be tested in the following ways.

a. The teacher gives the learners a noun from the text. The learners copy the whole noun group containing the noun. Alternatively the learners can just copy the first two and last two words of the noun group in the text.

b. The teacher gives the learners a verb from the text and they copy the subject and object of the verb from the text. Here are items based on the examples of noun groups given above.

_____ are no longer satisfactory.

_____ depends on _____

2 Co-ordination

The following sentence can be divided into three parts.

1
The main cables of all modern suspension
2
bridges/are fixed to the tower tops,/and subject
3
the towers to a very heavy vertical load (almost the whole weight of the bridge).

Parts 2 and 3 are parallel to each other and they are both connected to part 1. A problem in reading such a sentence is seeing the relationship between part 1 and part 3. This can be tested in the following ways.

a. The teacher instructs the learners to remove *and*, and rewrite the sentence as two sentences.

b. If part 3 begins with a verb, the teacher gives the learners the verb and they copy the subject and object of the verb from the text.

_____ subject _____

3 Reference words

This, that and *it* are the most difficult reference words because they can refer to items other than nouns or noun groups. There are however other factors which affect the difficulty of reference words. These include whether the reference word follows or precedes the item referred to, whether the item referred to is in a different sentence from the reference word or not, and whether there are other grammatically (although not semantically) possible items between the reference word and the item referred to. Barnitz (1980) found that the most difficult reference items were those that referred to a noun in the same sentence and followed the item referred to. Barnitz tried to make a ranking of the difficulty of different types of reference items. When such a ranking has been made, teachers can use tests of reference items to see how far a particular learner has gone on the way to mastering the items. Then suitable help and practice can be provided. Teachers can also use the tests described in this article to make their own rankings of difficulty. Examples of reference word items have already been given.

4 Verbs

Verbs typically enter into a relationship with a subject, and an object, adjunct, or complement. In a sentence like *The committee reached a decision*, the subject and object of the verb *reach* are quite apparent. These relationships are less apparent in a sentence like *After much deliberation by the committee a decision was finally reached*. Sometimes the relationships are even less apparent when the verb has become a noun. For example, in the following sentence, some learners will have difficulty in deciding what *uses* what and what *competes with* what.

> Sowing the orchard to grass will result in a temporary check to the vigour of the trees, due principally to the use of the available nitrogen by the grass and competition by the sward for the moisture.
> (NZDA, 1974, p. 50)

We have seen how the *What does what?* item can be used to test learners' understanding of noun groups and co-ordination. It is the most efficient way of testing whether learners see the subject verb (object/complement) relationship in different parts of a sentence. Here is a sample item.

> compete with   (line 3)

The rules to follow when answering a *What does what?* item are:

(*i*) Always make the verb active — not passive.

(*ii*) Copy only the headwords of the subject and object noun groups. That is, give short answers.

(*iii*) Do not use reference words when answering but answer using the item referred to.

Types of test items: problem solving strategies

In order to succeed in independent reading, learners need to be able to cope with unknown words and complicated sentences. It is not enough to know that a learner cannot cope with these difficulties. If help is to be given, the teacher must know where the learner is going wrong.

1 Words in context

Here is an item to test how well learners have mastered the strategy of guessing unknown words from context (Long & Nation, 1980).

> If the home orchard area is small, the problem of the large size to which most fruit trees grow can be met by planting dwarf or semi-dwarf trees . . . . . They can be grown conveniently along the edge of the vegetable garden without encroaching on it.
> (NZDA, 1974, p. 51)

> *encroaching*   a. What part of speech is it?
>   b. What does not encroach on what?
>   c. Which word could you put between the two sentences — *but, because* or *then*?
>   d. What does *encroach* mean in the text?

If the learners' guess at *d* is a different part of speech from *a* then they need to make a basic change in their strategy. Their guess must be the same part of speech as the unknown word. *b* tests whether the learners notice the immediate grammatical relationships. *c* tests the learners' appreciation of the wider context. A breakdown at any one of these points shows where further practice is needed.

2 Simplifying sentences

The steps in this strategy consist of items mentioned in the section on language features, namely

a. reference

b. co-ordination, and

c. noun groups.

Here is a sample item.

> Simplify the following sentence by replacing all reference words by the items referred to, by removing *and, but,* or *or* and rewriting as different sentences, and by removing the parts of the noun groups that follow the main noun in the group (relative and reduced relative clauses).

> The legs of the Severn towers, on the other hand, have no cells, and the visible outer plating, reinforced by internal longitudinal stiffeners, is carrying the whole of the tower load, and surrounds an otherwise open space, save for diaphragms, ladders and lifts.
> (Adamson & Lowe, 1971, p. 97)

Here is the answer.

> The legs of the Severn towers, on the other hand, have no cells. The visible outer plating is carrying the whole of the tower load. The visible outer plating surrounds an otherwise open space, save for diaphragms, ladders and lifts.

This strategy is used whenever the learners meet a sentence that they cannot understand in spite of knowing the vocabulary (Nation, 1979; Long & Nation, 1980).

Validity

The validity of the test items described in this

article depends on whether the items test real problems in advanced reading and whether the strategies work.

There is considerable evidence that the items test real problems. Most of the evidence however comes from studies of children learning their mother tongue. Researchers have found that children learn items like reference words, or noun groups, in a particular order. This order seems to reflect the difficulty of the items. So, children learn relative clauses attached to the object before relative clauses attached to the subject. In addition, comprehension tests reveal that children have more difficulty in interpreting sentences containing a relative clause attached to the subject. The small amount of experimentation done with learners of English as a foreign language supports the findings of first language learning research. But there is need for more research with foreign learners. Teachers can carry out much of this research in their own classroom by combining the use of the test items described in this article with translation checks and individual interviews with learners. Evidence about whether the strategies work can only come from their use. They have been useful in my teaching but teachers should not accept them uncritically. The question of validity should be the concern of all teachers.

Conclusion

The test items described in this article direct attention towards structural features of a reading text and to analytical strategies. There are several reasons for this. Firstly, performance on the items provides the teacher and learners with feedback which can result in appropriate help and practice with features that occur in almost every reading text. Secondly, the items allow teachers to investigate learning. That is, teachers can act as experimenters and develop and validate rankings of learning difficulty of structural features. Through their testing they can gain new insights into language and how it is learned. Thirdly, the items direct attention to language as a system. An important educational goal of language learning is the development of an interest in language for its own sake. An awareness of the system behind language is a step towards this goal.

It needs to be stressed that the items described in this article are not offered as substitutes for comprehension questions. They are useful additional tools which may lead to a greater understanding of learning and a corresponding improvement in teaching.

References

Adamson, V. and Lowe, M.J.B., *General Engineering Texts: English Studies Series 9*, Oxford University Press, London, 1971.

Barnitz, J.G., 'Syntactic effects on the reading comprehension of pronoun-referent structures by children in grades two, four and six', *Reading Research Quarterly* 15, no. 2, 1980, pp. 268–89.

Long and Nation, *Read Thru*, Longman, Singapore, 1980.

Nation, I.S.P., 'The curse of the comprehension question: some alternatives', *RELC Journal Guidelines* 2, 1979, pp. 85–103.

N.Z.D.A. (New Zealand Department of Agriculture), *The Home Orchard*, Government Printer, Wellington, 1974.

Brian Heaton

Writing in perspective: some comments on the testing and marking of written communication

The need to improve tests of writing does not seem to have received as much attention in the past decade as the need to improve techniques for testing grammar and lexis. However, even during the heyday of the psychometric and structural school of testing, composition writing, together with the oral interview, provided an essential balance to discrete point tests by laying stress on the more communicative tests of language use. For many years, the composition paper has been ostensibly concerned with the total effectiveness of the written message rather than with the correctness of the language forms comprising its various parts. Although such mechanical methods of scoring as the error-count method (in which one mark is deducted for each mistake made) were used at one time by some examiners in an overriding desire to achieve reliability, misguided and inhibiting methods of this nature were on the whole short-lived, and were soon replaced by analytical and impression methods of scoring. The advantage of setting two or more short realistic writing tasks in place of one literary type of essay has also been recognised for many years in several widely administered examinations.

Nevertheless, in spite of its many merits, free composition is by far from being the only means of testing the writing skills. Neither is it necessarily the most reliable means. Controlled composition testing, still in its infancy, offers a reliable way of measuring a limited number of identifiable skills at a time. Although by no means appropriate for every situation in which writing is tested, controlled composition may be useful in many progress and diagnostic tests, simply because it can help teachers to identify, and concentrate on, specific areas of difficulty. Moreover, the controlled writing task itself can be made far less time-consuming.

What does controlled composition measure which a test of grammar by definition does not usually measure? Most tests of grammar are concerned with the recognition and manipulation of correct forms of language and operate at the sentence level (though good grammar tests often operate beyond the level of the sentence). Tests of written composition, on the other hand, should concentrate

primarily on those aspects of grammar and syntax which relate to meaning in a piece of discourse rather than meaning in isolation: e.g. reference features, connectives, substitution devices, omission. In addition, a controlled composition test may seek to identify and measure such judgement skills as appropriacy of style, register, relevance and ordering.

Paragraphs for completion, stretches of language in which sentences are put in their correct order, pieces of continuous writing designed to test an awareness of style and register as well as relevance and appropriacy are all useful techniques for testing writing. However, not all tests of writing need consist of long pieces of connected discourse: there are also ways of testing writing beyond the level of the sentence, using much shorter stretches of language. Samonte and Sharwood-Smith cite the use of a two-sentence text which measures an ability to form a coherent unit of language. For example, candidates may be instructed to write a sentence to precede the statement 'Moreover, it was impossible to open the windows'. Example responses could be 'It was very hot in the small room', 'There was only one fan in the room, but it was broken', 'The door slammed behind John, and he realised he was locked in the room', etc. Though in all cases students are required to demonstrate an awareness of the communicative nature of language in general, and cohesive devices in particular, there is a large degree of subjectivity and freedom of response in this type of item, as can be seen from the following example stimuli.

(*i*) There is one here, too.
(*ii*) To do this, the water must first be boiled.
(*iii*) These should then be carefully sorted.
(*iv*) For wild life, however, there are even greater dangers in the pollution of rivers, lakes and seas.
(*v*) But there is no reason to be so pessimistic.

The degree of control (and objectivity) in testing composition writing can vary widely. The following is an example of a closely controlled composition task which resembles in many ways a test of grammar. However, it should be remembered that the composition is intended to test solely an ability to use appropriate connectives and reference devices in connected discourse.

A travel agency in Bangkok is now arranging day tours to foreign countries by jumbo jet. _____, you can leave Bangkok very early in the morning and have lunch at the Taj Mahal. _____ you can fly to New Delhi _____ do some shopping _____ returning to Bangkok at midnight. _____, you may leave Bangkok much later in the morning _____ spend a day shopping in Singapore, returning home in time to watch the evening news on television.

Control can be relaxed to varying degrees; at the other extreme, as illustrated by the following example of written work based on information given in tabular form, very little control need be exercised.

when carrying out the writing task. Indeed, in everyday situations in real life we rarely write without a particular purpose in mind, whether it is a letter, an article, a report, or notice. Consequently, even the two examples of controlled composition previously given would benefit from such rubrics as:

The following paragraph has been taken from a newspaper report. The writer hopes to interest his readers by giving surprising information about new kinds of day tours. Rewrite the paragraphs, inserting a suitable word or phrase in each blank.

and

Use the following table to provide information about the influence of propaganda. As your readers are largely ignorant about the effects of

Propaganda

	Means	Result
1	Loaded words	Influence people with no strong views on subject
2	Both sides of argument	Convert people originally opposed to idea
3	Repetition	Make people remember
4	Quotations from respected sources	Strengthen arguments

Regardless of the extent of the degree of control operated, however, it is important that controlled composition tests should never become unnatural exercises involving the performance of mental somersaults on the part of the students. Tasks requiring students to form sentences according to certain patterns (e.g. 'Combine the following sentences, using *which* and *although*.') often result in all kinds of errors simply by forcing students to guess what was in the examiner's mind, adopting unfamiliar and alien lines of thought.

All written work, whether free or controlled, should be carried out as far as possible in a communicative context. When we speak, we are generally aware that we are addressing another person: hence there is a basic desire — whether conscious or subconscious — to communicate with that person. Because the writer often finds himself addressing a general audience which is far less clearly identifiable than in normal speech situations, such a desire is not so apparent in writing. Consequently, it is all the more important in tests of writing to provide both a context and a purpose which the student can have uppermost in his mind

propaganda, try to convince them of its power over people.

Where it is important in the test to concentrate on a particular register, students can be instructed to write a letter to a friend, an article for a newspaper, a report drawing certain conclusions, a memorandum advising someone, etc. The following two topics from the Joint Matriculation Board Test in English Overseas illustrate how writing tasks can be put into a communicative context which provides both motivation and guidance for candidates. It is also worth noting that these items appeared many years ago.

Example (i)
Imagine that a British friend of yours has recently gone to live in your country. You have arranged for him to stay for a week-end with some relative of yours. They are eager to welcome your friend, but have never met any young people from Britain before.

Your friend is very frank, sincere and likeable, but he has many casual ways that you think might upset your relatives. Your friend is often untidy and unpunctual, treats older people as equals (in a very friendly way of course), and likes to argue about subjects such as politics and religion. Your friend will probably be ignorant of the customs observed in your country when visiting people.

Write a letter to your friend, who may be male or female, whichever you prefer. Describe your relatives briefly, and advise your friend how to behave towards them. Write between one and one-and-a-half pages.

Example (ii)

The following table gives information about the cost of sending 27 tons of office machinery from London to New York by air and by sea:

	TRANSPORT	DELIVERY TO THE NEW YORK CUSTOMER	INSURANCE	TOTAL
Sea	£5,610	£810	£1,660	£8,080
Air	£6,500	£840	£1,120	£8,460

Imagine that you work for the company that wishes to sell this machinery to America. You have been asked to write a short report advising your company whether to send it by sea or by air. In addition to the above information, you know that most other British companies that export office machinery send it by sea, and that the American customers want quick delivery. The delivery time by sea is six weeks; by air it is two weeks. Furthermore, the total value of the 27 tons of office machinery is £115,000.

Write your report to your company. It should not be in letter form. Write between one and one-and-a-half pages.

It is necessary, however, to sound a cautionary note when devising writing tasks which stress the communicative nature of language. Creating cultural obstacles should be avoided when devising realistic tasks: for example, however tempting it may be to instruct candidates to write notes for imaginary milkmen, such a writing situation would be quite alien to students in Thailand — or even in Germany.

In many compositions, assessment of writing performance is sometimes based largely on the number of grammatical errors made. As will be readily appreciated, the resulting score using this method bears little relation to the effectiveness of a student's ability to express himself freely in writing. The scoring of tests of free-writing has, in fact, long been the subject of considerable research. Briefly, marks may be awarded on what the testee has written; on what it is thought the testee meant by what he wrote; on handwriting and general appearance of the composition; or on previous knowledge of the student. Furthermore, it is possible (and not unusual) for two markers to differ widely in the spread of the marks they award, their strictness and their rank ordering of papers. Indeed, whether the analytical method or the multiple-marking method (often referred to as the impression method) is used, examiners award marks chiefly on the basis of their impression of the students' work.

Whatever method is used to assess written work, care should be taken to avoid an excessive concern with the manipulation of language forms. At the other extreme, of course, is the attitude typified by the statement 'I know what the candidate is trying to say' — an attitude which too frequently reflects a desire to interpret on behalf of the student at all costs and which results in a neglect of the grammatical and even the communicative aspects of the written language.

It is precisely in the attitude to grammatitical errors where the testing of the writing skills differs from the teaching of these skills. In the teaching of writing, attention may be concentrated on the correction of high-frequency errors or of those errors which are least acceptable to native-speakers. Alternatively, the teacher may wish to correct only those errors which are related to the particular language forms currently being taught. In tests of writing, however, attention ought to be paid primarily to those types of grammatical errors which impede written communication. As a result of examining such kinds of errors, Burt and Kiparsky (1972) advocate classifying errors according to whether they are global or local errors. They define global errors as those which involve the overall structure of a sentence, causing the reader to misunderstand a message or even fail to understand it at all. Misuse of connectives, relatives, pronouns and other reference devices, wrong sequence of tenses, incorrect word order and inadequate lexical knowledge as well as serious mis-spellings and wrong punctuation can usually be classed as global errors. Local errors, on the other hand, comprise those errors which cause trouble in a particular constituent or clause in a sentence and which do not significantly hinder the comprehension of the sentence. They include misuse of articles and prepositions, lack of agreement between subject and verb, incorrect affixes, wrong verb forms and the incorrect position of adverbs. Burt argues that this distinction between global and local errors provides the most useful criteria for determining the communicative importance of errors, claiming that the correction of one global error helps to clarify a message far more than the correction of several local errors.

In a study based on the work of Burt and Kiparsky, Tomiyana examines the various ways in which grammatical errors can distort written messages. The results indicate that such local errors as those caused by the omission and wrong choice of articles are easier to correct and hence less crucial to successful communication than the omission and wrong choice of connectives. However, the incorrect insertion of both articles and connectives does not cause any serious breakdown in communication. Hendrickson has modified Burt and Kiparsky's global/local error distinction, defining a global error as a communicative error which results in a proficient speaker misinterpreting or even failing to understand a message and a local error as a linguistic error which renders a structure, etc. awkward but which nevertheless does not give rise to any real difficulty in understanding the intended meaning of a sentence. The whole area of global/local or communicative/linguistic errors is a rich one for further research and may well provide a systematic method for assessing fre-written work with deeper insight.

Finally, the whole question of time should be considered when administering tests of writing. While it may be important to impose time limits in tests of reading, grammar and lexis, such constraints may well be very harmful in tests of writing, increasing the sense of artificiality and unreality. Moreover, the fact that candidates are expected to produce a finished piece of writing at their very first attempt adds to this sense of unreality. How often in real-life situations is anyone expected to write something without having a chance to produce one or more preliminary drafts first? Not only should students be given sufficient time to produce preliminary drafts of whatever they write but they should be actively encouraged to do this in any test of composition. If writing tests are made far more realistic and relevant to real-life situations, emphasis will automatically be placed on writing as a communicative activity.

References

Burt, M.K. and Kiparsky, C., *The Gooficon: a repair manual for English*, Rowley, Mass., Newbury House, 1972.

Hendrickson, J. (Ed.), *Error Analysis and Error Correction in Language Teaching*, RELC Occasional Papers, No. 10, 1979.

Joint Matriculation Board, Test in English (Overseas), March 1968, July 1968.

Samonte, Aurora L., 'Techniques in Teaching Writing', *RELC Journal*, Vol. 1, No. 1, 1970.

Sharwood-Smith, Michael, 'Courses in Written English — Some Comments and Words of Caution', *ELT Documents*, (73/1), 1973.

Sharwood-Smith, Michael, 'New Directions in Teaching Written English', *Forum*, Vol. XIV, No. 2, April, 1976.

Tomiyana, M., 'Grammatical Errors Communication Breakdown', *TESOL Quarterly*, Vol. 14, No. 1, March 1980.

J P Boyle

Testing language with students of literature in ESL situations

Passing your driving test means being able to drive the car well, not simply knowing the Highway Code and a manual on engine maintenance. Language testing nowadays, like language teaching, also stresses the ability to do something with the language, not merely to know about its formal characteristics: the rules of use are seen to be important as well as the rules of grammar. Alan Davies' Survey Articles in *Language Teaching and Linguistics: Abstracts* (*i*) outline well the new awareness of the problem of testing communicative competence as well as formal knowledge. Interestingly, he ends his careful and wide-ranging survey with the question: 'Is communicative testing feasible?'

Whatever our feelings on this, most people with experience in language testing would agree that a good test will contain both questions of a general nature and questions on more specific details, in other words integrative as well as discrete point. If we accept this general position and turn to the business of testing students of literature in ESL situations, some interesting test types, both of a general and specific nature, can be suggested.

But first, some preliminary remarks on the validity of considering students of literature as a special group. I am thinking of the type of situation which is not uncommon, especially in tertiary education in Commonwealth or former Commonwealth countries, where the students who choose to do a degree in English must study a great deal of literature. However, their language ability is often not too good, particularly in countries where English is being spoken less and less and the mother tongue is taking over. There is a tendency in such circumstances to play down the relevance of literature in language teaching. This tendency is reinforced when ESP becomes fashionable and the generalities of literature are considered less relevant to the students' needs than the more purpose-specific language of other disciplines – science, medicine, engineering.

More than half a century ago Ezra Pound refuted such thinking:

'And this function (of literature in the state) has to do with the clarity and vigour of any and every thought and opinion. It has to do with maintaining the very cleanliness of the tools, the health of the very matter of thought itself . . . . . When their (writers') work goes rotten – by that I do not mean when they express indecorous thoughts – but when their very medium, the very essence of their work, the application of word to thing, goes rotten, i.e. becomes slushy and inexact, or excessive and bloated, the whole machinery of social and individual thought and order goes to pot. This is a lesson of history, and a lesson not half learned.' (*ii*)

So the first justification for keeping language teaching – and therefore testing – in touch with literature is that literature, being language at its most vigorous and clearest, keeps language 'clean and healthy'.

A recent issue of *Forum* shows a renewed interest in returning to literature as a source of texts for enjoyable and stimulating language teaching. Admitting to a slight guilt-feeling about using literature, one writer says:

'Most of us teach literature in language class for exactly the same reason we are ashamed that we teach literature: stories and poetry are interesting. We enjoy them. The students enjoy them. Our attention is engaged, as it is rarely engaged by word-lists and exercises, for literature touches our common humanity.' (*iii*)

And in the conclusion to the first article of the same issue of *Forum*, Albert H. Marckwardt, the author of *The Place of Literature in the Teaching of English as a Second or Foreign Language* (1978), says:

'In our wholly justifiable concern with the language per se and with taking every possible advantage of the systematic study of language to facilitate the learning process, there is a danger of overlooking or undervaluing some of the uses to which language may be put, among them its function as a literary medium.' (*iv*)

J P Boyle

Teaching language to students of literature is in a sense ESP, with the paradoxical twist that the speciality of literature is the consideration of human nature at its broadest, its most general. In the medical field the specialist – the surgeon, the psychiatrist, the paediatrician – is considered the high-flyer; the poor old General Practitioner definitely a cut below. In language teaching ESP is felt by some to be more high-powered than general English. But with language, as with medicine, the specialist must first be an expert in his general field. And with language that general field is human nature in action – the realm of literature.

In this context, then, let us see what kind of tests would be appropriate to students of literature. Rather than speak in general terms, I will give examples where possible.

1. Reading

a. A short story is read, e.g. Frank O'Connor's *My Oedipus Complex*. Specific comprehension questions can be asked:

(*i*) What particular delight did climbing into his mother's bed in the morning give the boy?

(*ii*) What incident brought the boy and his father together?

Short passages can be quoted and their significance in the story as a whole questioned:

(*i*) 'You must be quiet while Daddy is reading, Larry,' Mother said impatiently. It was clear that she either. genuinely liked talking to Father better than talking to me, or else that he had some terrible hold on her which made her afraid to admit the truth. 'Mummy,' I said that night when she was tucking me up, 'do you think if I prayed hard God would send Daddy back to the war?'

(*ii*) I pretended to be talking to myself, and said in a loud voice: 'If another bloody baby comes into this house, I'm going out.' Father stopped dead and looked at me over his shoulder. 'What's that you said?' he asked sternly. 'I was only talking to myself,' I replied, trying to conceal my panic. 'It's private.'

b. The literature student must be able to discriminate in reading, between facts that are non-essential and others which are of central symbolic significance. In D.H. Lawrence's *The Horse Dealer's Daughter*, for example, the relevance of the pool (into which the doctor wades to rescue the attempted suicide) could be questioned. This type of question tests not simply accuracy in remembering all the facts of a story – 'vacuum-cleaner reading', as it has been called – but the power to appreciate the importance of certain facts – like the painting of the fence in *Tom Sawyer*.

c. Cloze/Modified cloze. The cloze test, together with dictation, has risen in the popularity polls. The Hong Kong Examining Board is happy with initial results from modified cloze (where the blank has three or four answers and the correct one has to be chosen – a multiple-choice question). All types of cloze test seem to be reliable: deleting every *n*th word, or deleting on a more rational basis; allowing only the exact word or accepting reasonable alternatives. For literature students the cloze is probably more valid, certainly more relevant, if something like the following can be given. It is taken from the text of an interview with Joyce Cary, the novelist, contained in the Paris Review Interviews, *Writers at Work*.

> INTERVIEWERS: Have you read *The Bostonians*? There was the spellbinder.
> CARY: No, I haven't read that.
> INTERVIEWERS: *The Princess Casamassima?*
> CARY: I'm afraid I haven't read that either. Cecil is always telling me to read her and I must. But I read James a good deal. There are times you need James, just as there are times when you must have Proust – in his very different _____ of change. The essential thing _____ James is that he came _____ a different, a highly organized, hieratic society, and for him ___ was not only a very _____ and highly civilized society, but _____ It was the best the _____ could do. But it was ___ subject to corruption. This was ___ center of James' moral idea – ___ everything good was, for that _____ specially liable to corruption. Any _____ of goodness, integrity of character, _____ that person to ruin. And ____ whole civilization, because it was ___ real civilization, cultivated and sensitive, ___ fearfully exposed to frauds and _____ brutes and grabbers. This was ___ tragic theme. But my world ___ quite different – it is intensely _____ a world in creation. In ___ world, politics is like navigation ___ a sea without charts and ____ men live the lives of pilgrims.

In this example I have deleted mechanically every sixth word. To guess the correct word in some cases may perhaps seem extremely difficult, even for the native speaker, e.g. 'static', which fills the seventh blank, or 'exposed', which fills the fourteenth. However, two things must be remembered: first, that such a short passage is not a real example of a cloze test; secondly, that with a longer passage, the same mental mechanics go on as in crossword puzzle solving — clue 3 across seems impossibly difficult, until you get helped by discovering the answer to clue 5 down. Similarly with cloze, a word guessed later on in the passage gives a clue to an earlier word, e.g. 'dynamic', which fills the fourth last blank, would not be impossible to get, particularly with the help of 'a world in creation' immediately following it. And once 'dynamic' has been guessed, in the context of the whole passage, the earlier seventh blank might well be correctly filled too, 'static'.

INTERVIEWERS: Have you read *The Bostonians*?

CARY: No, I haven't read that.

INTERVIEWERS: *The Princess Casamassima*?

CARY: I'm afraid I haven't read that either. Cecil is always telling me to read her and I must. But I read James a good deal. There are times you need James, just as there are times when you must have Proust — in his very different world of change. The essential thing about James is that he came into a different, a highly organized, a hieratic society, and for him it was not only a very good and highly civilized society, but static. It was the best the world could do. But it was already subject to corruption. This was the center of James' moral idea — that everything good was, for that reason, specially liable to corruption. Any kind of goodness, integrity of character, exposed that person to ruin. And the whole civilization, because it was a real civilization, cultivated and sensitive, was fearfully exposed to frauds and go-getters, brutes and grabbers. This was his tragic theme. But my world is quite different — it is intensely dynamic, a world in creation. In this world, politics is like navigation in a sea without charts and wise men live the lives of pilgrims.

---

2. Writing

a. Vocabulary. The literature student has to be more at home in words which describe the finer shades of human emotion. Basic feelings can be taken as the starting point. Then the student must find six words within the range of that broad feeling, and use the six words in a sentence. For example, ANGRY might turn up such words as: raging/cross/peeved/annoyed/furious/fuming. JOY: happy/glad/overjoyed/pleased/cheerful/delighted. FEAR: terrified / afraid / dreading / apprehensive / anxious/nervous. LOVE: adore/like/be fond of/be attached to/be devoted to/be infatuated with.

Another way is to give a picture of a face which expresses a complex of emotions. The Mona Lisa would be a good example. The student has to describe the face. Or a pair of pictures can be used, e.g. a self-portrait of Rembrandt and a self-portrait of Van Gogh. Works of art are usually more useful for this, in that they are more enigmatic, less explicit than most photographs. But good photographs can readily be found too.

b. Students of literature are no different from other ESL students in their tendency to make grammatical errors. I am concentrating here on test-types which seem to be particularly relevant, but by no means saying these are the only ones. In one type of test the grammatical accuracy may be the testing-point. In another, the student's power of imagination may be the important thing. 'The snow felled on the ground like flying-saucers landing' or 'The tree falled over like an oil-rig in the North Sea capsizing' should not be marked down, because of the slip, 'felled' or 'falled'. I am *not* saying the student should not be 'felled' for such errors in a *grammar* test. Since simile and metaphor are so important in literature, simple tests can be devised. The student has to complete the sentence imaginitively.

(*i*) 'His face was wrinkled like . . . . .
'Her hair was flowing like . . . . .
'The old lady's teeth were black like . . . . .

(*ii*) More difficult would be examples with two blanks:
'His face was . . . . . like . . . . .
'Her hair was . . . . . like . . . . .
'The old lady's teeth were . . . . . like . . . . .

(*iii*) With less control will come more variety and scope, as well as more difficulty:
'His . . . . . was . . . . . like . . . . .
'Her . . . . . was . . . . . like . . . . .
'The old lady's . . . . . was . . . . . like . . . . .

c. To test appreciation of register, discrete-point examples like the following are useful:

(*i*) 'This old (person/chap/individual/gentleman) comes up to me and he says . . . . .'

(*ii*) 'The butler bowed and (heaved/shoved/passed/donated) over the letter.'

More creatively, the student can be asked to write a short passage which deliberately aims at humour by means of mixing registers. P.G. Wodehouse is the master and model for this.

d. More global tests of writing would include composition, more or less controlled, or a free response to a text, tape or film.

J P Boyle

3. Listening

a. Drama on tape/radio. After a play has been listened to, response of a general nature can be required. What was the play really about? Or more specific answers could be demanded: Match each of the following with one of the characters in the play — wily/forthright/exuberant/discreet/retiring. A problem with this type of question, of course, is that words describing character tend to be subtle in their nuances. However, this brings us back to the type of exercise under Writing, *2a*.

b. Story. Again, after hearing a story, a global response can be required: briefly retell the story, making sure you include what seems to you to be the main point. A more specific question would be: Which of the following titles best suits the story you have heard? This would be a multiple-choice question, in effect, with one of the answers more obviously defensible objectively.

c. Poetry. I have said very little on the use of poetry in testing the language ability of literature students. It is of limited value, it seems to me, to use a poem for structural questions, asking the student to put the poem into 'plain English'. This can take the heart out of poetry, though in some cases, with extremely difficult poets (e.g. Hopkins), this exercise will be almost necessary for ESL students. A more relevant type of test question will test the literature student's ability to appreciate the way poetry charges words with different levels of meaning. 'To read poetry adequately a student must not only have a command of lexis in the sense that he knows how to use a number of words; he must also know a number of possible uses for any given word.' A good example would be W.B. Yeats' *The Song of the Old Mother*.

> I rise in the dawn, and I kneel and blow
> Till the seed of the fire flicker and glow:
> And then I must scrub and bake and sweep
> Till stars are beginning to blink and peep;
> And the young lie long and dream in their bed
> Of the matching of ribbons for bosom and head,
> And their day goes over in idleness,
> And they sigh if the wind but lift a tress:
> While I must work because I am old,
> And the seed of the fire gets feeble and cold.

The student can be asked what 'the seed of the fire' means in the poem. Many examples of this kind can easily be found. I have included this exercise under listening, because poetry is essentially an oral exercise, but clearly it could be a test-type for reading comprehension too.

d. Oller makes much of dictation as a reliable test-type. For straight dictation, probably such occasional essays as J.B. Priestley's *Delight*, for instance, would be the most suitable.

A more difficult test, of the Dicto-Comp type, would be to read a section from a modern play, preferably a radio-play, and then to ask the student to fill in the missing dialogue, as well as can be remembered. The following brief example may serve as an illustration. This example deletes too much in too short a space, and is therefore more difficult than a real test; it merely gives the idea of the test-type. It comes from a prize-winning radio play by Jennifer Phillips, *Daughters of Men*. *(vi)*

KATE: Age. Photos, of course you can have retouched.
ANNE: What?
KATE: Bahama had her photo taken every week.
ANNE: She told you?
KATE: No, Boy did. But he doesn't understand. You can't retouch the image in the mirror.
ANNE: But you have so much else to draw on, Kate . . . . . inner strengths.
KATE: And I shall be much freer.
ANNE: Oh, yes.
KATE: Without a child.
ANNE: But you won't be without.
KATE: Best to be prepared, isn't it? On the defensive. I always went round before exams at school saying I'd fail, didn't you? Saying I had to fail because I hadn't worked at it.
ANNE: The thought of exams struck me dumb.
KATE: Your driving test! Oh, I'll never forget that. And the lead up to it. And then I practically carried you there.

KATE: Age. Photos, of course, you can have retouched.
ANNE: What?
KATE: Bahama had her photo taken every week.
ANNE: _____
KATE: No, Boy did. But he doesn't understand. You can't retouch the image in the mirror.
ANNE: But you have so much else to draw on, Kate . . . . . inner strengths.
KATE: _____
ANNE: Oh, yes.
KATE: Without a child.
ANNE: But you won't be without.
KATE: _____ On the defensive. I always went round before exams

at school saying I'd fail, didn't you? Saying I had to fail because I hadn't worked at it.

ANNE: _____

KATE: Your driving test! Oh, I'll never forget that. And the lead up to it. And then I practically carried you there.

4. Speaking

a. Reading aloud. The difficulties of oral production tests are well outlined in J.B. Heaton's *Writing English Language Tests*. (*vii*) For testing appreciation of the meaning of a text, his recommendation of combining specific features with general fluency seems sound. For students of literature, the dimension of reproducing feeling or emotion in a text should also be tested, with some sort of dramatic reading. This kind of test will, of course, be affected by all sorts of extraneous factors, and these can hardly be overcome.

b. Conversation/Discussion. In ideal test conditions, with small numbers involved, the tester should be able, not so much to conduct a conversation with the student (this examiner/examinee situation can render real conversation pretty well impossible), but to observe two students conversing. With the importance which conversational dialogue has in both the novel and in drama, it is an area which should have a place in testing, but the problems of assessment are obvious. Probably as good a general test as any for literature students is to let them view a short play on video, after which the examiner asks them, pair by pair, to discuss the play while he sits in on the discussion. A library of suitable video plays can easily be built up.

c. Other suggestions could be short talks on the work/life and times of major literary figures; and here pictures or slides, useful in all sorts of ways in testing spoken English, could be assembled by the student, and the project assessed as a whole.

Conclusion

David Daiches claims that in literature students can achieve 'the fullest possible awareness of human relevance.' (*viii*) And an African writer to *ELT Journal* says: 'We have become so convinced that learning ESL means acquiring skills that the teaching of literature seems to have become of much less significance. ESL teachers do not seem to give much importance to the educational values of the literature they teach.' (*ix*) In a sense it is true of language teachers that, by their tests, you shall know them. This article has done no more than suggest a few test types which will show our students that we do respect the relevance of literature and that we do consider educational values in our teaching and our testing.

References

(*i*) Davies, A., Survey Articles on Language Testing, *Language Teaching and Linguistics: Abstracts*, Vol. 11, (1978).

(*ii*) Pound, Ezra, 'How to Read' (1928), *Literary Essays*, London, Faber & Faber, 1954, p. 21.

(*iii*) Power, H.W., 'Literature for Language Students: the Question of Value and Valuable Questions', *Forum*, XIX, 1, 1981.

(*iv*) Marckwardt, A.H., 'What Literature to Teach: Principles of Selection and Class Treatment', *Forum*, XIX, 1, 1981.

(*v*) Haynes, J., 'Polysemy and Association in Poetry', *ELT Journal*, XXX, 1, 1976.

(*vi*) Phillips, Jennifer, 'Daughters of Men', *Best Radio Plays of 1978*, Eyre Methuen.

(*vii*) Heaton, J.B., *Writing English Language Tests*, London, Longman, 1975, pp. 83–84.

(*viii*) Daiches, David, 'The Place of English in the Sussex Scheme', *The Idea of a New University*, Daiches, David (Ed.), MIT Press, 1970, p. 79.

(*ix*) Adeyanju, T.K., 'Teaching Literature and Human Values in ESL: Objectives and Selection', *ELT Journal*, XXXII, 2, 1978.

Patricia L McEldowney

A place for visuals in language testing

Introduction

If we consider the type of English that is currently used as a medium of education here and overseas and also as the medium of the day-to-day conduct of an English-speaking society, we find that, in both its spoken and written forms, verbal communication of information is commonly associated with the use of non-verbal communication devices. For instance, either in a text book or at a lecture, a geographical description of volcanos may be accompanied by photographs of typical examples, or by diagrams showing various types of core formation; an historical account of the Battle of Waterloo may be accompanied by a map summarising the progress of events; in biology, a tabulation summarising the characteristics of living organisms may be used to introduce a detailed discussion of each; in chemistry, a description of how to prepare and collect electrolytic gas may be accompanied by a diagram to show how to set up the relevant apparatus; or, in physics, a graph may be used to show how the volume of a fixed mass of water changes with temperature. Similarly, in the world outside the educational institution, a person asked to give a stranger directions to the Post Office may illustrate what he is saying with a rough sketch map; a set of instructions for operating a vacuum cleaner is usually accompanied by a set of diagrams to aid communication; a newspaper report of unrest in some part of the world may be illustrated by a map to pin-point the area and photographs of events; weather reports in newspapers or on television are commonly accompanied by weather maps; and so on.

This interdependence of verbal and non-verbal information devices would suggest that a test of the type of language involved might well not be complete without the inclusion of an element which will enable the candidate to demonstrate his familiarity with the typically associated range of non-verbal displays.

We note at this point, however, that the real-world relationship between the two types of information device must be altered if a valid language test is to be developed. In the examples cited above, the two stand side-by-side to supplement each other, the one rendering the other to some extent redundant. If our primary aim is to test linguistic behaviour, we must ensure that in a test of reading or listening comprehension, for instance, our candidates are responding to language rather than finding the meaning in accompanying visuals. This can be achieved by the separation of the two types of information device. So, for instance, candidates may read a text on the classification of different types of volcanic core and then be asked to label a set of blank diagrams as one type or another. Successful labelling would indicate understanding of the language of the text as well as demonstrating a familiarity with the type of diagram used.

It is the contention of this paper that visuals used in the way just described have a valuable role to play in the development of valid language tests, a role which extends far beyond a demonstration of familiarity with non-verbal information devices.

Let us now examine this role in more detail.

Comprehension

It is obvious that to produce a valid test we must be able to identify what it is exactly that we are testing. Towards this end, we note that in any piece of English there are two types of information and that a consideration of the relationship between the two highlights some central aspects of the comprehension skill. In the following extract, for instance, items communicating content or real-world knowledge are italicised:

Of the *perianth*, the *corolla* is inside the *calyx*. This *section* of the *flower* . . . . .

Now, though he may not 'know' the words *perianth*, *corolla* and *calyx*, the skilled reader can work out from the extract that they are parts of a flower. His main tool for doing this is the second type of information in the extract — the language information.

First of all, the marker *the*, together with its position in a preposition group, indicates that *perianth* refers to an object. Then, the linkers *this* and *of* associate it with the word *flower*. Similarly, *corolla* and *calyx* are marked as nouns by *the* and

86

their relative sentence positions while the language item *of* indicates that *corolla* and *calyx* are parts of the perianth. In addition, the language item *inside* indicates the relative positions of the calyx and the corolla. In this way, language information signals the type of referent of each content item and also indicates the relationships between them.

We note here that to have known the information about the perianth, calyx and corolla as expressed in the extract would indicate the possession of learning. Not to have known but to have been able to find out in the way described above indicates the possession of a tool for learning. Seen in this way, therefore, the ability to use language to discover content seems to be a very basic comprehension skill worthy of testing.

How might we go about developing such a test?

In light of the discussion above this can probably most clearly be illustrated with regard to a text like *Globbes* in which the content items are unknown to us.

Globbes

The four trug jigs of the globbe are the colls, the solls, the pals and the tals. They are in wongs, one inside the other. First, there are the colls in the centre with the solls around them. Outside the solls is the polnth. Where the polnth has two wongs, the jigs of the outer wong are the pals which tote the calyth. The jigs inside this are the tals toting the colnth.

In an attempt to test candidates' skills with regard to using their language knowledge to discover content, we might ask questions like:

Test Type A

(*i*) What are the four trug jigs of the globbe?
(*ii*) Where are the solls?
(*iii*) What totes the colnth?

It can be argued that success in finding the answers to such questions demonstrates some skill in using language knowledge. For instance, in (*i*), a solution word which provides a noun shows a response of the correct sort to the question word *what*; the provision of four nouns shows a response to the code item *four*; the solution *colls, solls, pals* and *tals* shows, in addition, an ability to match the general sentence structure of the question and the statement in the text. In (*ii*), the provision of a preposition group shows a response of the appropriate type to the question word *where*; the candidate who provides the group *around them* demonstrates further an awareness of general sentence structure; and the provision of *around the colls*

shows, in addition, an awareness of the function of *them* to refer back to *colls*.

In this way then we may be able to find some evidence of grammatical skill. Can we be sure, however, that the correct response necessarily demonstrates anything more than mechanical manipulation?

We note that it is quite possible that correct responses are triggered by information in the question and a familiarity with a manipulative technique rather than being a demonstration of any real processing of the information in the text. For instance, test questions of the type illustrated in A will be no problem to candidates who have had classroom practice (oral or written) similar to:

Answer the questions.
Example: Is the rope around the parcel?
         Yes, it's around the parcel.
Is the table in the corner?
Is the tree in the garden?

or *Look at the picture and answer the questions.*
Example: Where is the pond?
         The pond is in the park.
Where is the bird?
Where is the tree?

or *Make some questions.*
Example: The two boys are in the tree.
         Are the two boys in the tree?
The four cats are in the basket.
The three pencils are in the box.

Such practice constantly pairs question and statement forms so that, given one form, the correct response is to produce the other and it is not clear from a comprehension test incorporating the same principle whether a candidate is capable of producing the appropriate answer if he does not have the relevant information supplied in the question. That is, it is not clear to what extent he really 'understands' the text.

In an attempt, therefore, to ensure a demonstration of some processing of the information we might develop:

Test Type B

(*i*) List the components of the globbe.
(*ii*) What surrounds the colls?
(*iii*) Describe the construction of the colnth.

In these questions a rephrasing of the concepts expressed in the text demands a greater 'understanding' from the candidate. So, in (*i*), for instance, the use of the synonym *components* for *jigs* eliminates a direct clue from the question. The knowledge of the appropriate response to the instruction *List* . . . . . together with a response to the noun + *s* form (*components*), an awareness that the question is being asked about the globbe and a knowledge that, where *globbe* occurs before *are*, the relevant information follows the verb are all factors that will help a successful candidate to produce *colls, solls, pals* and *tals*. Thus, without a knowledge of the word *components*, a candidate who produces the appropriate response is more likely demonstrating a spontaneous use of his language knowledge than was the case in *Test Type A*.

We note, however, that if a candidate had known the meaning of *components* and if he had known that it is a synonym for *jigs*, he would have had a content clue in the question to direct him to the relevant sentence in the text. Now, it is clear that though language information is the basic tool for finding content, the more content items a reader or listener has at his command, the more efficient is his comprehension. For instance, if in the first sentence of the *Globbes* text we know two more of the content items:

The four trug parts of the flower are the colls . . . . .

our comprehension task would have been much easier. That is, in real-life the efficient reader uses a combination of language information and known content to discover unknown content. It would seem, therefore, that a clue in the question of the type illustrated by *components* in *B(i)* and *surrounds* in *B(ii)* is justifiable in a way that the one-to-one relationship illustrated in *Test Type A* is not.

We note now that *B(iii)* (*Describe the colnth*) goes even further than *B(i)* and *B(ii)* in eliminating clues from the question. The candidate must here, in response to the instruction *Describe* . . . . ., gather several pieces of relevant information and put them together in his own form:

There are sometimes two wongs in the polnth. The outside one is the colnth. It is toted by the tals.

This, however, highlights a difficulty for the examiner that is inherent, to a lesser degree, in all of the other items illustrated in *A* and *B*. In *B(iii)*, though we might agree on the relevant number of points, different candidates will express them in very different ways and examiners' responses to these will also be very different. This situation is likely to demand subjective judgements from individual examiners as to whether responses are correct or not. Moreover, the questions demand a verbal response. Many candidates may make grammatical mistakes — a further potentially subjective decision for the examiner. We can ignore such grammatical mistakes in our marking and so go some way towards isolating the comprehension skill. Even if we do this, however, we are not going far enough towards ensuring that poor productive skills do not hinder the demonstration of comprehension. Though certain candidates may 'understand' the text, their productive skills may be too weak to enable them to demonstrate even a small proportion of their understanding.

It can be seen, therefore, that the rephrased question type of *B* should be made objective. A common solution is that demonstrated below:

Test Type C
Tick the appropriate box.

(*i*) The main parts of the globbe are the:

wongs, solls, polnth, jigs ☐

colls, solls, pals, tals ☐

calyth, jigs, tals, colnth ☐

pals, tals, calyth, colnth ☐

(*ii*) In the globbe the sols surround the:

tals ☐

colls ☐

polnth ☐

calyth ☐

(*iii*) The colnth is formed by a circle of:

tals ☐

pals ☐

polnths ☐

calyths ☐

Though we have, in this way, allowed for objectivity, *Test Type C* embodies another problem also inherent in *A* and *B*. All three types of questioning are fragmentary.

On the whole, we read and listen for two main reasons. At times we wish to follow exactly what is being said. On other occasions we wish to find information that is incidental to the speaker or writer's purpose. In the latter case we might, for instance, skim through an outline of the events leading up to the sinking of *Bismarck* in World War II merely to find the names of the ships involved, ignoring the sequence of events. In this case the skill of isolating fragmentary detail seems to be of relevance and it may well be that *Test Type C* is valid from this point of view.

It seems clear, however, that we also need to test whether candidates can follow a writer or speaker's intent. In this case, we require a demonstration of an awareness of the whole — some demonstration of how individual parts fit together.

Let us now consider the passage *Globbes* from this point of view.

It seems that, in this description of the jigs of the globbe, the writer is concerned to show
> *both* a set of relationships of parts to the whole
> *and* a spatial arrangement.

In *Test Type C* items (*i*) and (*iii*) emphasise the first concept while (*ii*) deals with spatial arrangement. The same is true of *A* and *B*(*i*) and (*ii*). We note in *B*(*iii*), however, there is an attempt to broaden the question so that it covers both of the author's purposes. The constraints of objectivity already discussed, however, make it very difficult to construct global questions in the genre illustrated by *C*.

It is, however, possible to get closer to an awareness of the whole:

Test Type D
(*i*) *Use the words in the box to complete the diagram*:

> calyth, colls, colnth,
> pals, polnth, solls, tals

globbe

Inside   Outside

(*ii*) *a. Complete the key. To do this use words from the box below*:

> calyth, colls
> colnth, pals, polnth
> solls, tals

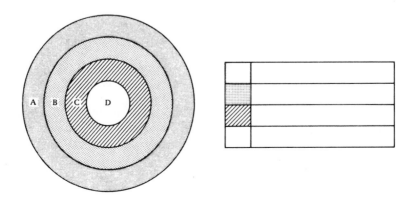

(ii) b. Find suitable words for the circles labelled A, B, C and D in the diagram. Use words from the box above to complete the following. Write X if there is no suitable word.

Circle A =

Circle B =

Circle C =

Circle D =

Circles A + B =

Circles B + C =

Circles C + D =

We note, at this point, that the display for (*i*) is more abstract than that for (*ii*). We could offer a third alternative which would be even less abstract. We could provide a drawing of a flower and ask candidates to label the parts.

In this way, we can test an awareness of the whole as well as that of spatial arrangement at whatever level of abstractness seems appropriate to our particular candidates. Moreover, *Test Type D* does this while still maintaining the criteria of the elimination of overt clues from the question, of objectivity and of the elimination of verbal production.

We now note a further important advantage of *Test Type D*. With appropriate language skill it is possible to produce correct verbal responses to questions like those illustrated in *C* without there being any assurance of a real-world knowledge of the forms being used. For instance, we might read

John drew a rectangle, coloured it green and added a cross flunger the bottom trig corner.

and respond correctly with *flunger the bottom trig corner* to the question
Where did John draw the cross?
We would, however, be at a loss if asked to draw John's diagram.

The move from verbal to non-verbal information illustrated in *Test Type D* thus gives the candidate the opportunity to demonstrate his ability to 'visualise' the relevant spatial relationship and so indicate a degree of real-world or content understanding.

Production

If comprehension can be defined as a means of using language and known content to discover new content either for one's own purpose or to mirror the author's purpose, production, in both the spoken and written modes, can be defined as the skill of using language and content information to fulfil a specific purpose. For instance, given a body of information about coracles, the production of instructions for making one, or a description of its appearance, or a classification of various types, or a narration of how one was used on a particular occasion will each require use of a cluster of different language items and a different organisation of the content information (see McEldowney, P., *Test in English (Overseas) The position after ten years*, Joint Matriculation Board, OP 36, September 1976).

If we wish to assess the tools of such expression, it is important, as indicated above in the discussion about the testing of comprehension, that we isolate the thing we wish to test in such a way that our impression of linguistic performance is not blurred by any extraneous factors.

Let us consider how this might be carried out.

Test Type E
(*i*) Describe how to make a coracle.
(*ii*) Describe what a coracle looks like.

Items like this, though directed towards a specific purpose, demand a prior knowledge of coracles. If we intend to test such knowledge, then these items might well be valid — perhaps in a local history or general studies paper. If, however, we intend to test language proficiency, a candidate who has no knowledge of coracles has nothing to write about and so cannot demonstrate his productive skills.

Does this mean our choice of topic is at fault? Can we, rather, choose topics previously prepared or topics known to be within the experience of our candidates? In either case we are asking candidates to depend on memory of content and cannot, in fact, be sure that a lucky 'question-spotter' has not learned an essay or speech off by heart. We have not, in fact, isolated the ability to use production tools from some closely associated assessment of content knowledge.

It would seem, from this point of view, that, as is implicit in the discussion of comprehension testing above, the choice of a topic which is largely unfamiliar to our candidates might well provide us with a better means of isolating the language tools we wish to test. This suggests that our test item needs to provide the basic information to be used in the production task.

We might do this by providing a text and asking questions of the type illustrated above in *B(iii)*, or by asking candidates to write a precis of the text. Such tasks, however, place too great a reliance on comprehension skills and are no more valid, therefore, than *Test Type E* in isolating production skills. Moreover, they allow for the (verbatim) copying of stretches of the original, and the organisation of the original more often than not provides the framework of organisation for the candidate to follow. This is not likely to allow the candidate to demonstrate spontaneously language and organisation skills appropriate to a specific task.

Valuable alternatives seem to be

(i) supply a set of construction diagrams together with the rubric:

Say how to make a coracle

or (ii) supply a picture of a coracle with the rubric:

Describe what a coracle looks like

or (iii) supply a sequence of pictures outlining a story with the rubric:

Tell the story of Old Joe and his coracle

It is the contention of this paper that, when the basic information is provided for candidates in a non-verbal form, they are more able to demonstrate their spontaneous use of language forms and their ability to organise information in a manner appropriate to the task indicated by the rubric and that they are able to do this with minimum reliance on verbal comprehension in such a way that they demonstrate their familiarity with non-verbal information devices.

Arthur Godman

Competence in English used for academic subject examinations

Introduction

Nobody can write in a language without a content. The evaluation of written sentences in English depends on the reader assessing both the language and the content of a sentence. Unless the written material is subject specific, the content may be vague, or the concepts diffuse. The aim of this paper is to discuss competence in English using material which is extended to include communication in academic subjects. Final exemplification will be given from science subjects, as, in these subjects, the content of a sentence must conform with known concepts in relation.

1.1 Lexis

An academic subject has a linguistic register expressed in grammar and a restricted vocabulary. A sound knowledge of the lexis is the first requisite of competence in an academic subject. Each academic subject has its own lexis, and the same term can have different denotations in different subjects. It is thus important to ascertain whether a student associates the correct concept with a particular term when he meets it in a specific situation. In para. 5.2, question 1 contains the term 'blood pressure'. The term 'pressure' varies with the subject under discussion. In general speech it describes the concept of a force applied by means of an area, e.g. as in a trouser press. In politics it describes, these days, the lobbying of politicians and acts which endeavour to influence them, but the meaning is diffuse. In science it describes force per unit area, and force per unit area can be expressed in millimetres of mercury. When confronted with question 1, how will the student react to the term 'pressure'? In order to be competent in science, for example, he must know the precise definition.

1.2 Grammar

Competence in language depends on the understanding of the semantic implications of grammar. Firstly, an understanding of the morphological processes words can undergo is necessary. Secondly, the syntax of clause and sentence must be understood. A sentence is a statement corresponding to a state of affairs. The state of affairs consists of a set of concepts in relation to each other in a person's mind. The structure of a sentence can thus be incorrect because the concepts are inadequately known, or the relation is inadequately formulated. In general speech, it is often difficult to distinguish between these two sources of error. Question 1 in para. 5.2 affords an example of the semantic implication of grammar in a science register. The passive voice is used to indicate measurement irrespective of the observer, hence the question requires an answer describing an accepted method. Answers 1 *b,, c., d., e.* show that this has been understood.

1.3 Cohesion

Cohesion in a text necessitates several factors, mainly expressed in grammatical functions and by the use of adjuncts. As this paper puts forward a tentative suggestion for the analysis of sentences and not for the analysis of discourse, the subject is not discussed further. The evaluation of competence in the construction of sentences must be determined before discourse can be analysed.

2.1 The question

In most tests a question is presented to a student, who then supplies an answer. The first stage of this process involves the student understanding the question, and this, too, has to be evaluated. The student is required to understand the lexis and the implication of the grammar. These two interact to produce a semantic content. This interaction can be illustrated by question 1 in para. 5.2. The key lexemes are obviously 'measure' 'blood' 'pressure' with 'blood' and 'pressure' interacting. In several Oriental languages, the sentence would be reduced to 'How measure blood pressure?' and the answer reduced to 'Doctor measure blood pressure', indicating specialist knowledge is required and shifting responsibility on to an acceptable observer. In English, the answer would be, baldly stated, 'By a sphygmomanometer' (SPHYGMO — pulse; MANOMETER — a pressure measurer). This, too, really evades the question, but would be an acceptable answer. If, on the other hand, the question was 'Describe the measurement of blood pressure', then a fuller answer would be obligatory. The framing of a question, therefore, depends on the answer which is required. Sufficient length is required in the answer to ensure that it is possible to detect the student's understanding of the question.

2.2 The answer
Having understood the question, does the student know the answer? Response can be at three levels: recall, application of knowledge, or solution of a problem. The answer thus depends on the student's conceptual knowledge and his ability to reason, with these two factors forming the limits of a spectrum of application.

2.3 Composing the written answer
The student must first marshal his concepts and choose suitable terms for such concepts. He must then select the necessary interrelationships between the terms and choose suitable syntax and morphological structures to express the interrelationship. The reader of the answer, for perfect communication, should have complete congruity of concepts with the writer. The sum total of the answer includes not only the lexis and the individual items of grammar, but also their interaction. The whole of the answer is thus greater than the sum of the parts, and this provides a semantic content which is in addition to lexis and grammar.

3.1 Difficulties encountered in evaluation
Objective-type questions produce an objective score; they test passive as well as active vocabulary, but they do not test the student's ability to express himself. Structured questions can be used to test active vocabulary alone, and also to test sentence structure. Structured questions do involve a degree of subjectivity in scoring. Essay-type questions always test all stages of sentence composition, but are highly subjective for scoring. Cloze tests examine lexis and syntax to some degree, but tend to test passive knowledge rather than active application.

3.2
The brief summary of basic testing procedures outlined in para. 3.1 points to structured questions as the best compromise in testing the basic elements of language, with essay-type questions as the sole means of testing connected and logical discourse. The structured questions must be of a type to produce a positive response. The set of questions in para. 5.2 indicates the degrees of success that can be obtained in eliciting a positive response.

4.1 Evaluation
The concept in an answer must be capable of being marked objectively, and then the interrelationships of the concepts, as expressed in language, can be evaluated with some degree of success. Questions should preferably be selected from academic subjects, particularly where the lexis is defined accurately. The lexis in a sentence in an answer can then be examined to see whether it is correct, bears some relation to the question, or is completely irrelevant. For example, in answer 1a. of para. 5.2, apart from the repetition of the question, the lexis is mainly irrelevant. An answer can be evaluated using different criteria. Is the scientific accuracy of an answer (in para. 5.2) being evaluated or is it the student's competence in language? Both evaluations will contain an element of the other, and hence different methods of scoring the evaluation could be produced. If competence in language is to be evaluated, then it is first necessary to ascertain the student's knowledge of scientific concepts in the semantic area to be examined. For example, in question 1 of para. 5.2, does the student have any knowledge about blood pressure and its measurement? Such knowledge can be pretested by simple recall, using objective-type questions. This reduces the possibility of incorrect lexis through ignorance if the subject is shown to be known to the student.

4.2 Subjective evaluation
Evaluation of language competence needs quantitative measurement. Looking at the range of answers in para. 5.2, a quantitative evaluation would seem extremely difficult. Yet there is a parallel in the evaluation of oral English in which a subjective rating is made of different qualities. The factors to be measured in evaluating competence in written language are (a) lexis, (b) syntax, (c) morphology and (d) semantic content. Factors (b) and (c) comprise grammar, (a) and (d) comprise the content of communication. Competence in content is more important than competence in grammar as the following two sentences illustrate.

(A) Hookworm penetrate the not wearing shoes feet.
(B) He is a male with normal vision because his mother has a sex-linked characteristic.

In (A) communication is excellent but the grammar is bad. In (B) the grammar is good, and even the lexis is correct, but the communication is bad. In (A) the student knows the correct state of affairs in relation to the question. In (B) the student has no idea of the state of affairs in relation to the question.

On the basis of the facts outlined so far, it is suggested that 60% of a score should be given to content and 40% to grammar. The mark for grammar can be split equally, 20%–20% for each of morphology and syntax. The mark for content has to be split between lexis and semantic competence in indicating interrelationships. Three schemes are suggested for experiment. Lexis is considered for focal lexemes in a sentence. Syntax is considered for logical order, and the use of prepositions. Morphology is considered for tense, aspect, voice, and agreement of verbs, together with correct paradigms for other terms. Semantic content is considered from the point of view of whether the sentence is correct in its interrelationships and whether communication is adequate. These factors can be measured only on a subjective scale, and it is suggested that a total score of 10 be allotted to a sentence. The distribution of scores for the factors in the three schemes is:

	Scheme A	Scheme B	Scheme C
Lexis	2	3	4
Syntax	2	2	2
Morphology	2	2	2
Semantic content	4	3	2

Scheme A maximises content, perhaps more suitable for evaluation of an academic subject. Scheme C minimises content, perhaps more suitable for evaluating language competence.

5.1

The questions and answers in para. 5.2 have been selected to show average performance by overseas students. With a mark out of 2, 3 or 4, and eliminating half-marks, a simple subjective scale is formed for each factor. By examining ten sentences, a subjective pattern of a student's performance can be ascertained. By examining the average score for a class, each factor can be evaluated to see which of them is weak or strong in sentence structure. Evaluations of the questions in para. 5.2 are given in para. 6.2.

5.2 Questions and answer in science examinations

Q.1 How is the blood pressure of a man measured?

Answers:

a. The blood pressure of a man measured is cooler than the woman's blood. Because the blood in the man body is very little than the woman's blood.

b. The blood pressure of a man measured is by a special of measurement which is put along muscle of our arm.

c. The blood pressure of a man measured is by using the checking of the diabetes disease instruments.

d. The blood pressure of a man measure by tieing a place of cloth like thing to the person arm and plump it tie where it is related to a thermatore in the other box where it is show.

e. It is measured by a pumping artificial organ controlled by a device. Usually it is green in colour.

f. A man measured of the blood pressure is 37°C.

Q.2 Why may it be dangerous to use human urine as a fertilizer?

Answers:

a. Because it contain salts.

b. Human urine contain large of salts this make the plant death.

c. When a human being eating the plant (vegetables) with human urine that person will easily be injected by a disease.

d. Because harmful germs are presented in urine, and it has not been properly washed before cooking it may transmit disease.

e. It may be dangerous because if that person may have any infectious disease.

f. Because in human urine it consists of mineral salts.

Q.3 Why does Table 2 (No. female mosquitoes trapped/time of day) give results for female mosquitoes only?
(*Note*: diseases are spread only by female mosquitoes.)

Answers:

a. Female gives more mosquitoes and more son.

b. Because the mosquito landed on human beings to take their meals.

Q.4 Why does a farmer use a nitrogen fertilizer for the cereal crop under these conditions?

Answers:

a. Because they need fertile soil to growth.

b. Can grow better after long time. the long the time is the more the crop grow.

c. To enable the cereal crop for consumption.

Q.5 Why did the water not rise to the 600cm^3 mark?

(*Note*: 25 cm^3 of air in 100 cm^3 of soil added to 500 cm^3 water in a measuring cylinder)

Answers:

a. Because the water fill up the soil hole.

b. Because the soil completely press due to the water which are shake.

Q.6 What would be a suitable precaution to be taken by most people to avoid being bitten by this species of mosquito?

(*Note*: this species bites in the middle of the night.)

Answers:

a. Throw unwanted can which contain water.

b. Most people would use mosquito nets before they sleep.

c. By used a blanket to cover before went to bed.

Q.7 Explain why the information given by the graph and histogram agrees with a suggestion that female mosquitoes lay their eggs before seeking a blood meal.

Answer:

Because the time lowest number of mosquitoes are trapped has the highest number of eggs laid and verse-visa.

Q.8 What is the effect of a nitrogen fertilizer on the root crop under these conditions?

(*Note*: progressive use decreased crop yield.)

Answers:

a. The root crop does not take nitrogen fertilizer and after six years it has drops to −10%.

b. The root crops under a nitrogen fertilizer will grow fewer than the phosphorus fertilizer.

c. It yield is very low and worst some times.

Q.9 What is the function of a *mesentery*?

Answer:

It flows the blood to the arms.

Q. 10 Why does a female mosquito need a blood meal from a human being or other mammal?

Answer:

A female mosquito rely human being for blood for reproduction.

The candidates answering these questions were overseas students and had been exposed to eleven years' teaching of English language.

6.1

In para. 4.1 it was stated that the students' knowledge of related concepts should be tested by objective-type tests. The following test questions illustrate how this is envisaged.

Q.1 In what units is the blood pressure of a man measured?

a. calories

b. degrees Celsius

c. millimetres of mercury

d. newtons per square metre

This objective-type question tests the background knowledge required for question 1 in para. 5.2. The answers from such a question would show that answers 1*a.* and *f.* in para. 5.2 could be anticipated, as these students would have chosen answer *b.* above.

Q.2 What danger is there in eating unwashed vegetables?

a. The disease of scurvy may be spread

b. The high salt content can increase blood pressure

c. Intestinal diseases may be spread

d. The dirt on the vegetables can cause gangrene.

The choice of answer would show whether pupils are aware of the method of transmission of intestinal diseases, knowledge necessary to formulate a correct response to question 2.

6.2

Using *Scheme C*, the answers to questions 1 and 2 were evaluated, and the average score found. Results were:

	Question 1	*Question 2*
Lexis	2.0	2.5
Syntactical order	1.0	1.2
Morphology	1.1	1.0
Semantic content	0.4	0.7
Total	4.5	5.4
Maximum	10	10

Arthur Godman

The small number of items does not permit any useful analysis to be made. With more students, each contributing ten sentences, a qualitative evaluation of basic weaknesses in the four areas under investigation could be made for the entire set of students. This information would be in addition to the evaluation of the efforts of individual students.

6.3

Any academic subject could be used for the purpose of evaluation of language competence. Certain restrictions arise, however, in the evaluation of language for overseas students or non-native speakers of English. The questions must be culture-free, which eliminates English literature, particularly for non-Indo-European students. For native English speakers, a wide range of academic subjects would be most suitable, as this follows the advice of Halliday *et al.* (*i*), in which he stated that the teaching of English should not be limited to an exclusively arts subject.

(*i*) Halliday, M.A.K., McIntosh, Angus, Strevens, Peter, *The Linguistic Sciences and Language Teaching*, Longmans, London, 1964.

Evaluation

To evaluate is to make a judgement of the worth or value of something. The dictionary definition is useful in high-lighting the subjective nature of the evaluative process. Different evaluators will not necessarily arrive at similar judgements of the same educational programme. One may endorse a mathematical syllabus because it produces high levels of concept mastery. Another may retort that children who have been exposed to it still cannot add, subtract, multiply or divide. A foreign language course may be commended for the command of vocabulary and control of structures it offers to students. It may be open to criticism if it affords them few opportunities to develop communicative skills. Much depends on the values the evaluator brings to bear in arriving at his/her judgements.

We begin by asking three questions. *What* are we to evaluate? *How* do we set about it? *When* do we do it? *What* we are to evaluate — to judge the value or worth of — is an educational programme or project defined, with Astin and Panos, as 'Any ongoing educational activity which is designed to produce specified changes in the behaviour of the individuals exposed to it'. (*i*)

Traditionally, educational evaluation has been identified with curriculum evaluation. The definition proposed above is both broader and narrower. Examples of educational programmes are: a single classroom lesson; a visit to a museum or factory; a particular method of instruction; the content of a particular text-book; a remedial programme; the environment in which learning occurs; the study of parental attitudes to the education of their children; the re-organisation of a school system.

Clearly, a massive programme such as the last mentioned above will comprise a whole range of smaller and different programmes or sub-programmes, designed to modify people's behaviour in different ways; and since the programmes are different, the methods used to evaluate them will also be different.

This brings us to our second question. *How* do we evaluate? We start from the premise that *evaluation involves the collection of information about the impact of the educational programme.* How should we collect this information? What tools are available? Which are appropriate in evaluating which programmes or sub-programmes?

There is no doubt that for many educators and researchers the task of evaluating educational programmes is associated mainly with the construction and administration of achievement tests. It goes without saying that the assessment of student achievement or progress is an essential component of the evaluation process and that well-constructed achievement tests can contribute importantly to such evaluation. In this context, evaluators need to consider which of the two test styles, norm-referenced or criterion-referenced, is the more suitable for their purpose. Unless that purpose is to rank students (which is scarcely an educational objective), the evaluator will normally opt for criterion-referencing procedures.

To repeat, assessment of achievement is an important element in the evaluative process. But it is only one such element. Others may have an equal claim to importance: attitude scales, questionnaires, probes of opinions of students, parents, teachers, communities; and explorations of other non-cognitive aspects. All or some of these several modes of obtaining information may need to be deployed in the global task of evaluation. Otherwise, the danger exists of painting an incomplete or even a distorted picture if the search for information is restricted to those aspects of the educational programme which are more readily measurable at the expense of those less so. In technical terms, validity may be sacrificed to reliability. Stake makes the point cogently: 'It is a great misfortune that the best-trained evaluators have been looking at education with a microscope, rather than with a panoramic viewfinder'. (*ii*)

The third question was concerned with *when* evaluation should take place. In an important seminal article Scriven (*iii*) has distinguished between evaluation occurring during the educational programmes — he calls it *formative* evaluation — and evaluation deferred until its conclusion — *summative* evaluation. Broadly speaking, the distinction he makes is between 'How are we doing?' and 'How did we do?' More specifically, formative evaluation refers to data emerging on taking stock at some intermediate stage, leading probably to slight modification or possibly even to substantial design of subsequent procedures. Summative evaluation, on the other hand, refers to an evaluation of the effectiveness or success of the programme as a whole after it has been completed. Particularly with extensive programmes, both formative and summative styles are essential. It would be unrealistic to suppose that no change need ever be made from initial plans. The programme would be pointless if no-one were concerned to establish its overall and final effectiveness.

The roles of the formative and summative evaluator are in strong contrast. Though both are concerned in making judgements, their standpoints are very different. The essential thing in formative evaluation is close cooperation between evaluator and programme developer, interplay and involvement in smoothing out difficulties as they occur and in maintaining momentum. The essential thing in summative evaluation is total independence on the part of the evaluator, disinterest and uninvolvement and commitment only to dispassionate analysis and reporting.

Let us sum up so far. Evaluation was defined as judging worth. We have discussed what is to be evaluated — an educational programme defined as an on-going activity designed to modify people's behaviour in desirable ways. We have noted some (but by no means all) of the tools available for evaluating a programme. We have drawn a distinction between formative and summative evaluation, the first occurring during the operation of the programme, the second at its conclusion.

So much for 'what', 'how' and 'when'. There remains the question '*Why* evaluate?'

The fundamental purpose of evaluation is to produce information and use it to make decisions about an educational programme. The operative word is *decisions*, stressed here in order to bring out the distinction between, on the one hand, educational evaluation used in making decisions which may directly affect the futures of many people, and, on the other hand, educational experimentations aimed at extending the boundaries of knowledge but without special regard to its immediate practical utility.

Evaluation, then, is about decision-making. A decision might be to continue an existing programme, to terminate it, or perhaps to modify it. Or it might be to develop a new programme with a view to possible adoption.

In principle, the process of decision-making should go something like this. First, the programme planners should specify some educational objective or set of objectives and in due course devise and implement some means of accomplishing these objectives. Second, the evaluator should bring to bear whatever tools are deemed appropriate to assess the extent to which these objectives have in fact been accomplished. Third, decision-making should occur either during (formative) or at the conclusion (summative) of the programme.

Let us look a little more closely at what is involved here. In regard to the first point, the planner assumes an implicit causal realationship between the stated objectives and the means proposed to promote them. In regard to the second point, the evaluator assumes that the tools used in assessment are valid indicators of the extent to which this causal relationship exists and the objectives are achieved.

In practice, neither of these assumptions is necessarily valid. On the planning side, the provision of a computer in every classroom will not necessarily lead to an enhanced grasp of mathematical concepts or better mathematics learning in general — though it may do so. The installation of a well-equipped language laboratory may or may not lead to an improvement in students' language performance. Again, it is part of the folk-lore that a more favourable staff-student ratio will improve the quality of school education. It may, or it may not. On the evaluation side, it might be concluded, as a result of applying achievement tests alone, that education has failed to benefit from the provision of a new area school when there are in fact handsome dividends in the way of improved relationships between community and school staffs which other assessment techniques might have brought to light.

Let us summarise again. An evaluation procedure has three aspects: *an educational programme* in which there is an assumed causal relationship between the stated objectives and the means proposed to achieve them; *an accumulation of relevant information* about the extent to which the objectives are achieved by these means; and the *use* of this information to reach a *decision* about how best to operate the programme in the future.

An educational programme comprises three components which for evaluation purposes it is useful to keep conceptually distinct. These are: *inputs*, *process* and *outputs*.

Inputs, sometimes called *antecedents*, include the talents, skills and other potentials for growth and learning that the students bring with them to the educational programme. They also include the characteristics of the students' families and of the culture in which they live. The child who comes from a family or culture which values educational achievement is more likely to benefit from school than one less fortunate in this respect. Regional or cultural differences in input may give rise to quite different outcomes even with the same programme.

Process, sometimes called *operations*, includes those characteristics of the educational programme itself which affect, or could affect, the outcome. Process includes curricula, experimental treatments, learning strategies, instructional techniques, teacher styles, educational interventions, environmental experiences — in short, the whole range of environmental variables that characterise the educational programme — the means by which the educational ends are to be achieved.

Outputs are the ends or objectives of the programme, otherwise referred to as *criteria, outcomes, goals, achievements* or *dependent variables*. They are sometimes expressed at a high level of abstraction (for example, the development of critical thinking). The trouble with such outcomes, desirable though they are, is the practical difficulty of assessing the extent to which they are achieved. Evaluation is likely to be more efficient if the outcomes are capable of more specific statement — pupil achievement, knowledge, skills, attitudes, aptitude for future learning, inter-personal relationships. Such outcomes are more readily assessed using currently available instruments — achievement tests, attitude scales, questionnaires, interviews and the like.

These are strictly pupil-oriented outcomes, needing little justification. But there are other outcomes best described as intermediate: a reduction in operational cost, recruitment of highly qualified staff. These tend, only too easily, to become regarded as ends in themselves. There are two reasons for this. First, they are more readily specified. Second, their achievement is more easily measured. It is easier to demonstrate a per pupil reduction in expenditure than to monitor the possibly unfavourable consequences for the pupils. Administrators may proudly announce an increase in the proportion of graduate teachers. They have yet to show that pupils' development has improved in consequence.

Also to be taken into account are unintended outcomes or 'side-effects'. For instance, loss of identity with family or community is perhaps too high a price to pay for high academic achievement. Again, class grouping by ability, while enabling the brighter children to achieve their potential may discourage those in lower groups to the extent that their performance is uncharacteristically poor. On the other hand, mixed ability grouping on egalitarian grounds may hold back the brighter child. The conclusions drawn from an evaluative study may be incomplete or even misleading unless the possibility of such unintended outcomes is taken into account.

To summarise once more: an educational programme has three components. First, an *input*: a condition existing at the start, the status of the student — his/her aptitude, previous experience, interest, willingness. Second, *process*: encounters of student with teacher, student with student, student with environment, the succession of engagements which the educational process comprises. Third, *outputs*: student achievements, attitudes, aspirations, resulting from the educational experience: the consequences of education, immediate and long-range, cognitive and effective, personal and community wide.

Analysing the programme in this way helps evaluators to pay due regard to each of these three components. They have a dual role to play: first, through accumulating information about the programme in all its aspects, they must provide a full description of it; and secondly, on the basis of this description, they must arrive at judgements on the programme in order to reach decisions about it: whether to recommend its continuation, modification or abandonment.

Robert Stake (*ii*) has proposed a model which brings together all of these aspects of evaluation. The diagram shows a layout of statements and data to be completed by the evaluator.

	Intents	Observations
1		4
2		5
3		6

Objectives

Description Matrix

	Standards	Judgements
Inputs	7	10
Process	8	11
Outputs	9	12

Judgement Matrix

Inputs, Process and *Outputs*, the components of the programme already discussed, have their place in both matrices, *Description* and *Judgement*. The Description matrix is further divided into *Intents* and *Observations*; and the Judgement matrix into *Standards* and *Judgements*. Each matrix thus contains six cells.

The first column in the *Description* matrix is a declaration of the educational programmer's intent, a statement of the programme as originally planned so as to achieve the global objectives specified in the box on the left. Cell 1, input, describes the students to be included, their number and distribution, their prior achievements, their backgrounds, their environments and any other information about them he/she considers should be seen as *Input*. Cell 2, process, indicates the processes he/she intends to operate with these students: the special teaching he/she hopes they will receive, the new equipment, materials and text-books he/she hopes will be available to assist this special teaching: in short, the whole range of processes he/she hopes to engage the students in so as to achieve the output hopefully specified in Cell 3.

The chief concern of the evaluator with the *Intents* column will be the logical relationships vertically displayed in this column. Are the intended processes specified in Cell 2 logical in the light of the intended input in Cell 1? That is, are the lessons, learning experiences, equipment, etc. specified in Cell 2 appropriate for the students described in Cell 1? Moreover, is it logical to expect the outputs specified in Cell 3 if the operations listed in Cell 2 are conducted with the students described in Cell 1?

Still in the *Description* matrix we move from the hopeful statements of the *Intents* column to the harsh realities of the *Observations* column, which is a statement of what, in the event, actually happened. Horizontal comparison of Cells 4, 5 and 6 with the corresponding Cells 1, 2 and 3 will indicate the extent to which original intentions were or were not achieved in input, process and output. Cells 4 to 6 should indicate not only the extent of these short-falls but also the modifications and adaptations of the original plan these short-falls made necessary.

In making these horizontal comparisons, Cells 1 and 4, 2 and 5, 3 and 6, the evaluator should have in mind these questions. How far adrift is actuality from intention? How different from those originally intended are the inputs, processes and outputs that actually occurred? Has the programme been so materially altered as to be no longer capable of providing answers to the questions originally asked?

In summary, the descriptive aspects of the evaluator's task are: *First*, to assess the extent to which the educational programme as analysed in the *Intents* column reflects the basic educational purpose stated in the *Objectives* box.

Second, to assess the extent to which the three *Intents* aspects are logically connected — the extent to which the intended programme makes sense. *Third*, to describe the extent to which intended inputs, process and outputs correspond to what actually happened.

We now turn to the *Judgement* matrix.

First, the *Standards* column. Its purpose is to indicate *acceptable* levels or standards for inputs, process and outputs. What is acceptable is partly a matter of experience and partly one of judgement. The declaration of intent in Cells 1–3 of the *Description* matrix is translated, in this *Standards* column, into a statement of what the evaluator is prepared to accept. However carefully planned the original programme may have been, it is unlikely that all contingencies will have been foreseen and that no problems will be encountered in practice.

The *Standards* column is a statement of the extent to which the evaluator is prepared to settle for less than perfection — always provided that the success of the programme is not materially prejudiced by this degree of tolerance. In the *inputs* cell (7), a limited departure from the complete randomisation of student input envisaged in the corresponding cell in the *intents* column (1) may not be disastrous. In the *process* cell (8) a slight fall below the specified teacher student ratio (2) may be tolerated. In the *output* cell (9) 85 per cent of students achieving mastery in a criterion-referenced achievement test instead of the 90 per cent hopefully specified in the *intents* column (3) is not to be despised. In short, the *standards* column is a realistic statement from the evaluator of the several criteria by which the educational programme's success or failure is to be judged.

Finally, *Judgements* in the last column are based on the degree of matching between *Observation* entries in the *Description* matrix and *Standards* entries in the *Judgements* matrix. The procedure is first, to compare, then, to judge. To what extent does the actual course of events, as recorded in the *Observation* column cells, measure up to the criteria supplied by the corresponding *Standards* cells? Against all the odds, maybe, some, though not all, of the parents in a rural community have been persuaded that their daughters would benefit from formal education. A hostel is built to accommodate women teachers. Potential success or certain failure of this educational programme will depend on whether women teachers can be persuaded to live and work within the community.

The word 'criteria' has just been used in the context of comparisons between *Observations* and *Standards*. We are becoming increasingly familiar with the notion of criterion-referenced testing and the underlying concepts. It is suggested that an extension of the notion of criterion-referencing be made to the present wider context. It may be helpful to think of the comparison between corresponding cells in the *Observations* and *Standards* columns as criterion-referenced.

It is not to be expected that every evaluation plan will take account of every aspect of the Stake model. The point is that this analysis indicates twelve sub-areas within which and among which evaluation can take place. Emphasis will vary from one educational programme to another. The evaluator must clarify his responsibility by answering questions such as these: is the evaluation to be primarily descriptive, primarily judgemental, or both? Is it to emphasise input conditions, processes or outputs alone, or a combination of all three, and their logical connections? Is it to be concerned with the degree of correspondence between what is intended and what occurs? In seeking answers to questions such as these, the evaluator may hope to keep all his options in mind and to establish priorities among them.

References

(i) Astin, A.W., and Panos, R.J., 'The Evaluation of Educational Programmes'. In *Educational Measurement*, (Ed. Thorndyke, R.L.), American Council of Education, Washington D.C., 1971, pp. 733–751.

(ii) Stake, R.E., *The Countenance of Educational Evaluation*, Teachers College Record, 1967, Vol. 68, pp. 523–40.

(iii) Scriven, M., 'The Methodology of Evaluation'. In *Perspectives of Curriculum Evaluation: AERA monograph series on curriculum evaluation*, Chicago, Rang-McNally, 1967, pp. 39–83.

Frank Chaplen

Measuring student achievement:
some practical considerations

1. Introduction

This article summarises some of our experience gathered over the past 5 years with the ESP programmes for premedical and paramedical students in Kuwait University. In our teaching situation, the yearly intake of each group of students is divided into 5 classes taught by different teachers, each class following the same weekly teaching/study programme as the others, and each class taking the same tests and examinations as the others. Thus, each semester in the 4-semester premedical and paramedical English programme each premedical student and each paramedical student is assessed on virtually the same scale of achievement as every other premedical and paramedical student. To achieve this requires a rather more complex and systematized approach to evaluation than is necessary in some teaching situations. Nevertheless, our experience should be of interest to any teacher or administrator who is responsible for developing assessment procedures.

2. Setting Target Dates for Tests and Examinations

For several reasons the dates for examinations need to be fixed far in advance. Teachers prefer this, students demand it, and administrators can be extremely unsympathetic if you try to give them only one week's warning of the fact that you need a large examination room with film projection or video facilities from 8.00 to 10.00 a.m. In our experience, a host of problems can be alleviated if a list of target dates and responsibilities such as that in Table 2.1, is routinely prepared at the beginning of each course. It reduces arguments later if this is prepared during a meeting of all the teachers involved in the course.

3. Weighting the different parts of the assessment component

The term 'assessment component' is intended to encompass all the forms of assessment on the basis of which a student's final grade for a course is decided. In our teaching situation, these include the following:

(a) teacher's assessment based on a student's achievement in class activities (oral and written), in delivering a prepared talk, in homework, etc.

(b) tests and examinations.

For the first 15-week course in our programme the weighting of the different components is as follows:

Test 1 (after 30 class hours)	10%
Mid-semester Exam (after 70 class hours)	20%
Test 2 (after 110 class hours)	20%
Final Examination (after 150 class hours)	40%
Teacher's assessment	10%
	100%

The difference in the weighting of Test 1 (10%) and the Final Examination (40%) is intended to take account of two facts. First, the students come straight from secondary school, so few of them know what is expected of them at university for at least the first several weeks. Second, the comparatively heavy weighting of the Final enables slow starters to compensate for low achievement earlier in the course.

The teacher's assessment is intended to provide students with some incentive for working continuously both in and out of class throughout the course. It also provides the teacher with an opportunity to evaluate elements of the course which it is difficult to measure in a formal test or exam, e.g. oral communication. In earlier years, we gave a weighting of 20% to the teacher's assessment, but this tended to have an adverse effect: the weaker students copied their homework assignments from those written by the more proficient students (usually in other classes so that a direct check by the teacher was impossible). Since this defeated the purpose of the teacher's assessment element, the weighting was dropped to 10%. This seems sufficient to persuade the weaker students to work reasonably consistently while not being enough to encourage them to go to the trouble of copying the work of more proficient students.

In the second, third and fourth courses, the teacher's assessment element is increased to 20% because by this time all but a few students recognise that they will make little progress except through their own unaided efforts.

The number of marks for each element in the assessment component will vary, of course. The maximum mark for Test 1 might be 115, that for Test 2, 95, and that for the Final, 135. Therefore, to obtain the desired weighting, the marks obtained by students in each element must be converted.

Let us assume that the assessment component of a course consists of the 3 elements listed in Table 3.1, and that their maximum marks and desired weightings are as entered in columns 2 and 3. (see page 105).

To convert Test 1 marks to the required weighting (20%), multiply each student's mark by 20, then divide the result by 115. To convert Test 2 marks, multiply by 30, then divide by 95. To convert Final Exam marks, multiply by 50, then divide by 135.

The task of calculating these conversions (i) is considerably lightened if a class mark grid like the one in Table 3.2 on page 105 is constructed at the beginning of each course. This grid also simplifies record keeping, and makes it relatively easy for a second person to check each teacher's calculations. A cheap electronic calculator is an essential tool in these operations.

4. Deciding a student's final grade for a course

End-of-course results are rarely expressed as percentages or raw marks because these are not very meaningful. A mark of 80%, for example, may represent an outstanding achievement in one course, but only an average achievement in another. For this reason, course results are commonly reported on a letter scale: a grade of A representing an outstanding achievement, B representing an excellent achievement, etc.

In our teaching situation, we are required to report course grades on the following 10-point letter scale:

A	
A—	OUTSTANDING
B+	EXCELLENT
B	GOOD
B—	QUITE GOOD
C+	
C	CLEAR PASS
D+	BORDERLINE PASS
D	BORDERLINE FAIL
F	FAIL

Consequently, when the students' total marks for a course have been calculated (column G in Table 3.2), these have to be converted to letter grades. grades.

When only one teacher is involved in deciding which students should receive A's, which should receive B's, etc., the conversion of marks to letter grades is a relatively painless process. However, when 4 or more teachers are involved, each responsible for 15 or more of the total number of students, decisions are far more difficult to make. Most teachers identify very strongly with their students, and would like to see the majority receive high grades; but this is not always possible, particularly if the students are assigned to classes on the basis of placement test results in order to produce fairly homogeneous groups. The procedure that we have evolved over the past 5 years to decide the students' final grades seems to satisfy both teachers and students.

The first step in this procedure is to prepare a distribution of final marks for each class (columns 1, 2, 3 and 4 in Table 4.1), and for the entire intake (column 5). Column 6 contains the cumulative frequency of final marks, e.g. 43 students scored 73% or above, 56 scored 61% or above. Column 7 contains the cumulative frequency percentage of the final marks, e.g. 66.2% of the 65 students scored 73% or above, 86.2% scored 61% or above. Column 7 provides a convenient check in later years on the comparative standards of successive intakes of students.

Note that columns 1, 2, 3 and 4 contain tallies. These are entered on the distribution sheet in the following manner: one person reads out the final marks from each class mark grid (Table 3.2, column G), a second person makes a tally on the distribution sheet in the appropriate class column as each mark is called out. A decimal of .5 or above is rounded up to the next whole number, e.g. 64.51 becomes 65. A decimal of .49 or below is rounded down, e.g. 71.47 becomes 71.

The first person calls out the mark as it appears on the class mark grid, e.g. 71.49. The second person calls out the rounded-up or rounded-down figure, e.g. 71, before entering the tally on the distribution sheet. The first person listens to provide a check on the calculation.

Column 6 on the distribution sheet, the cumulative frequency column, provides a check that all the final marks have been tallied, then added correctly horizontally. For example, if the cumulative frequency total is 64, and if there are 65 students, it is clear that an error has been made either in calling out final marks, or entering tallies, or totalling tallies, or calculating the cumulative frequency. This error needs to be rectified.

The distribution of final marks is considered at a meeting of all teachers, and initial decisions taken on where to set the boundaries between the letter grades on the mark scale. The first year that a course is taught, these initial decisions are necessarily somewhat arbitrary. It might be decided, for example, to base the initial tentative distribution of grades approximately on the normal distribution curve, that is, to determine by purely statistical means what proportion of the students should fall between each grade boundary. Diederich (i) suggests that teachers use a modified stannine score scale for this purpose; applying his suggestion to the letter grade scale described above, we get something like this:

their final examination papers are studied before a final decision is taken. In this case, it is decided to leave the boundary where it is: between 84% and 85%, but in other cases the boundary will be moved.

The most painful decisions concern the placing of the lower boundaries, particularly that between D+ and C. Inevitably there will be one or two students just below this borderline who have made extraordinary efforts during the course, and one or two students who have done very little work. Does one give all 4 a grade of C, and thereby risk convincing the lazy ones that they really do not need to work in the remainder of the English language programme courses? Or does one give all 4 a grade of D+, and risk convincing the serious students that no amount of effort is worthwhile? However

Letter Grade	A	A−	B+	B	B−	C+	C	D+	D and F
% of Students in each Grade	4%	8%	12%	16%	20%	16%	12%	8%	4%
Cumulative %	4%	12%	24%	40%	60%	76%	88%	96%	100%

The second year that the course is taught, the tentative grade boundaries can be based on those finally decided the previous year. On whatever basis the initial setting of the grade boundaries is done, however, the next stage in the grading procedure is the critical one: the initial grades for each individual student are written on the class mark grid lightly in pencil, and each teacher considers each student's tentative grade in the light of his knowledge of that student's work. Now comes the time-consuming discussion of borderline students that usually leads to the shifting of the tentative grade boundaries up or down 1, 2 or even 3 percentage points.

Look at the distribution of tallies in Fig. 4.1 on either side of the boundary between the grades B+ and B. The teacher of class II may feel that his student who gained 84% deserves a B+, but a student in class III and one in class IV have also gained 84%; therefore the teachers of those classes are necessarily involved in this decision about where the B+/B boundary shall be placed. They feel that their two students merit B's, not B+'s. The teacher of class II admits that because he has only one other student with a grade higher than B, this may be affecting his judgement. Nevertheless, all the marks that the 5 students on 84% and 85% gained in all tests are examined and discussed, and

painful these decisions may be, one must resist the temptation to 'find an extra mark somewhere' for the serious students; that would be certain to create all manner of problems in the future.

The main point to notice is that final decisions about where to place grade boundaries are based on consensus, and that this consensus arises only after considerable discussion of the individual students concerned. It seems to us that it is only in this way that one can come as close as possible to measuring each student's achievement with the same yardstick, no matter who his teacher is, while at the same time retaining an intense concern for the individual student. It is perhaps an indication of our students' recognition of the objectivity yet fairness of the grading system employed that during the past five years we have not had one serious complaint about the grades that we award.

(i) The conversions demonstrated here take no account of the standard deviation of the scores for each element. Therefore, only an approximate weighting is obtained. But it is certainly a considerable improvement over simply adding the raw scores for each evaluation element to obtain a final mark for the course.

(i) Paul B. Diederich, *Short-cut Statistics for Teacher-Made Tests*, Evaluation Advisory Series No. 5, Educational Testing Service, 1960, p. 37.

Table 2.1: Example of a Target Dates Information Sheet

Assessment and Count-Down Dates, Semester 1, 1980–1981

Course	Assessment and person responsible	Date, time and place of assessment	Posting of notice for students	Preliminary drafting meeting	1st Draft	Final Draft for typing	Completion of marks processing	Posting of provisional grades
101	Test One: A.M.	Mon. Oct. 6 10.00 Room 101	Wed. Oct. 1	Tues. Sept. 10	Wed. Oct. 1	Sat. Oct. 4	Sat. Oct. 11	Sun. Oct. 12
	Mid-Sem P.S.	Wed. Nov. 12 9.00 Room 312	Wed. Nov. 5	Sun. Nov. 2	Tues. Nov. 2	Sat. Nov. 8	Wed. Nov. 19	Sat. Nov. 22
	Test Two G.L.	Tues. Dec. 9 10.00 Room 102	Tues. Dec. 2	Wed. Nov. 26	Sun. Nov. 30	Wed. Dec. 3	Sun. Dec. 14	Mon. Dec. 15
	Final S.A. + A.M.	Sun. Jan. 4 9.00 Room 213	Sun. Dec. 28	Tues. Dec. 23	Sat. Dec. 27	Mon. Dec. 29	Sat. Jan. 10	Mon. Jan. 12

Table 3.1

	maximum marks	desired weightings
Test 1	115	20%
Test 2	95	30%
Final Exam	135	50%

Table 3.2: Example of a Class Mark Grid

Course 101   Semester 1, 1980–81   Class IV   Teacher: J. Doe

STUDENT	TEST 1 Max. = 115	$\frac{A \times 20}{115}$	TEST 2 Max. = 95	$\frac{C \times 30}{95}$	FINAL EXAM Max. = 135	$\frac{E \times 50}{135}$	TOTAL B + D + F	FINAL GRADE
	A	B	C	D	E	F	G	H
1. Ahmed	85	14.78	81	25.58	101	37.41	77.77%	B
2. Ali	49	8.52	51	16.11	86	31.85	56.48%	D+
3. Fareed	53	9.2	60	18.95	89	32.96	61.11%	C
etc.	etc.	etc.	etc.	etc.	etc.	etc.	etc.	etc.
15. Mohammed	87	15.13	83	26.21	114	42.22	83.56%	B+

Table 4.1: Example of a Mark Distribution Sheet

English Language Division   Course 101   Semester 1, 1981–82

Final Mark Distribution and Grade Boundaries

	1	2	3	4	5	6	7	
MARK	CLASSES				TOTAL I–IV	c.f.	c.f.%	GRADE BOUNDS
	I	II	III	IV				
95			/	/	2	2	3.1	A
94			/	/	2	4	6.2	
93								A−
92				/	1	5	7.7	
91			/	/	2	7	10.8	
90								B+
89			///		3	10	15.4	
88			/		1	11	16.9	
87		/			1	12	18.5	
86				//	2	14	21.5	
85			/	/	2	16	24.6	
84		/	/	/	3	19	29.2	B
83			//		2	21	32.3	
82		/		//	3	24	36.9	
81								B−
80		/		//	3	27	41.5	
79			/		1	28	43.1	
78	/			/	2	30	46.2	
77		/	//		3	33	50.8	C+
76	/		/	/	3	36	55.4	
75	/				1	37	56.9	
74	/		/	/	3	40	61.5	
73			/	//	3	43	66.2	
72								C
71		/			1	44	67.7	
70								
69		/			1	45	69.2	
68		/			1	46	70.8	
67	/				1	47	72.3	
66		/			1	48	73.8	
65		///			3	51	78.5	
64	/	//			3	54	83.1	
63								
62	/				1	55	84.6	
61	/				1	56	86.2	
60								D+
59	//	//			4	60	92.3	
58								
57	/				1	61	93.8	
56								D
55								
54								
53								
52		/			1	62	95.4	
51								F
50	/				1	63	96.9	
49								
48	//				2	65	100%	

Appendix: Research

A comment on specific variance versus global variance in certain EFL tests

Perhaps the basic statistical problem in the determination of what a test measures is the assessment of the sources of the variance across individuals that the test produces. Put in nontechnical terms, the deeper problem is to find out what factors in the behaviour of test-takers result in differences in the performances of various individuals and groups. According to the classical factoring model (cf. Harman 1976: 18–20), the standardized unit variance of any test j can be composed (at least theoretically) into three uncorrelated components: 1) variance that is common to other tests, referred to as the *communality* which is designated h_j^2; 2) variance that is unique to j but nonrandom, known as the *specificity* designated b_j^2; and 3) variance which is unique to j but random, referred to as *error* or *unreliability* designated e_j^2. These three terms must add up to 100% of the total variance in j if the assumptions underlying the classical model are correct. According to that model, in order for a test to achieve a satisfactory level of validity, we should expect its communality with tests aimed at the same construct(s) to be high while its communality with tests aimed at disparate constructs should be low. When we examine tests aimed at distinct constructs, we expect them to have relatively high specificities and low communalities. Always we hope for low unreliabilities.

It is generally conceded (not quite gleefully) that there is no determinate single best solution for any given factoring problem. The variance in any given test may be partitioned in an infinitude of ways, as has been demonstrated in theory, and arguments about the best possible solution are probably misguided (Harman 1976: 27f). However, this is not the same as saying that all possible solutions are equal for all purposes. In some cases it is possible to show that one solution is decidedly better than a number of others. In most cases, the arguments must be thrashed out by appealing to theoretical reasoning that goes beyond statistics per se. Nevertheless, the application of statistical methods seems indispensable.

With the foregoing as background, this note will respond briefly to claims by Abu-Sayf, Herbolich, and Spurling (1979) concerning 'unique nonchance variance' (which, according to the classical factor model, is specificity) in each of four parts of an EFL proficiency exam recently developed by them at Kuwait University. In subscores of 139 adult non-native speakers of English, they claimed to have identified (using a method recommended by Davis 1968, 1972) four specificities — Grammar 22%, Listening Comprehension 41%, Reading Comprehension 32%, and Translation 24%. They further suggested that these findings were in conflict with 'Oller's hypothesis (1973) of there being only one global proficiency [test] such as a cloze or a dictation' (p. 117).[1]

Actually, their paper raises two substantive issues. First there is the question of test specificities in relation to the global factor, and second, there is the question of what is the most plausible tentative conclusion regarding such a global factor. In the first matter we may ask whether the claimed specificities actually exist in the reported magnitudes, and in the second what the implication is for the existence of a large global factor of language proficiency.

In regard to the question of specificities, Oller and Khan (1980) demonstrate that the application of the modified Davis method of obtaining estimates of unique nonchance variance (or specificity) which was applied by Abu-Sayf *et al.*, is flawed in two ways: first it overestimates specificity by conflating it with error variance, and second, it underestimates communalities by overcorrecting for bias in squared multiple correlations. In fact, squared multiple correlations are already conservative estimates of communalities due to the fact that they are known to constitute the lower bounds of true communalities. Oller and Khan show that the more probable limits of the specificities properly obtainable from the correlations in the Abu-Sayf *et al.* study are near zero — this compared with a large global factor accounting for as much as 95% of the variance in the Grammar Test by one method and never less than 75% of the variance

107

in any of the tests by any one of three different methods (squared multiple correlations corrected for bias, communalities estimated by principal factoring with iterations, and communalities estimated by Rao's canonical factoring with iterations). Even by the most conservative method of estimating communalities, the respective specificities were Grammar −.01, Listening Comprehension .04, Reading Comprehension .00, and Translation −.11. In no case did the specificity estimated for any test by any method amount to as much as half the error variance in the test in question.[2]

Coming now to the second question concerning the global factor of language proficiency, what does the foregoing mean? In practical terms can we conclude that there is only one factor, a general factor? It seems to me that we cannot. The evidence suggests that following the classical factor model there is no reason to believe that any of the four tests produced by Abu-Sayf *et al.* generates a reliable specific variance. The variance generated by any triplet of the tests pretty much exhausts the variance generated by the remaining single test. That is, most of the reliable variance in each of these four tests is common to the remaining three. But these four tests do not by any means exhaust the universe of possible language tests! Therefore, we cannot on the basis of this study or any previous study conclude that there is only one factor underlying the variance in all language tests. On the other hand, on the basis of many previous studies (see Oller, 1979, Appendix for a brief and already somewhat dated review), we can say that there appears to be a large general factor of language proficiency in nearly all of the tests so far studied (an exception is a narrowly defined spelling score, see Oller, 1979: 281).

There is no basis, in spite of these findings, to conclude that a single test such as a dictation or a cloze test, is the best way to measure that general factor. In isolated cases of certain sets of tests, results favour the interpretation that one or more of the input tests are better at measuring the general factor than other tests, but the only way we could even theoretically find the single best test would be to obtain all possible data on all possible tests — a clear impossibility. In fact, all of the evidence that I know of points to the conclusion that a multitude of language processing tasks aimed at the kinds of things language users will actually be expected to do with language makes the best language test in any given set of circumstances. If students are expected to learn to use the target language in contexts where they will be required to listen, speak, read, and write the language, it makes sense to use a plurality of testing procedures for many reasons. I also still believe the remark that was written in 1977 though not published until 1979, that 'it is . . . . . probably safe to say that the best pragmatic testing procedures have yet to be invented' (Oller, 1979: 416).

The exigencies of practical life often force us to leap beyond the empirical evidence. Theories in general are not based exclusively on substantiated empirical findings either. Even if it turned out that there were only one general factor of language proficiency, it would still make sense to use a multiplicity of testing methods (as John Carroll, 1980, and others have recently observed). Moreover, in spite of the pervasiveness and general strength of a global factor of language proficiency underlying educational and psychological tests of all sorts, there is recent evidence that suggests a multiplicity of specific factors will yet be found (see Bachman and Palmer, 1980, and Upshur and Homburg, 1980). However, I personally doubt (at this moment) that the general factor can be explained away satisfactorily by even the newer and more powerful methods of confirmatory factor analysis. Nor have I seen any evidence as yet that would refute the claim that Spearman's general factor of intelligence may indeed turn out to be indistinguishable from proficiency in one's primary or strongest language (see Streiff and Oller in press). Still, we are speaking here of hypotheses rather than proven facts, and it is my belief that one should not place too much weight on hypotheses and hunches but carefully regard them as precisely what they are.

1 Perhaps the cited remark can be reasonably inferred from things I have said or written, but I do not believe that I have ever actually advocated the use of any single test or pair of tests as measures of language proficiency in an all encompassing general sense. While the evidence seems to suggest that dictation and cloze procedure along with a number of other integrative tests, or more specifically pragmatic tests, are useful practical tools for assessing language proficiency (whatever it may turn out to be), I have long tried to stress that the concept of pragmatic testing extends to an implicit infinitude of test procedures (so do the terms cloze and dictation). While some tests appear to be better measures of general language proficiency than others, there is no reason to suppose that the class of best tests has yet been identified. Nevertheless, in the article referred to by Abu-Sayf et al., I indicated my advocacy (at that time) of 'integrative testing' and suggested that 'some of the types of tests that qualify as belonging to the integrative family besides dictation, cloze procedure, composition, and oral interview, ... are Upshur's test of productive communication (Upshur, 1969), reading aloud, and some multiple choice tests of reading comprehension and other skills' (1973: 11). In the reference to multiple choice tests I intended to include some of those developed in connection with the testing of foreign students at UCLA during my three years there, as well as tests like the Listening Comprehension and Reading Comprehension sections of the TOEFL. Parish's Grammar Test (see Oller and Perkins, 1980, Appendix, item 22) is an integrative or pragmatic test in this sense.

2 By contrast, communality estimates (which may be read as indicants of a global factor in this case and many similar studies) ranged from a low of 60% to a high above 85%. Further, in this particular case we are referring to estimates based on the squares of multiple correlations, a lower bound for the true values.

References

Abu-Sayf, F.K., Herbolich, James B., and Spurling, S., 1979, 'The identification of the major components for testing English as a foreign language', *TESOL Quarterly* 13, pp. 117-20.

Bachman, Lyle F. and Palmer, Adrian S., 1980, 'The construct validation of oral proficiency tests'. Paper presented at the Fourteenth Annual TESOL Convention, San Francisco, March 1980. Also in *TESL Studies* 3, pp. 1-20 (University of Illinois at Urbana-Champaign). To appear in Oller (in press).

Carroll, John B., 1980, 'Language testing and psychometric theory'. Closing plenary lecture at the Second International Language Testing Symposium, Darmstadt, West Germany, May 1980. Also presented at the Language Testing Conference, Albuquerque, New Mexico, University of New Mexico, June 1980. To appear in Oller (in press).

Davis, Frederick B., 1968, 'Research in comprehension in reading'. *Reading Research Quarterly* 3, pp. 499-545.

Davis, Frederick B., 1972, 'Psychometric research on comprehension in reading', *Reading Research Quarterly* 7, pp. 628-78.

Guilford, J.P. and Fruchter, B., 1978, 'Fundamental statistics in psychology and education', 6th edition revised, New York, McGraw Hill.

Harman, Harry H., 1976, *Modern factor analysis*, 3rd revised edition, Chicago, University of Chicago.

Oller, J.W., Jr., 1973, 'Pragmatic language testing', *Language Sciences* 28, pp. 7-12.

Oller, J.W., Jr., 1979, *Language tests at school: a pragmatic approach*, London, Longman.

Oller, J.W., Jr. (Ed.). In press, *Issues in Language Testing Research*, Rowley, Massachusetts, Newbury House.

Oller, J.W., Jr., and Khan, R., 1980, 'Is there a global factor of language proficiency?' Paper presented by the first author at the 15th Regional Seminar sponsored by the South East Asian Ministers of Education Organization, at the Regional English Language Center, Singapore, April 1980. In the proceedings edited by John Read (to appear).

Oller, J.W., Jr. and Perkins, Kyle, 1980, *Research in language testing*, Rowley, Massachusetts, Newbury House.

Oller, J.W., Jr. and Streiff, Virginia A. In press, *The language factor: more tests of tests*, Rowley, Massachusetts, Newbury House.

Upshur, John A., 1969, 'Productive communication testing'. Paper presented at the Second International Congress of Applied Linguistics, Cambridge, England. In G. Perren and J.L.M. Trim (Eds.), *Applications of linguistics*, Cambridge, England, Cambridge University, 1971, pp. 435-42. Also in Oller, J. and Richards, J. (Eds.), *Focus on the learner*, Rowley, Massachusetts, Newbury House, 1973, pp. 177-83.

Upshur, John A. and Homburg, Taco J., 1980, 'Some language test relations at successive ability levels'. Paper presented at the Second International Language Testing Symposium, Darmstadt, West Germany, May 1980. To appear in Oller (in press).

Profiles

JOSEPH BOYLE *teaches in the English Department of the Chinese University of Hong Kong. He has previously taught in South America, India and the Philippines. He studied English Language and Literature at Oxford and has done the Leeds ESL Postgraduate Diploma Course. He works with Chinese students who have chosen English as their major subject. He also runs extra-mural courses in Business English and Medical English.*

BRENDAN CARROLL *had extensive ELT experience in Kenya, India and Nigeria before becoming Director of the British Council English Language Teaching Institute in London. He left his last post in the Council as head of their English Language Testing Service Liaison Unit to take charge of Pergamon English Testing, Oxford. He also works as a private consultant and is the author of several books, his most recent being* Testing Communicative Performance *(Pergamon Press, 1980).*

FRANK CHAPLEN *has been Director of the English Language Division, Faculty of Medicine, Kuwait University since 1975. Previously, whilst Research Officer to the University of Cambridge Local Examinations Syndicate, he was responsible for developing the new form of the Proficiency and First Certificate examinations. He has also been engaged as a tests and examinations consultant by the UN, the FAO, UNESCO, and the Council of Europe. Dr. Chaplen is the author of several EFL textbooks, his latest being a course in scientific English.*

ALAN DAVIES *teaches Applied Linguistics in the Department of Linguistics, University of Edinburgh, where he is a senior lecturer. He is the author of the English Proficiency Test Battery (used for some years by the British Council) and has edited 'Language Testing Symposium' (1968) and the 'Testing and Experimental Studies' volume of the Edinburgh Course in Applied Linguistics (1977) as well as numerous articles on language testing. He is currently carrying out a validation study of the new British Council-Cambridge ELTS (English Language Testing Service).*

PETER FABIAN. *Co-founder of Arels and its chairman, 1962–64, he has been in EFL for 42 years, interrupted by 10 years in industry. Soon after becoming owner-principal of the London School of English (1960), he led a team of enthusiasts to develop the Arels Oral Examinations; he has been Chairman of the Arels Examination Trust*

since 1976. Listening comprehension is to him the most fundamental of all four language skills. Language acquisition he regards as an essentially intuitive, emotional and non-cerebral experience. He is suspicious of 'academic postures'. Being himself a linguist, he prefers to call the other kind 'linguisticians'.

PENNY FRANTZIS *has taught English in Spain and Saudi Arabia, and directed an English Language Course in Switzerland. For the last eight years she has been lecturing and teaching at the University of Leeds. Her work has involved the preparation of course materials for the academic needs of overseas students in Britain and ESP (English for Specific Purposes) programmes for such diverse groups as Kuwaiti hospital administrators, overseas psychiatrists, engineering students from the Middle East, etc.*

ARTHUR GODMAN *is in the Department of South-East Asian Studies, University of Kent. He has been a consultant for the British Council on EST, and has written on that subject for the Regional Language Centre, Singapore. He has examined science subjects for overseas' examinations in both English and Malay, and was science consultant for the* Nucleus *series (Longman). Current publications include the* Longman Dictionary of Scientific Usage *and the* Longman Illustrated Science Dictionary.

BRIAN HEATON *is Lecturer in English for Overseas Students at the University of Leeds and is the author of several books concerned with English as a second and foreign language. His experience includes teaching and lecturing throughout Europe and Asia. He taught and lectured in Hong Kong for twelve years, becoming Senior Inspector for English, and was Visiting Professor in Education in Singapore from 1976 to 1979.*

ROBERT KEITH JOHNSON *is Senior Lecturer in the School of Education, University of Hong Kong. He taught English in Zambia before completing an M.A. in Applied Linguistics at Essex in 1970. Since then, he has been involved in ESL teacher-training and Applied Linguistics Programmes, first with the Faculty of Education, University of Papua New Guinea, for nine years, and since 1979 in Hong Kong.*

PAT McELDOWNEY *taught in New Zealand and Libya before joining the University of Manchester in 1971. She is now a Lecturer in Teaching English*

Overseas in the Department of Adult and Higher Education at the University. Apart from various short courses, she also runs the In-Service teacher-training course for the Lancashire Education Authority. She is Chief Examiner for the Joint Matriculation Board's Test in English (Overseas), the North West Regional Examinations Board's English as a Second Language and is Moderator for the Yorkshire Regional Examinations Board's English as a Second Language. Her new book English in Context is due for publication early in 1982, published by Thomas Nelson & Sons, Walton on Thames.

KEITH MORROW is an Assistant Director of the Bell Educational Trust, based in Norwich. He was formerly a lecturer at the University of Reading. He is the Chief Examiner for the Royal Society of Arts 'Examinations in the Communicative Use of English as a Foreign Language'.

PAUL NATION is a senior lecturer at Victoria University in Wellington, New Zealand. He has also taught in Indonesia and Thailand. His special interests are in teaching techniques and code-based approaches to language teaching.

JOHN W. OLLER, Jr. received his doctorate in general linguistics from the University of Rochester, in Rochester, New York in 1969. He has served on the faculty at UCLA and the University of New Mexico and has held visiting appointments at Southern Illinois University and Concordia (in Montreal). From 1971 to 1976 he served on the Committee of Examiners for the Test of English as a Foreign Language at ETS. Presently, he is Professor of Linguistics at the University of New Mexico.

ALBERT PILLINER was, until his retiral in 1978, Director of the Godfrey Thomson Unit for Educational Research and Senior Lecturer in the Department of Education, University of Edinburgh. He is especially interested in the testing of English as a foreign or second language. Sponsored by UNESCO and by the British Council, he has taught (and continues to teach) in Europe, West Africa, South America and in the Middle and Far East. He has also directed language testing courses for international groups in UK on behalf of the British Council and, more recently, the University of Edinburgh Institute of Applied Language Studies.

PAULINE M. REA is Senior Lecturer in the Department of Foreign Languages and Linguistics, and Co-ordinator of the Communication Skills Unit at the University of Dar es Salaam. She has EFL experience at secondary level and in teacher training programmes in Africa and Europe. She has worked on the General Medical Council's English language testing project for overseas doctors. Her current research interests are related to language testing, curriculum development, and ESP materials production.

JOHN ROGERS is a Senior Lecturer at the English Language Institute, Victoria University, Wellington, New Zealand, where he has been teaching on Dip. TESL courses for teachers from Southeast Asia, the South Pacific and New Zealand since 1971. He spent two years teaching English to adults and secondary school students in Sweden from 1955 to 1957, and from 1957 to 1961 he helped to train secondary school English teachers at Universitas Airlangga, Indonesia. He worked for the British Council in Nigeria (1961–1963) and in Ethiopia (1963–1969), where he was the co-adaptor of several books. From 1976 to 1978 he was seconded to the SEAMEO Regional Language Centre, Singapore, as Specialist in the Psychology of Second Language Learning and Applied Linguistics. In Singapore he compiled Group Activities for Language Learning (RELC Occasional Papers).

IAN SEATON is Head of the Liaison Unit for the English Language Testing Service in the British Council. He taught ESP programmes for two years at the University of Tripoli, Libya and for two years at the University of Helsinki, Finland before joining the Council in 1976.

BILL SHEPHARD. Academic training consisted of systematic escape from the Cambridge English course via non-compulsory Old English, linguistic gossip (no department at that time), phonetics and dialect research at Leeds. This was followed by EFL teaching and finally adminstration of the Cambridge EFL examinations. With colleague Harold Otter, he has tried to absorb usefully into the examination structure the successive waves of revolution and counter-revolution in EFL teaching and testing.

NIC UNDERHILL. Educational Co-ordinator, International Language Centres. Taught EFL at various schools in London and Sussex and then worked for ILC for two years at the Kuwait Oil Company Training Centre before returning to England to do an M.A. in Applied Linguistics at the University of Reading.

CHRISTOPHER WARD is head of the Testing Department, International Language Centre (Japan) in Tokyo. After obtaining a Diploma in English as a Second Language at Leeds University, he taught immigrants in Bradford, Yorkshire for two years. Then he went to Japan and taught at ILC for three years before taking up his present post six years ago.

SIDNEY WHITAKER has directed the TESL

training course at University College, Bangor, since 1964. He previously taught French at Glasgow University, and English and language-teaching methodology in Vietnam and Venezuela, with shorter assignments in India, Bangladesh, China, Egypt, Jordan, and Yugoslavia. He regularly collaborates with English teachers in Spain as well as with teachers of immigrant pupils in Britain.

Bibliography

Alderson, C. and Hughes, A. (Eds.) (1981) *Issues in Language Testing*, ELT Documents 111. London: British Council

Allen, J.P.B. and Davies, A. (Eds.) (1977) 'Testing and experimental methods', *Edinburgh Course in Applied Linguistics*, Vol. 4. London: O.U.P.

Beardsmore, H.B. (1974) 'Testing oral fluency', *IRAL*, 12, 4, pp. 317–26

Brière, E.J. (1971) 'Are we really measuring proficiency with our foreign language tests?', *Foreign Language Annals*, 4, May

Burstall, Clare (1969) 'The main stages in the development of language tests', Stern, H.H. (Ed.) *Languages and the Young School Child*, London: O.U.P.

Carroll, B.J. (1980) *Testing Communicative Performance*, Oxford: Pergamon

Clark, J.L.D. (1972) *Foreign Language Testing: Theory and Practice*, Philadelphia, Pa, Centre for Curriculum Research

Crocker, A.C. (1969) *Statistics for the Teacher (or How To Put Figures in their Place)*, Harmondsworth: Penguin

Davies, A. (1968) *Language Testing Symposium*, London: O.U.P.

Davies, A. (1978) 'Language Testing (Survey Articles)' *Language Teaching and Linguistics: Abstracts*, Cambridge: Cambridge University Press, Vol. II

Davies. S. and West, R. (1981) *The Pitman Guide to English Language Examinations for Overseas Candidates*, London: Pitman

Douglas, D. (1978) 'Gain in reading proficiency in English as a Foreign Language measured by three cloze scoring methods', *Journal of Research in Reading*, 1, 1, pp. 67–73

English Speaking Board (1981), *Oral Assessments in Spoken English as an Acquired Language*, Southport

Fok, A.; Lord, R.; Low, G.; T'sou, B.K.; and Lee, Y.P. (1981) *Working Papers in Linguistics and Language Teaching*, Special Issue on Language Testing, No. 4, Hong Kong: Language Centre, University of Hong Kong

Grieve, D.W. (1964) *English Language Examining : Report of an Inquiry into English Language Examining*, Lagos: African Universities Press

Harris, D.P. (1969) *Testing English as a Second Language*, New York: McGraw-Hill

Heaton, J.B. (1975) *Writing English Language Tests*, London: Longman

Ibe, M.D. (1975) 'A comparison of cloze and multiple-choice tests for measuring the English reading comprehension of South-East Asian teachers of English', *RELC Journal*, 6.2. Singapore: SEAMEO Regional Language Centre

Jones, R.L. and Spolsky, B. (Eds.) (1975) *Testing Language Proficiency*, Washington, D.C.: Centre for Applied Linguistics

Lado, R. (1961) *Language Testing: the Construction and Use of Foreign Language Tests*, London: Longman

Lee, Y.P. and Low, G.D. (1981) 'Classifying tests of language use'. Paper presented at 6th AILA World Congress, Lund, Sweden

Moller, A. (1975) 'Validity in Proficiency Testing', *ELT Documents*, 3, pp. 5–18, London: British Council

Morrow, K.E. (1977) *Techniques of Evaluation for a Notional Syllabus*, Reading: Centre for Applied Language Studies, University of Reading (for the Royal Society of Arts)

Morrow, K.E. (1979) 'Communicative language testing: revolution or evolution', C.J. Brumfit and K.J. Johnson (Eds.) *The Communicative Approach to Language Teaching*, London: O.U.P.

Munby, J.L. (1978) *Communicative syllabus design*, Cambridge: Cambridge University Press

Oller, J.W. (1971) 'Dictation as a device for testing foreign-language proficiency', *English Language Teaching*, 25, 3, pp. 254–9

Oller, J.W. (1972) 'Cloze tests of second language proficiency and what they measure', *Language Learning*, 23, 1, pp. 105–18

Oller, J.W. (1979) *Language Tests at School*, London: Longman

Oller, J.W. & Streiff, Virginia (1975) 'Dictation: a test of grammar-based expectancies', *English Language Teaching Journal*, 30, 1, pp. 25–36

Palmer, A.S. (1972) 'Testing communication', *IRAL*, 10, pp. 35–45

Palmer, A.S. (1981) 'Measures of achievement, communication, incorporation, and integration for two classes of formal EFL learners', *RELC Journal*, 12, 1, pp. 37–61

Bibliography

Palmer, L. & Spolsky, B. (Eds.) (1975) *Papers on Language Testing, 1967–1974*, Washington D.C.: TESOL

Perren, G.E. (1967) 'Testing ability in English as a second language', *English Language Teaching*; 21, 1, pp. 129–36; 21, 2, pp. 99–106; 21, 2, pp. 197–202

Perren, G.E. (Ed.) (1977) *Foreign Language Testing: Specialised Bibliography*, Centre for Information on Language Teaching and Research

Rea, Pauline M. (1978) 'Assessing language as communication', *MALS Journal*, New series, No. 3, University of Birmingham, Department of English

Read, J.A.S. (Ed.) (1981), *Directions in Language Testing, RELC Anthology Series 9*, Singapore: SEAMEO Regional Language Centre

Schulz, Renate A. (1977) 'Discrete-point versus simulated communication testing in foreign languages', *Modern Language Journal*, 61, 3, pp. 91–101

Spolsky, B., Murphy, P., Holm, W. and Ferrel, A. (1972) 'Functional tests of oral fluency', *TESOL Quarterly*, September

Stein, Oswald (1972) 'Was Prufen Wir Eigentlich?', *Verlag Lambert Lensing GmbH*, Dortmund, pp. 357–65

Stubbs, J.B. & Tucker, G.R. (1974) 'The cloze test as a measure of English proficiency', *Modern Language Journal*, 58, 5/6, pp. 239–41

Upshur, J.A. & Fata, J. (1968) 'Problems in foreign language testing', *Language Learning*, Special Issue, No. 3

Upshur, John A. (1971) 'Objective evaluation of oral proficiency in the ESOL classroom', *TESOL Quarterly*, 5, pp. 47–60

Valette, R.M. (1977) *Modern Language Testing* (2nd ed.), New York: Harcourt Bruce Jovanovich

Valette, R.M. & Disick, R.S. (1972) *Modern Language Performance Objectives and Individualization*, New York: Harcourt Bruce Jovanovich

THOMAS NELSON & SONS
English Language Teaching

The first name in language testing

PRACTICE TESTS FOR CAMBRIDGE FIRST CERTIFICATE IN ENGLISH

M Archer and E Nolan-Woods
Two new sets of five practice tests in the format of the revised examination. They provide complete practice in examination techniques for all five papers.

PRACTICE TESTS FOR CAMBRIDGE CERTIFICATE OF PROFICIENCY IN ENGLISH

M Archer and E Nolan-Woods
Five new tests with sections on Reading Comprehension, Composition, Use of English, Listening Comprehension and Interview, providing complete preparation and practice for the new examination.

PRACTICE FOR THE JMB TEST IN ENGLISH (OVERSEAS)

P L McEldowney
Comprehensive practice material to prepare students for, and monitor their progress towards, the *JMB Test in English (Overseas)*. A cassette and answer key accompany the Students' Book.

PRACTICE TESTS FOR RSA

S Edmonds, R Frizell and D Kindler
A series of three books each containing nine tests for Stages I, II and III of the *Royal Society of Arts* examination. Part I of each test is an Objective Test and Part II involves an aural comprehension test, reading comprehension and composition work.

PRACTICE TESTS FOR MICHIGAN CERTIFICATE ENGLISH

G P McCallum
Three practice tests in examination format provide valuable practice material for students preparing for the *University of Michigan Certificate of Proficiency in English* examination.

PRACTICE TESTS FOR TOEIC

G W Pifer
A complete package for students taking the *Test of English for International Communication*. It includes three examination-format tests, answer check sheets, a set of three cassettes and an instruction booklet in Japanese.

BUILDING SKILLS FOR THE TOEFL

C King and N Stanley
A complete course with a key and cassettes which builds and practises the academic skills and examination techniques needed for the *Test of English as a Foreign Language*.

PRACTICE TESTS FOR THE TOEFL

V W Mason
A set of four practice tests identical to those in the examination. Exact timings and separate answer sheets reproduce, as closely as possible, examination conditions. A key and two cassettes are also available.

NELSON ENGLISH LANGUAGE TESTS

W S Fowler and N Coe
A complete range of easily-administered tests graded at all levels from beginner to advanced. The Teacher's Book includes an easy-to-use answer key and guidance on using the tests.

TEST YOUR ENGLISH

W S Fowler and N Coe
A three-book series of progress tests at beginner, intermediate (to Cambridge First Certificate) and advanced (to Cambridge Proficiency) levels. They are fully cross-referenced, for remedial work, with Practise Your English by the same authors.

ENGLISH TESTS FOR DOCTORS

D Alderson and V Ward
Six practice tests for doctors and medical students who wish to assess their aural and written skill in the English language. The Students' Book is accompanied by a Teacher's Book and a set of three cassettes.

For more information about Nelson examination materials, please write to:
ELT Promotions, (MEPTs/84), Thomas Nelson & Sons Ltd., Nelson House, Mayfield Road, Walton-on-Thames, Surrey KT12 5PL, England.